SKELMERSDALE

FICTION RESERVE STOCK

THE STALKING OF EVE

Also by Louise Pennington

Jessica's Lover

THE STALKING OF EVE

Louise Pennington

Hodder & Stoughton

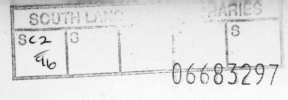

First published in Great Britain in 1996
by Hodder and Stoughton
A division of Hodder Headline PLC

10 9 8 7 6 5 4 3 2 1

British Library Cataloguing in Publication Data

Pennington, Louise
Stalking of Eve
I. Title
823.914 [F]

ISBN 0-340-63961-X

Typeset by Avon Dataset Ltd, Bidford-on-Avon, Warks

Printed and bound in Great Britain by
Mackays of Chatham PLC, Chatham, Kent

Hodder and Stoughton
A division of Hodder Headline PLC
338 Euston Road
London NW1 3BH

In memory of my father, Alan Pennington –
for your wit, your gentle humour, your fruit cakes
– and for making me change the ending . . .

His sister was his guard . . . The mighty Isis who protected her brother, seeking him without tiring, not resting until she found him . . . She received his seed and bore his heir, raising their child in solitude in an unknown hiding place . . .

New Kingdom hymn to Osiris

One

For the first time in years she thought of him, but there was no conjuring up of his face in her mind – or his name, or the place she had last seen him. Nothing as simple as that.

Her eyes flinched and she leaned her weary head back, lapping up the hypnotic drone of all-night cabs speeding down the drizzle-soaked Fulham Road as she shuddered away from the memory.

He would come back though, somehow, some way. He would.

'Eve?'

She wheeled round. Andrew was sitting up in bed, watching her. Usually he slept deeply, like a baby, and it soothed her to hear the soft snory murmur of his breathing, it helped quell the nasty thud of her heart.

'What's the matter?' he said. Even in the half-light she could see the worry creasing his face: a nice face, a warm face, a face she needed.

'I couldn't sleep.'

'Again?'

'Again.'

'Nothing else?'

She crossed the room, sat on the edge of the bed. 'What more could there be?'

He shook his head, but it was an odd sort of answer, he thought, even at three o'clock in the morning. 'Come back to bed.'

Wordlessly she climbed in beside him, felt his body close up against her, his arm snake around her waist, knowing what would come. And she didn't want to, not now, not tomorrow, or the day after that. Sometimes she thought that never having sex again would be too soon.

He was pulling up her nightie, lifting it gently over her head. Andrew

1

liked her naked, he wanted to see everything, love everything – because he did love and much more than her. 'With this body I thee worship'. And he did.

She stiffened just perceptibly, tried to suppress her revulsion as he crouched above her, but made her lips move as he leaned down to kiss her, made her body go limp and opened her legs enough to let him inside. Even when he prolonged the lovemaking with foreplay designed to please, it did nothing to arouse or excite; but she would play the game – moaning a little, sighing a little, keeping up the pretence, silently praying for it to be over.

She could not tell him because it would hurt him too much and he had never guessed, or, if he had, he'd said nothing and that would bother her if she cared to think about it, except that Andrew wouldn't keep something like that to himself. He would want to talk about it, understand, for heaven's sake. And she didn't want that. God, no.

He was playing with her now, teasing her, and she was astonished that he was unable to detect her disgust. It seemed horrible to her then, a travesty, that they could be so physically close, that their sweat, saliva and sexual juices could mingle and run together, yet in the purest sense of the word they still remained apart.

But something was happening inside.

Something inside her rising up in eagerness. He was straddling her, his body silhouetted against the dull light of a lamp so that she couldn't see his face.

He could be anyone.

She watched him for a long moment, then reached up and began raking her nails across his chest, down, until her hand closed around his erect penis, felt it pulsate beneath her fingers.

Her tongue passed along her lips.

It was like the sudden remembrance of some dark, delicious promise, a black secret put away long ago and then lost. And she was actually giving in to it, savouring it, and the savouring was somehow an inexpressible relief. She wanted him – it – wanted to be filled up, made complete in some bizarre way and she didn't know why. Except it didn't seem like Andrew, it seemed like someone else, and she knew who it was. Really she did, if she made herself look.

Rain was still spitting at the window when she awoke, but the sky was brightening and she wondered if the sun was going to come out; the weatherman had said it would and Andrew deserved a good day for the surprise party he had arranged for her birthday. No real surprise, of course, Eve had found out from Pansy in the end, and it would have been churlish to make a fuss after all the trouble he was taking. A shadow momentarily dimmed her eyes and she brought her knees up to her belly, arms crossed against her chest, and turned her face to the wall.

She should have foreseen the lake house, it was perfect for a party, even if Andrew knew of her dislike of the place. He had never been able to understand her reluctance to spend time there and so she hid behind the feeble excuse of its remoteness, its neglect, the overgrown garden and crumbling walls – as if that was all she found distasteful – but he had taken care of all that, apparently. Andrew was very good at taking care of things. He thought he was taking care of her now.

She slid a hand between her legs and held it there for comfort; it was tender there, a little bruised, and she closed her eyes.

Andrew was on the phone, she could hear his voice floating up from the study. Perhaps he regretted all the extra work involved, no matter how beautiful the outcome: three rambling sixteenth century cottages knocked into one and bordering on a small piece of water. The plumbing was bad, the wiring worse. If something should go wrong after all his efforts there was probably very little they could do, because it was so far off the beaten track, practically in the middle of nowhere. The Fulham house wasn't big enough, of course, not for two hundred people.

And she didn't like the water, that great pond which her mother had ostentatiously christened a lake. She snapped her eyes open and abruptly pushed back the bed clothes.

For an instant her expression was both wary and perplexed and when she looked down at her hands she saw that they were shaking.

'Nerves,' Eve murmured soothingly to herself, 'just nerves,' and walked into the bathroom where she turned on a tap and let the crystal-clear water run through her fingers.

Andrew had once managed to coax her into the lake. It had been very late and he was sober and she a little the worse for several glasses of champagne – a naughty, naked swim designed to drive her dislike away. He had held out his hands to her as she stood on the jetty and she had slipped effortlessly into his arms and with no protest, not even the ghost of a frown. Odd, that.

Now she could only remember how cold it had been, how the moon had carved an alabaster path across the water, how she had stared with disbelief at the whiteness of their bodies against the blackness of the water, her breasts lying on the surface, glistening, like two silver orbs; beneath and between them a clump of weeds, tendrils streaming eerily like human hair.

And that thick slimy mud squirming up between her toes.

Nothing after that, because she had blanked out.

Eve began to pour scented oil into the running bathwater, trailed her fingers across the surface.

Poor Andrew. The experience had really frightened him and he blamed himself, but it had only been the result of a lethal combination of tiredness and champagne.

Yet it made her wonder. Sometimes during those endless waking moments she wondered a lot.

'Thought you might like a tea . . .'

Eve swung round, startled.

'Hey,' Andrew said gently and put the cup and saucer down, 'it's only me.'

'Sorry.'

'You're tired, that's all.' He slipped his arms around her, felt the curves of her body through the silk of her kimono. 'That's why I let you sleep on – after yet another of your broken nights.'

She nodded.

'But this time I can't say I'm entirely sorry . . .' He stroked her hair and felt the outline of her skull beneath his fingers, caught the sweet warm fragrance of her and thought of their feverish lovemaking. Eve's uncharacteristic reaction to his caresses had surprised, no, stunned him because generally she was a passive partner: pliant, amenable, but passive. Perhaps he had unwittingly stumbled upon some invisible switch in her that neither of them had suspected existed. He frowned softly, trying to comprehend this mystery, but wondered whether he hadn't simply and finally got it right with her. These things took time, hadn't he told himself that often enough?

He cupped his wife's face in his hands. Even the grey smudges beneath her eyes did nothing to reduce her attraction. Eve was an innocent voluptuary, if there was such a thing: dark and opulent and sensitive, perhaps too sensitive.

'You do love me?' she said suddenly. 'Don't you?' The words tumbled out from nowhere and Eve sent a hand to her mouth as if to catch and bring the clumsy words back.

Andrew gaped at her and when he spoke his voice was gentle, disbelieving. 'How can you ask that? And after last night? What is it, Eve – what's the matter?'

But sex wasn't love. She wrinkled her brow; one of the nuns at school had told her that sex was bad because God hated it. Sister Rosemary with her white shiny moon face and big mannish shoes who thought that sexual sin was worse than murder. 'I'm sorry. That was a stupid thing to say.'

'Very.'

'And there's nothing the matter. Really. I just need to make up some sleep.'

'No,' he said. 'You're worried about something.'

'I'm not,' she protested,

He scrutinised her sharply. 'Sure?'

'Yes.' Eve smiled a little, her luminous eyes never leaving his.

Andrew sucked in a breath. 'Well, thank God for Pansy. Now at least Jack shouldn't be disturbing your sleep so much. Our gorgeous little son has hardly given you a decent night since he was born.'

'It's not been as bad as that.'

'It's been pretty bad.' More than that, Eve was different somehow, and he couldn't explain exactly why. The post-natal depression seemed to be passing, but she didn't spend enough time with Jack now that Pansy was here. In fact, she seemed to avoid him, which was crazy and probably an exaggeration when he remembered how much she had wanted their child. Andrew sighed softly; maybe he was tired, too.

'All right,' she said with a trace of impatience. 'But let's not dwell on it.' Perhaps Andrew was right, she told herself and it was as simple as that: lack of regular sleep, followed by the depression which had dogged her since Jack's birth.

'Perhaps you stopped taking the tablets too soon?' he queried gently.

'You mean good old Prozac?' she replied dryly. 'No. I don't think so. I hate taking pills.'

'I understand all that,' he said. 'But just watch points. Okay?'

'Okay.' If things didn't get any better, perhaps she would see the doctor and get something to help her sleep. Nothing long-term, just something mild, to tide her over.

And the feeling would go.

'Better now?'

She nodded.

Andrew's gaze came to rest on her mouth, lips that could still tantalise and arouse with startling ease. He thought back to last night and heat flooded him again; she had abased herself, that was the only word that seemed to fit. There had been a sickening sensation of power having her on her knees before him. Yet what bothered him most about her behaviour, and his subsequent reaction, was the fact that he had liked it.

'Wow!' Pansy exclaimed. 'I had no idea it was so dreamy.'

'Your father's obviously been doing a lot of work on the place,' Eve said quietly. It was her stepdaughter's first visit to the lake house, and she had forgotten how beguiling its charms could seem to a newcomer. It had beguiled her once; it had been her home, everything.

'Do you like it?' Andrew darted a glance at her as he drove further up the long gravelled drive, drawing them closer to the house. She knew he was anxious, it was all there: in his voice, the expression on his face.

'Yes, of course,' she said with an effort. 'You've done a wonderful job.'

'I wasn't sure . . .' he said. 'I knew you weren't keen on the place, but I thought after a bit of renovation . . .' He shrugged. 'It seemed such a waste to let it sit here and rot.'

'Don't you like it?' Pansy sounded incredulous. Eve could feel her stepdaughter's eyes boring into the back of her head.

'Memories, I suppose,' Eve answered with a shrug. 'I don't know really.'

Andrew looked at his wife out of the corner of his eye, but her face was closed. She never spoke of the past, not in any real sense. Her father was dead, her mother had lived in the States for years, and there was a brother, James, somewhere in the Far East who never wrote, never came home.

'There used to be a pair of swans,' Eve said abruptly. 'They used to come every year, nesting beneath one of the willows until the cygnets hatched.'

Andrew stopped in front of the house just as Eve finished speaking and he and Pansy followed the direction of her gaze to the water.

It was very quiet and a little lonely because of the silence. There were no other buildings close enough to desecrate the skyline and no noise, not even birdsong, any animal life sheltering from the heat of the day. The trees still crowded thick and dark to the water's edge where the moss would be succulent and green and where an odd ring of mushrooms grew: red-capped brilliant things with white, pulpy stems. Eve drew in a breath, caught the old clinging, earthy scents in her nostrils. She had often walked there in that other time, sat on the bank and trailed her toes in the water, watched for tadpoles, water-snails and the birth of dragonflies.

Later came other things: the stench of cigarette smoke, a pair of monster feet striding through long grass.

She licked her lips, slowly, carefully.

Amongst the reeds there were probably moorhens and ducks, furtively rustling the tall stems alongside the other things – the small, unknown and nameless ones that only come out into the world at night to live for a while, and breathe, and have their moment.

Baby Jack began to grizzle as if the stillness of everything had snapped him out of his dreams.

'He'll need his nappy changing,' Pansy said and wrinkled her nose.

'If you'll do that for me,' Eve suggested, 'I'll make up a picnic lunch. You can have it down by the water.'

'No problem,' Pansy enthused. 'And I love eating outdoors.'

'Can't stand the bugs myself,' Andrew remarked, pulling a face. 'They never leave you alone long enough to get your teeth into a good sandwich.' He started rummaging in his pockets. 'Now let me see – I've got the keys here – somewhere.' When he found them he held them up in the air and grinned as if he had just won a prize.

Eve watched Pansy as she walked with her father to the house, Jack swinging gently in his baby-seat by her side. She wore a bright yellow waistcoat with red tassels and a long black skirt from which huge Doc Martens protruded like clowns' feet. On her head perched a wide floppy-brimmed hat, pinned up at the front with a cameo brooch; beneath the hat her hair sprang forth, a mass of tiny dark-brown plaits into which she had woven gold thread. Eve liked Pansy, she was almost as nice as her father, a little wild maybe, but good-hearted. Eve wanted her to stay with them as long as possible, and hoped that Pansy's burning desire to obtain an Equity card, and hopefully commence an acting career, would not materialise for a very long time.

She felt very guilty about this secret wish and found herself over-paying and over-indulging her stepdaughter to salve her conscience. It had done wonders for their once thorny relationship, but not much for Eve's guilt. That was always there in some shape or form, clinging to her back, her very own *bête noire*.

She slammed the door of the car and stood on the path for a moment, looking up at the house. All the paintwork had been renewed, the brasswork on the front door cleaned of verdigris and polished, a wall rebuilt, an old cracked pane of glass which had sat in the leaded windows for years replaced. It looked strange and familiar at the same time and she wondered if that was a good thing.

Andrew had not removed the parasitic creeper and wistaria climbing the walls because the bricks were probably held together as much by this as by the ancient mortar. Her mother had pointed that out the last time she had come. Eve sucked in a breath and thought of September, the next time she made her annual pilgrimage from the States. Did her mother really think he would care whether she were there or not?

Eve felt uncomfortable suddenly, hot and sweaty, and she brought a hand up to sweep her hair away from her flushed face before realising Andrew was standing in the doorway watching her, a trace of that funny, worried look on his face. She forced a smile and walked towards the house.

There was a flagged-stone terrace which met a sloping lawn leading down to the water – a black rippleless pool, blacker where trees crowded thickly to the bank and willows trailed their leaves in the water. Magical. Pansy loved it, loved it even before she had taken a step outside the confines of the car.

After dumping her bags and changing Jack's nappy she had brought him straight down, leaving her father and Eve to sort out the preparations for the party.

The sun was strong now, as if the weather had finally made up its mind to stay fine, and Jack was sleeping on feather cushions set down on the red and blue car rug, curled in a ball, like a little hibernating animal.

Pansy was sitting up, hands clasped around her knees, staring out across the water.

This was Eve's childhood home, she had even been born here apparently. Pansy's eyebrows drew together in a frown; her own father would have been fourteen then. When Eve reached the same age he was already a director of a very successful advertising agency, and married to her mother, Minty.

Pansy winced inwardly and wondered if she would make an appearance at the party. She would be drunk, of course, and it would be cringingly embarrassing – which was why she intended staying in her room. No doubt she would also be hanging on the arm of that wanker, Tony, he of the flashing choppers and coke-glazed eyeballs. He looked used-up and worn out, she thought meanly – penis probably withered and redundant like some ageing chipolata sausage – but then felt a little disgusted with herself for speculating on the state of her mother's boyfriend's genitals. No, she didn't want to think about that at all.

Instead she thought of Frank and what he had told her at the weekend. Hadn't it been a little cowardly to wait until they had slept together several times before informing her that he was polygamous? And what was that supposed to mean, exactly? That he wanted two women in his life – three? Thirty-three? Or perhaps it was simply a sophisticated way of telling her that he preferred sleeping around.

What a shit.

And he called her his 'Little Flower' because of her ludicrously twee name. Her mother must have been in orbit when she thought that one up.

Unfortunately Pansy liked Frank, she liked him a lot and she didn't know if that meant she was stupid, or in love.

She took a deep breath and looked down at Jack. She would try and focus all her attention on her half-brother (who was she kidding?) and he was a handful all by himself, even if he was only five months old. A very demanding, lusty baby who reminded her of her father, which was probably just wishful thinking. She'd always wanted a brother. Eve had a brother, apparently, and a real loner by the sound of it. At their wedding, no one from Eve's family had attended, not even her mother, and that must have hurt, surely?

Pansy threw a stone into the still water, watched it disappear and the ripples wash away into the bent reeds until they hit the bank.

The water was supposed to be very deep in certain places, so her father had told her with a warning note in his voice, particularly on the far side where the inflow, or stream, entered the lake. Here, too, the water silted up rapidly, several feet in only a few years, so there would be a wall of mud, like a sandbank, out there somewhere. Pansy grimaced, but the mud was out of sight and almost instantly out of mind. There was nothing to disturb the dreaming landscape, only the endless flitting butterflies. She had never seen so many: cabbage whites, red admirals, blues and peacocks all dancing among the swaying seed-headed grass and creamy foxgloves.

The water and the land and the house all seemed faultless and serene as they slumbered ever so peacefully beneath that pale summer sun. There was nothing visible to disenchant.

Eve had told her that there was a small grove of trees close to the boundary of the grounds, but it would be overgrown now, she thought, clotted with saplings, brambles and thorn bushes left to run riot. Eve said it was old, older than the house.

She felt a sudden chill as if a breeze had bitten the back of her exposed neck and pulled a cardigan up around her shoulders. Jack stirred in his sleep and rolled over on to his back, arms outstretched now, little chubby palms open to the sky. He would wake soon and probably grumble and cry until she fed and watered him and made him smile.

She glanced again at the water. They would have to be careful once Jack started to walk because little ones had a way of finding danger, self-made or otherwise. She was beginning to realise that there was not a lot of peace of mind to be had once children came along. Sometimes she actually leaned into Jack's crib just to check that he was still breathing.

That, she supposed, was the way of things, but when little ones were suddenly quiet or out of sight for too long that was different. That was when worry crept in and fright, and all the other dreaming horrors that never cease to haunt the guardians of children.

Almost all the guests had come, even Andrew's first wife, Minty, who was notorious for being late. She had swept through the door in a blur of devastating bronze lamé, the colour of orange gold, her white-blonde hair which had hung right down her back in her modelling days, now cropped into an elfin cut that framed her finely-boned face in wisps of platinum. Around her neck hung a huge Aztec-style choker dripping with fine chains matching the pieces circling her wrists, and on her arm was Tony, an old colleague of Andrew's and Minty's new man – tall, tanned and in Armani; a man who grinned a lot.

It struck Eve that they looked like something plucked out of the pages of *Hello* magazine and she longed to laugh, except the spectacle of them both leaning against each other was hardly funny. Minty swayed because Minty had already been drinking, and at the height of Eve's scrutiny her husband's ex-wife met her steady gaze, casting an ironic, knowing look which lingered and made Eve's heart sink because Minty would come over – she just couldn't resist.

'Eve,' she said, approaching, an unconvincing smile lifting her mouth. 'How lovely to see you.'

'And you, Minty.'

'I take it this splendid celebration is all in aid of your birthday,' she said dryly, 'isn't it?'

'Yes.'

'How thoughtful of Andrew.' She paused. 'How very, very thoughtful.'

Behind her, Tony sidled up and placed a predatory hand on her lower back, let it slide down further so that it came to rest on one of the cheeks of Minty's pert bottom.

'Hi, Eve,' he smarmed, his eyes travelling over her with great avidity. 'Are you the one whose so very thoughtful – I couldn't help overhearing . . .'

'Andrew.'

'Ah,' he said, nodding, fixing his eyes on her breasts. 'Of course. Such a thoughtful guy. One of the best.'

Minty caught Tony's gaze and their eyes gleamed with shared amusement. She began to giggle, huskily, and Eve found herself wondering whether it was natural or contrived.

What a remarkably tiring scene. She sighed inwardly and looked beyond them, relieved to see one of the caterers cross the hall, which would give her the excuse she needed.

'I must go . . .' She nodded vaguely in the direction of the kitchen. 'Duty calls.'

They said nothing as she moved away, but she could hear Tony start to chortle and Minty's bitchy giggle turn to bitchy laughter. Par for the course, really.

The two women were very different, of course. Notwithstanding the age difference, ten years, Eve was as dark as Minty was fair and possessed the sort of curves Andrew's ex-wife termed derisively as 'Rubenesque' which was not entirely fair, since Minty considered anyone a size removed from her rapier-thin frame almost abnormal.

Theirs had not been an amicable divorce. Towards the end bickering and name-calling had become an accepted part of their relationship, but apparently none of that mattered any longer – so much water under the proverbial divorcees' bridge.

Yet, ironically, Minty seemed to appreciate Andrew – his thoughtfulness – far more now than she ever had when they were together, which rankled Eve somewhat. In fact it rankled Eve a great deal when Minty was playing her 'helpless woman act' and leaning on Andrew to sort out a tedious time-consuming problem she had dreamed up. She did it to annoy, of course, which didn't make it any the less annoying. Eve wondered why she let it bother her; there was no real love lost between them. It was stupid, childish even.

She paused for a moment in the narrow passageway between hall and kitchen and glanced through a window at the sky; at least the weather had stayed fine for the party, like an omen, and the air was almost balmy. Andrew had wanted to hold it at the end of July, but had changed his mind; which was just as well because it had rained nearly every day.

From where she stood she could see the lake very clearly, her parents' pride and joy. During the 1880s her maternal grandparents had enlarged it and landscaped the surrounding area, but nature had taken over long since. Now it seemed semi-wild and beneath its black silent skin the water teemed with minuscule animal life: tiny creatures living in the silt and mud and amongst an abundance of weeds – starwort, watermoss, blanket weed, taking up every inch of space and absorbing huge quantities of life-giving oxygen so that larger living things like trout and carp could not survive. Yet frogs thrived and at certain times the reeds and lily-pads seethed with them and their harsh ugly cry, grinding in chorus as the sun went down.

She switched her gaze to a covered walkway, strung with fairylights, leading down to the jetty from a marquee which had been erected on the lawn. Along the water's edge Chinese lanterns on sticks swayed a little in the early evening breeze. Surprisingly, all the preparations had gone off without a hitch, and later they would all congregate in the marquee, when the cake would be wheeled in proclaiming her thirtieth birthday, if a little late.

Hands forked around her waist and she caught a startled breath.

'What are you doing here? I thought you'd be in the garden somewhere, not hiding in the house.'

'I wasn't hiding.' She leaned her head back against her husband. 'I was merely observing from the sidelines.'

'Liar,' he said. 'Going well, isn't it?'

'Yes, very.'

'How are you feeling?'

'Fine.'

'Really?'

'Yes,' she said a little impatiently.

He sighed.

'No sighs tonight,' she said firmly. 'I know what you're thinking and I want you to stop. You see,' she continued earnestly, 'I don't want to go into it all again, Andrew, it's just not necessary.'

'I thought I was being terribly clever holding the party here, now I'm not so sure, which is a bloody stupid thing to say at this stage.' He gazed uselessly at the crowded lawn.

'Can't we forget it – once and for all?' She was pleading, trying to shrug everything off.

He regarded her steadily for a moment, then, 'All right, if that's what you want.' But it wasn't as simple as that for him, nor, he suspected, for her.

'You worry too much.'

'Maybe.' He could never tell her how their unhappy excursion into the lake still haunted and horrified him. How an abrupt and frighteningly powerful urge to couple with his wife had nearly driven reason away. And her face – what had he seen – desolation, grief? A sense of loss so great had shaken him that he thought she had died.

'I don't want you developing another ulcer, and all because of me,' Eve said, taking his arm and tugging him gently towards a side door. They stepped out and into benevolent evening sunshine and walked towards the marquee. She slowed and made him stop, as if she still had not done, or said enough, and looked into his eyes, large and pale brown, almost honey coloured, eyes alight with a sharp and delightful intelligence. Below them was the nose that so amused her. He had broken it playing rugby, the scar was still there and it made him look less than respectable, more some street-wise conman. 'I'm all right.' She kissed him lightly. 'Really. Now stop fussing.'

'Oh, take no notice, it's probably just my mood, or maybe I'm having my mid-life crisis. It is a little overdue, you know.'

'Don't be absurd,' she said with a wry smile.

'Just a joke.' Except, just lately, he did wonder.

They took each step together and when she shot a glance at him from the corner of her eye his face was still set and that stung, made her feel guilty because nothing she said or did ever seemed enough to reassure him. 'Hey,' she said gently, 'this is supposed to be my birthday party. Remember?' There was a throng on the lawn, a kaleidoscope of beautifully clad people. 'And if we're not careful Bob might catch us looking glum on his damned video camera. Couldn't he have left it at home, just once?'

'He's into filming in a big way, I'm afraid.'

13

'So I've noticed.'

'Have no fear – you look mouthwateringly desirable.'

She laughed, but suddenly thought of Minty all in amber. Her own black velvet seemed tame beside it.

'Have I also told you that you have a very sexy laugh?'

'Yes.'

'– sort of low and throaty, almost edible.'

'Like Minty.'

Andrew sighed and wondered why today of all days their talk constantly seemed to turn sour. 'I wasn't thinking of my ex-wife, I was thinking of you.'

'She looks wonderful.'

'She looks halfway to be being drunk. Stop being polite.'

'Well,' Eve said obligingly, 'if she wasn't drunk she'd look wonderful.'

'Thank you,' he said. 'Besides, in case you hadn't noticed I'm not married to her any more, so why on earth should I be interested in how she looks? I had twelve years of it, my dear, and that was more than enough. All that's over, was over in fact long before I met you.'

'I know, I know.'

'And she'd bristle with pleasure if she knew that you were even the tiniest bit insecure.'

'I'm not.'

'Liar.'

'I'm not, but sometimes I'm simply curious. It seems a long time to spend with someone only to part and live separate lives. A waste, if you like.'

'It is a waste, but I don't wish for it back. Most of it was sheer hell. I've rarely met a woman as insecure as Minty, but she hides it all beneath that brittle, if dazzling, exterior. At least when she's not drunk.'

'Do you think she could stop drinking? I mean, if she really wanted to?'

'I'll say no to the first part of your question and yes to the second.' He shrugged. 'Frankly, I think it's too late and frankly I wish she hadn't come. Needless to say I didn't invite her. Poor Pansy let the cat out of the bag.'

For a few slow steps they fell silent.

'She doesn't like me.'

'You're my lovely new wife and substantially younger than she is, I don't think you can expect anything else.' He squeezed her hand. 'Besides, she doesn't like anyone much.'

Impossible to explain how the person one marries changes into some-one else. It was like a tale plucked from a dark Germanic legend which told of doppelgangers and shape-changers. Except it was never as simple as that; there were always clues, little things that one didn't choose to notice and the sex, of course, that was a blind in itself. Minty had been very good at that. But even that had gone, in the end, just like everything else.

Now he could only remember the rages, the depressions, the bitterness. God, the misery of it all.

'One of the times I broached the subject of a separation she tried to kill herself. Cut her wrists in the bath.'

He had never seen quite so much blood. Clouds of it, staining the water.

'We'd had a row, you see, and I'd stalked out of the house – the usual – and by the time I'd got to work something . . . I don't know what . . . told me to get home.' He'd almost lost an account worth three million. Just walked in and out of that boardroom as if it were of no importance at all. He supposed, on the scale of things, a life was worth more than a new brand of figure-hugging blue jeans, even one badly fraying around the edges.

She had still been partially conscious, a parchment-white thirty-five year old woman lying in a bath who looked more like some pitiful starving child – except for the joint in one hand and a broken whisky glass in the other. 'She meant to do it, there's no doubt about that.'

If he hadn't found her when he did he would have had her on his conscience for the rest of his life; she would have been there, always, contaminating everything he touched. There would have been no sense of relief, no secret joy like that which comes when a burden dies and leaves you safe.

'Poor Minty.'

'Yes. But don't, for God's sake, ever let on that I told you.'

His wife, his ex-wife, hated pity.

'I won't.'

Eve scanned the garden, saw her on the terrace watching them and, caught out, Minty waved in a lacklustre sort of way. 'Maybe she'll remarry.'

'God – I hope so.'

The accident happened much later, just as some of the guests were deciding the night had been long enough. It was perhaps one in the

15

morning, but the band was still playing and waiters and waitresses in black and white still flitted amongst the thinning throng on the lawn, carrying trays of drinks.

Eve had left for a few minutes to ensure that all was well with Jack, she had hardly seen him all day, but she'd been busy, hadn't she? Occupied with other things. In the peace and quiet she had slipped the shoes from her aching feet and stood by his cot, run her fingers along the bars of his little wooden cage. He was a beautiful baby. Sometimes there was no avoiding echoes.

Her eyes narrowed in puzzlement, but then she moved to the window and looked down on the party.

Andrew was standing in the entrance to the marquee with some friends, unaware that he was being filmed by Bob and his faithful video camera. Further down the garden stood Minty's man, Tony, and he was alone, or rather Minty wasn't with him. He was talking animatedly to another female, a very young thing, the daughter of a neighbour as far as she could recall, and he was still grinning, expertly. Eve could see the glow of his flashing white teeth even from where she stood. No wonder Minty had wandered off.

She was standing at the end of the jetty and in the shadowy half-light Minty seemed almost ethereal. It was the fragility of her body, of course, and the bronze she wore reflected in the moonshine on the water . . . something in the tilt of her partly bowed head.

She wasn't contemplating a swim? Surely not.

Eve hesitated, but only for a moment before moving quickly out of the room and down the staircase to make her way back into the garden. She abruptly slowed on reaching the terrace because now Minty was only sitting on the edge of the jetty, dangling her feet in the water. Eve looked down at her own feet; she had forgotten her shoes. She sighed heavily in exasperation and walked down to the lake just the same, but nevertheless approached her husband's ex-wife with the usual irritating trepidation.

'You're not thinking of going in, I hope?'

Minty was smoking a cigarette. She shrugged, blew out a slow cloud of smoke and said, 'I might.'

'The water's freezing.'

'How do you know? Been in, have you?'

Eve coloured. 'You know I haven't.'

'No,' she said dryly and with one eyebrow cocked-up. 'I suppose not.'

Eve closed her eyes for a moment and wondered why she'd bothered.

'Andrew looks well,' Minty said tapping ash into the water. 'How's his ulcer?'

'Better.'

Minty stared out across the lake. 'Must be your calming influence. When he was mine . . .' she said, 'he was mostly creased-up in agony.' She paused. 'I did that. I nearly drove him insane.'

Eve said nothing.

'Anyway,' she continued, 'it hardly matters now – does it?'

'Why don't you come back to the house? I could make some coffee.'

'You think I'm pissed, don't you?'

'No.'

'Yes, you do. Or doped up . . .'

'I could do with a cup myself, that's all.'

'Well,' Minty said mockingly, 'you go and have your nice cup of coffee while I have a swim. Then I might join you.' She threw her cigarette into the water, stood up and began slipping the delicate straps of her dress from her shoulders. The rest was easy, the garment simply rippled down her narrow body to fall in a pool of liquid bronze at her feet.

'You can't, Minty,' Eve protested, 'it's too cold. And there are weeds, masses of them . . .' So easy to get a limb caught in the eager grasp of those lush green tentacles.

'Don't be such a baby. It's a beautiful night for a swim.'

'It's also freezing and black as pitch.'

She was just standing there, completely naked, except for the elaborate jewellery she favoured so much still adorning neck and wrists. In the unsettling half-light these pieces seemed to hint at the primitive, at metal collars and prison chains once worn by slaves and serfs and chattels.

'You're quite right. It is very cold and visibility is at a minimum,' Minty responded sarcastically, 'but I'm very hot blooded and I do a lot of things with my eyes closed,' she laughed drunkenly.

Eve averted her eyes, darted an uneasy glance at the water. 'Look it's very late and . . .'

' . . . I've been drinking.' Minty raised her eyes to heaven. 'Or snorting. Frankly, your touching concern surprises me. I didn't know you cared.'

'I do, as it happens.' Pity had come for her, finally, just as it had come to Andrew she supposed.

Minty looked back at her warily, then jerked her head in the direction of the party. 'No one else has noticed that I'm standing here stark naked. That's funny when you think about it – not even randy old Tony, he's too busy chatting up that little tart. He's almost fifty, you know, but looks more like forty, don't you think? And he swears he hasn't had a facelift.' She grinned unpleasantly, 'But he has trouble in the loins department, you know, his precious-great-bloody-prick . . . can't keep it up.'

'Come into the house.'

'I think he really believes that a young girl will make him feel young – be young – in some pathetic way. Then, maybe his big dick will stay horizontal long enough to let him do it.'

'Minty,' Eve pleaded. 'Come on.'

'He says I don't turn him on enough – says I'm hopeless in bed.' She shook her head and mumbled something Eve did not understand, then – 'I suppose if I was twenty instead of forty, or even thirty instead of forty, it might inspire his uninspired cock. Why is it some men, some men just won't . . . ?' Her words faded for a moment and her mouth drooped like a little girl's. 'I just bloody wish I could be . . .'

Different?

She stopped abruptly as if she had said too much and gazed into the black water. Like a tar-pit full of bleached bones and husks of decaying things. She blinked the image away and shot a dark glance at the woman who stood beside her. 'Well, what do you think, Eve? Aren't you going to give me the benefit of your infinite wisdom?'

'Wisdom? I'm not sure I have any, infinite or otherwise.'

'You're too modest. Do you know, Andrew talks about you with such reverence you'd think he'd married the Virgin-bloody-Mary.'

'Stop it, Minty,' Eve said wearily. 'Not funny.'

'Well, you do have Andrew.' Her eyes were set and cold. 'And I suppose you'll keep him.'

'Are we getting to the point now?'

Minty shrugged her fragile shoulders. 'I don't think so,' she said, feigning innocence. 'After all, I thought I began this conversation with Tony in mind.'

Eve looked back at her, puzzled.

'About Tony and his need for a young body.'

'For God's sake, Minty. I don't know.'

'You can do better than that. Try a bit harder. Indulge me. Use your imagination.'

They stared at each other, full in the eyes. Somewhere far away a door was banging.

'This is silly, and I'm getting tired.'

'What's the matter?'

'Nothing's the matter.'

'Well, then . . .'

Finish this, Eve's mind said. Get it over with. She tilted her head back and stared at the night sky, shifted her gaze slowly back to Minty. 'Perhaps,' she began haltingly, 'it's the lure of innocence.'

'Yes,' Minty coaxed.

'And power.'

'Power?'

Eve swallowed hard. 'It's easy for an older, more experienced man to have power over a young girl, hold someone in thrall with intelligence and sexual guile – easy to impress your image on an empty page . . .'

'Interesting. Go on.'

'Something forbidden,' Eve said flatly. 'There are men, people – who cannot resist breaking the rules and upsetting the established order of things. It is the risk, you see, the exhilaration of defying the norm.'

'But Tony . . .'

'Something missing inside them,' she sighed dreadfully, 'a void they can never fill.'

'Eve?'

'Ignorance,' Eve continued in that same dull monotone as if she had not heard, 'and misplaced trust.' She was staring blankly into the water. 'Misplaced love even . . . because the older man is so good at deceit and she is all unknowing. Sweet,' she said in a soft, grieving voice, 'so sweet.'

She shook her head agonisingly slowly. 'But he never stops – not with his words . . . nor with the touching.'

Minty was watching her with surprise and something close to astonishment. 'You sound as if you've been there.' And tasted it.

But Eve was silent, her face pale and her dark eyes unnaturally fixed.

'Eve?'

She jumped and in two deep and steadying breaths the tension was released. 'What?'

'Who was he?'

Eve rubbed at her temples, her expression one of bewilderment, even momentary fear. 'I don't know what you mean.'

Minty opened her mouth to speak, then closed it again.

The band had started up once more and automatically they both turned their heads in the direction of the house and the moment was gone.

Minty swore as her eyes came to rest on Tony. 'Christ,' she seethed, 'just look at him. He's still at it. Do you think he even bloody-well remembers he came with me?'

'Maybe he feels you're neglecting him,' Eve offered feebly, not caring very much. She was so tired suddenly, exhausted.

'Oh, sure,' Minty said with a sneer. 'And he's trying to make me jealous? Pull the other leg.' She shook her head in disbelief. 'He'll soon get bored. I don't see his new little friend performing the sort of tricks I do for him, somehow. He's into S and M, you know, likes the bizarre does good old Tony . . .'

She let off a peal of joyless laughter. 'I let him pee on me, I even let him make me bleed if that's what he wants. If you look closely at my nipples you might see the teeth marks, you might see the holes at the tip through which he puts a little gold hoop and then a little gold chain and then he pulls. Hard.' She was looking directly into the other woman's appalled gaze. 'Life is shit, Eve, but people are worse.'

'Come into the house. Please.'

'No,' Minty said. 'I like it here.' Tears were very close now and she blinked, quickly, snapping her eyes shut on her weakness. 'Besides, that other guy I was talking to said it's perfect in there – not really cold at all.'

'What guy?'

'The man in the water.'

'There's no one in the water, Minty.'

'Yes there bloody is. I was talking to him just before you came and interrupted things.' She was all sullenness now, but there was distant pleasure in her eyes as her gaze wandered back to the lake.

Eve frowned, perplexed. The surface of the water was flat and still and empty.

'Very tall, very lean . . .' Minty continued wistfully, 'with the most wonderful voice. Sort of seductive.' The things he had said had made her tremble inside. Dreadful, dark, exciting things, but then he had gone and a sort of bleakness crept up and gathered her in.

'There's no one there.' But for no reason at all Eve felt a chill; something wrong, something in the atmosphere, seeping into her pores.

'I'll prove it to you.'

'Minty, don't.'

'Watch me.'

She slid into the water. Disappeared.

Eve held her breath, but a moment later Minty reappeared a few yards away.

'It's fantastic,' she gasped. 'Why don't you join me?'

'Come out.' Eve peered anxiously over her shoulder at the now almost deserted lawn. Where was Andrew, or even Tony for that matter?

'What are you afraid of, Eve?' Minty was close now, one hand resting on the jetty, beads of water lying like sweat on her upturned face. 'What is it, exactly, that bugs you so much?'

'I don't think right now we should really be concerned about me. Do you?'

'Only trying to help.'

'No,' Eve said suddenly. 'Not help – hurt.'

Minty didn't reply. She only stared for what seemed like a long time and then moved away.

'Minty?'

Minty's head was cocked to one side and her expression had changed, seemed touched by wonder and then rapthess, as if she were listening to a voice only she could hear. It was not unlike the expression Eve herself had worn only minutes before.

And the voice was insisting that things changed in the dark – and in the water – that, freed of the suffocating chains of this world, everyone, everything could take on a different shape, a different name, a different meaning.

'Come in. Join me,' Minty said seductively.

'Don't be ridiculous.'

Minty moved back, snaked a hand around Eve's ankle. Tugged her gently. Drawing. Slid wet fingers over her flesh. 'Come in.' She was smiling, a full sweet smile of such peculiar and angelic brightness that Eve wondered if she'd suddenly gone mad.

She snatched her foot away. 'Stop it.' She felt obscurely frightened, looked again over her shoulder. 'Get out of there, Minty, for God's sake. This is crazy.'

They looked back at each other.

'Perhaps we could have been friends,' Minty said quietly. 'In another time, another place.'

Eve felt an odd, vague anguish. In another time, another place it had been darker than this.

Minty was swimming away, and so smoothly it was beautiful to watch, even then. She turned on her back and stared up at the stars, floating: like a piece of flotsam or a fragile insect; a water sprite with delicate papery wings.

'Minty?' Her voice tailed off flat and echoeless in the darkness.

Eve followed her with her eyes for a few moments, then turned back and ran along the jetty towards the waning party. A waiter appeared from inside the marquee and she waved at him. 'Fetch my husband, please.' The man looked blank. 'Hurry!' She tried to prevent the shrillness of panic from creeping into her voice, but knew it was there. She returned to the edge of the lake and squinted into the blackness, searching for Minty.

And there she was, a blonde wraith, nestling close to the bank on the far side.

Minty waved and Eve found herself waving helplessly back, like a half-wit or an impotent child who has no control over the events that are speeding towards it.

Minty shrieked at her and she was jolted out of her thoughts.

'*He's* here, Eve,' she screamed feverishly, joyously. '*He's* here.'

As if she should know who it was.

She was trying to frighten her, that was all. Bad joke, Minty. Bad, bloody joke.

Suddenly Minty was jerked up out of the water and a shadow swung across her upper torso, enfolding her.

Eve felt a kind of dreamy terror wash over her, a feeling both languid and repellent.

That wet sound, suction tight, flesh against flesh.

Sex in the water.

The blonde head was thrown back, the eyes closed tight, but flashed open again as Minty's mouth stretched wide into a permanent gasp. Bug-eyed and frantic she screamed at the moon, 'Yes, oh yes, oh yes . . ,'

A naked limpid dance. A squirm. A twitch.

Minty went under and Minty didn't come up.

Pansy squeezed her eyes shut before opening them slowly and staring again at the spectacle of her mother standing naked at the end of the jetty. She obviously intended outdoing herself tonight. Thank God she hadn't invited Frank, although he wouldn't have been shocked, nothing phased him, but that was hardly the point. And how would her father react to Frank? He would be fair, wouldn't he? Her father always tried to be fair, even if it almost killed him in the process.

And Eve? Sometimes she had the distinct impression that, like Frank, nothing much would phase her rather enigmatic stepmother either, but she had no idea why she should think this.

She was beautiful, but not like her mother had been beautiful. Pansy frowned, realising she had used the past tense, yet her mother still retained beauty, it was still there and perhaps it would always be there, even when she was old and time had done its work. People would look and know, somehow, that she had been beautiful once.

But I am not like her, Pansy thought. I wasn't even given her white-blonde hair; I am dark like Daddy and pretty would be stretching it a bit. Cute, Frank had called her. Sweet. She didn't want to be sweet.

Eve was dark, too, but sensual and somehow earthy despite her outward cool; it came off her in waves and men shot greedy glances at her when she walked by. Did she know? She must, surely, it would be difficult not to know that about oneself, wouldn't it? Pansy had no idea.

She blinked and refocused on her mother, but she was no longer standing at the end of the jetty, she was in the water, her blonde head the only part of her body visible now.

Was this another attention-grabbing exercise? With a sinking heart, Pansy began pulling on a pair of jeans; she'd better go down and make sure her mother wasn't intent on something more profound than mere skinnydipping.

She glanced again out of the window and felt a flicker of unease. The darkness was different beyond the perimeter of the house, deeper. Pansy found her eyes tracing the trees which hugged the bank, their shadows black without shading, and only the light from the moon relieving the darkness in spooky half-tones as it glanced off the face of the water.

Like mystical symbols in an old book of magic.

Two

There was light suddenly, harsh beams from lamps and torches blanching the trees and undergrowth white – and people, of course, as if they had just been conjured out of the night air. Eve saw them running towards her, felt a dangerous giddiness as she looked back at the place where Minty had disappeared.

'Where?' It was Andrew. His voice sounded oddly calm, but she sensed the fear and urgency pulsing beneath.

She pointed. 'The far side, where the trees meet over the water.' She heard him swear, then he was running back along the jetty, pushing carelessly through the long grass and for a moment the dark swallowed him, but then he reappeared armed with a torch, Pansy beside him. How had she got there? How had she known?

'Here?' He yelled at Eve across the water and she nodded, calling back at him in a voice that did not sound like her own, as if it came from someone else, not her at all.

He was pulling off his clothes, wading through the rim of reeds and into the water. He seemed to pause and she thought he looked back at her for an instant before he plunged downwards.

There would be no light in that still, dark underworld. There would only be blackness and the caress of the weeds as they raked his skin – oh, and the mud, of course. He must be careful of the mud.

He came up, thrashing for air and as he went under again, Pansy threw herself in. So much love for Minty. Or was it duty? Except duty wasn't frantic like this; there was no panic, no grief in duty. Eve's face crumpled just perceptibly because she belonged to no part of it.

Someone was shouting about a rope, or was it a boat? And she was doing nothing. She turned and ran; they would need an ambulance, wouldn't they? A doctor at least. And blankets because the water was so impossibly cold. Deathly even. She knew that, more than anyone, and the thought made her cringe inside herself.

The telephone was sitting in the hallway and as she reached for the receiver she froze; there was something, someone in the sitting-room.

Her bare feet made no sound on the flagstones as she approached the doorway and she breathed a heady sigh of relief because she needed to go no further to discover the origin of the noise that had so startled her. Tony was leaning with his back against the fireplace, trousers around his ankles, and the girl from the garden knelt, half-naked, before him.

As if Tony were some horny old god from a time long past, but gods don't grunt and groan and make strange noises of lust.

Moonlight was falling through the window on to his tanned face, turning it an unappetising yellow, his features pulled into an odd grimace, stretched and taut as if the skin might break.

He looked old somehow, an old man.

Eve padded quietly back to the telephone and picked up the receiver and when it was necessary for her to speak she did so loudly and then glanced behind her into the sitting-room. Tony was frantically pushing his shirt back into his trousers and the girl was busy hoisting the upper part of her dress over her exposed breasts.

And was it good? Eve wondered abstractedly – sucking Tony's worn-out and well-used penis? If the impossible had happened and the sun had come out just then, it would have invaded that room of so many memories with its flawless light and shamed them both.

Just as it had shamed her once.

She put a hand up to her face and covered her eyes.

'Eve!' It was Pansy, standing wet and dishevelled on the doorstep. 'Have you called an ambulance?'

'Yes – of course.'

'Thank God.'

'You found her?'

'Yes.' Pansy slumped down on to the stairs. 'Oh, yes. She even has a pulse. Can you believe that? I was so sure she'd . . . I thought, this time, this time she'd really done it.'

When her father had dragged his ex-wife from under the water he had lifted her up and out with pathetic ease. He had pulled her mouth open with his fingers and jerked her head back before putting his own mouth over hers, forcing air into her lungs, pumped her chest with his hands – waited – pumped again. Suddenly her limbs had spasmed and water, the colour of mud, began spurting from her mouth in violent bursts.

'It's probably something to do with the temperature.'

'What do you mean?'

'Of the water, it's so cold – the theory is that it slows things down, preserves them if you like.'

'For how long?'

Eve regarded Pansy steadily, found herself not wanting to think about it. 'I don't know,' she shrugged, 'a relatively short time, I suppose.'

'Yes,' Pansy said vaguely. 'I think I've read about it somewhere.'

'They'll need blankets,' Eve said abruptly and lifted the lid of a large wooden chest which sat in the hallway and took out several car rugs. 'I'll drop them down.'

'No,' Pansy stood up. 'I will.'

'You're wet through.'

'I want to.'

'Put one around your shoulders, then, and I'll put some coffee on. For everyone.'

'Good idea.' Pansy gave her a wan smile and turned back to the garden.

Eve followed her with her eyes and thought of the offer of coffee she had made to Minty. Half an hour ago? Wondered what had been in her mind when she had slipped into the water and said those odd, disconcerting things.

That nonsense about a man.

She walked slowly down the narrow passage to the kitchen where a light was burning and the kettle already boiling quietly away, in fact a cloud of steam was rising into the air. Eve stood very still. Had she, in the chaos and confusion, put the water on earlier? Had she?

Or Pansy perhaps?

She would ask her when she returned, just to be sure. Yet there was timid puzzlement about her eyes as she watched the shining chrome kettle do its work, a reminder of something.

'Are you okay?'

'God,' Eve exclaimed. 'You made me jump.'

'Sorry,' Pansy said and by way of explanation – 'I ran all the way . . . but you were standing so still, I wondered . . .'

'Must be my nerves.' Eve moved over to the boiling kettle. 'How's Minty?'

'Not conscious and she looks awful, but Daddy gave me a wink, so maybe it's not as bad as it seems.' But he would do that anyway, just to protect her, even if her mother had been dying.

'The ambulance should be here soon.'

'I hope so.' Pansy sagged on one of the breakfast stools.

Eve brought some mugs down from a cupboard and placed them on a tray. 'You didn't put the kettle on before you took the blankets, did you?' She had her back to Pansy, so the girl couldn't read her expression.

'No. I thought you were going to do that.'

'Doesn't matter,' Eve said quickly, 'I must be going mad.'

'Well,' Pansy said with a big sigh, 'it's been a weird sort of evening and not much of a way to celebrate your birthday.'

'It really doesn't matter. Honestly.' And it wasn't important to her, birthdays never had been. Her parents had never made a fuss; there had never been any secret surprises, or fantastic birthday cakes sculpted into the shape of teddy bears, dinosaurs or Peter Rabbits.

Not even for James.

She found herself gripping the large enamel sink with both hands, felt a little sick.

'Birthdays should be special.' Pansy's voice ran on behind her. 'After all, we're really celebrating the fact that we actually exist.'

Eve took a deep breath to steady herself. 'Why don't you go and take off those wet things?'

'Yes. I suppose I should.' But Pansy didn't move, she fell silent and watched Eve pour scalding water into the waiting mugs, her thoughts inevitably switching to her mother. 'Why does she do these things, Eve?' she said abruptly. 'I mean, what does she think she'll achieve?'

Eve turned and looked at her stepdaughter. Pansy was very pale, there was a dull half-questioning look on her face. She seemed very young just then, much less than twenty. 'I don't think she knows. I don't think she thinks at all.'

'It's so selfish,' Pansy said and so softly she could barely be heard, 'and she'll do it one day, won't she? Kill herself, I mean . . .'

'Your mother has nine lives, or haven't you noticed?' Eve smiled and came and stood beside her, put an arm around her shoulders. 'She'd been drinking; it was stupid to go for a swim.'

'You were there,' Pansy said helplessly. 'What did she do? What did she say?'

'Just that she wanted a swim.' Eve lied as a vision of Minty's face in the water took shape, that plaintive searching of eyes asking her to listen to some sound, some call in the dark. 'Not much more than that, really.'

'She must be terribly unhappy.'

'I don't know, Pansy.' In truth, Minty had seemed more strange than unhappy.

'She needs help, of course,' Pansy wiped her eyes with the back of her hand, 'Daddy and I should have done more.'

'You couldn't do more than you have. In the end the responsibility for your mother's life lies with her.'

Pansy shook her head, then shot a glance in the direction of the doorway. Tony was standing there, he swayed a little, a piece of shirt was sticking through a small opening left in his almost-zippered flies. He attempted a grin, but his mouth only wavered unconvincingly as if it computed, before his mind did, the startled, unlaughing expressions staring back at him.

'Something up?'

If the circumstances had been different, Eve might have laughed at his unfortunate choice of words.

'Only the fact that Mum nearly drowned,' Pansy said accusingly.

'Mum?' he repeated stupidly.

'MY MOTHER – you insensitive shit.' Pansy's hands balled into fists. 'Oh, of course, I forgot – you're not only insensitive, but senile as well.'

'Pardon?'

'Just looking at you makes my stomach turn.'

'Hey,' he began, 'steady on.'

'Well,' Pansy spat, 'where were you?' She scrutinised him sharply: his shirt was partially undone and his tie was hanging loosely around his naked neck; his surprisingly thick hair was a mess, it gleamed wetly with gel and in places stood up in tufts; and he was shoeless; there was still that hapless piece of shirt poking slyly through his fly-zip like a flag. 'I'm here', it seemed to say, 'brains and all'.

Tony frowned in confusion, still unable to comprehend what Pansy was saying.

'What does she see in you? What would any woman see in you?' Pansy's unsparing attack continued.

'Look . . .' he began hopelessly, 'perhaps you could tell me . . . ?'

'You're a seedy, disgusting, dirty old man.'

'There's no need for that sort of talk.'

'Just stay away from my mother.'

'Where is she, by the way?'

Pansy gaped, felt outrage boil up inside. 'I don't believe this. I really, really don't . . .'

'I think you'd better go, Tony,' Eve said.

'Why?' he protested. 'Christ. I know she's never liked me, but there's no need for this.'

'I'll call you a cab.'

His mouth fell open, he was sobering up fast. 'At this time of night? Do you think any self-respecting cab driver's going to drive all the way out here? In the middle-of-bloody-nowhere?'

'Why don't you walk then.' Pansy said coldly. 'The fresh air might clear your addled brain.'

'Well,' he said with an attempt at humour, at least you admit I have one.'

Eve raised her eyes heavenward and placed a restraining hand on Pansy's arm.

Pansy turned suddenly and ran to the window; the blue flickering light of an ambulance was heralding its passage up the gravelled drive. 'It's here. Thank God.' She pushed past Tony as if he no longer existed, and Eve only hesitated for an instant before following her stepdaughter out into the grounds.

'What's here?' Tony asked no one in particular.

And no one answered.

God. How he hated hospitals.

Andrew gazed wearily up at the white polystyrene tiles of the ceiling and wondered how Eve's carefully planned birthday party had come to this. It was down to Minty, of course. Once he knew she was intent on coming, he should have realised that she would manage to wreck what should have been a beautiful evening. Wasn't it something to do with jealousy and her resentment of Eve? Except that was just an excuse.

Minty had learned nothing from their disastrous marriage and had learned nothing since and, he supposed helplessly, she would go on learning nothing until in another irrational moment she actually would manage to snuff out her sad little life.

And a part of him wished she would. Oh, yes. If he was honest. Andrew closed his eyes.

'Coffee, Daddy?'

He shook his head, then looked up at his daughter. Pansy was standing over him, that sweet, concerned expression on her face. Sometimes she had a look of Minty about her, lovely even, and he wasn't sure he liked that.

'You could go back to Fulham, if you wanted.'

'And leave you?' she protested. 'And what about Jack? No. I'll go back with you.'

'There's nothing you can do here. I'm only staying until they get her up to the ward. Your mother's in no danger, you know that. As to Jack, Eve's perfectly capable of taking care of her own son until tomorrow.' Even if she doesn't want to. He winced inwardly because that wasn't quite fair – a bit below the belt that one, Andrew. He flushed and rubbed his face with his hands to conceal his discomfort.

'I know. I just don't like leaving you on your own.'

'I'll leave as soon as I can.'

'Are you driving back to Marlow?'

'Eve's on her own.'

'You're exhausted.'

'I'll take it easy.' He smiled tiredly. 'And that's a promise.'

'What time will you be back in Fulham?'

He shrugged. 'Mid-afternoon probably,' then looked up at her and said very firmly, 'so we'll see you then.'

'If you say so.'

'I do say so,' Andrew grinned. 'You'd better take my house-keys.'

'Thanks, Daddy.'

'And some money.'

It was her turn to grin and she leaned down and kissed him.

'See you tomorrow.'

'Your clothes are still damp.'

She shook her head as if he were a simpleton. 'So are yours.'

Pansy had not yet decided whether she liked Soho or not. Frank had once remarked that you can only 'love or hate her, there is no in between'. Even at three in the morning flashing neon proclaimed clubs and peep shows, men and women negotiated in doorways, and shop windows were still lit and illuminating their displays of tortured underwear.

And when she walked into TJ's Frank would be wearing a variation of one of them, except his underwear was usually covered with sequins and frills and lace, and there would be plumes and feather boas to add to the girly illusion. The attention to detail was almost touching. Like the other 'girls', Frank's chest would be shaved – just down to nipple level – eyebrows plucked, false talon-like nails glued on, rude bits tucked neatly up and away, and finally enough layers of make-up applied to cover any trace of giveaway beard.

Oh, but Frank would be beautiful. A little large maybe (he was six foot two), but nevertheless beautiful, as if that might take the sting out of the humiliation. And he had a voice, too – big and mellow and syrupy that could make your mouth fall open. He could also play the piano, and the sax and the trumpet and the clarinet, but at TJ's he was only a token black 'girl' in a pack of drag artists, and on nights like this he was called Sugarcane.

Sugarcane. She didn't know whether to laugh or cry. Sometimes she didn't even know what she was doing here, and tonight he wasn't expecting her and she was almost afraid to search his eyes out and see that look which told her he wished she hadn't come.

He was wearing a cat's mask of black and silver, a matching silver bra and G-string and thigh-length silver boots; nothing more, apart from a black furry tail hanging down the back that he pulled through his legs and rubbed suggestively up and down in time with the music.

Her father would be appalled, most fathers would, Pansy supposed bleakly, but he would understand, surely, that in this business working sometimes meant swallowing more than just a little pride. Frank called it 'eating shit', but she hadn't yet found the courage and sometimes she wondered if she ever would. She wasn't tough enough, of course, not the stuff hard-nosed ambitious actresses were supposed to be made of.

A cloud of smoke wafted into her eyes and she blinked through the haze, the routine had ended and the stage was momentarily empty until Milly's 'My Boy Lollipop' heralded the 'girls' ' return, their faces peeping through a halo of pink paper petals and the audience ooohing and aaahing, roused to hysteria by any innuendo of action or word or rampant wriggle of the hips.

But the pink petals' routine was almost the last. It was just as well, because Pansy wasn't sure how much longer she could remain standing without falling over with exhaustion. Her tired eyes flitted disinterestedly over the packed room; getting a seat was out of the question. She turned round and began making her way out into the glare of the foyer and pay-desk. From there she would take the door leading to the dressing-rooms, and no one would stop her, they knew her by now.

Once there, she took refuge in the shadows of an alcove, sank to the floor and hugged her knees, waiting for the final curtain, the encore and the elephant thumps of the troupe's feet as they left the stage. When they eventually swept down the narrow passage, not one noticed her, not even Frank, he was too preoccupied removing his head-dress, pulling a blond wig and top-hat from his head with a gesture of impatience, wiping sweat from beneath his beautiful, slightly slanting, brown eyes.

His mother was a black American, half Red-Indian, and it showed strongly in her son. He liked that, it made him different, even if he didn't much like his mother; something else he wouldn't talk about.

Pansy sat resignedly in the grey alcove waiting for him to appear. Don't be cross, she pleaded silently, don't put me down with that look you have.

But Frank only sighed, and he wasn't cross, he didn't even seem very surprised.

'You can tell me about it when we get back to my place.'

And she did. After he had undressed her, thrown her damp clothes in the drier and climbed into bed beside her with two coffees spiked with duty-free whisky. She had spoken slowly, stumbling here and there as her story unfolded. His warmth against her dragged up her loneliness so that she cried in front of him, something she had never done before. A first, and how ironic that it should be because of her wayward mother.

'At least she feels,' he said at last.

'What do you mean?' She was lying with one leg draped across him, her head nestling beneath his jaw.

'She feels that her life is useless, purposeless – she cares too much, if you like, or in the wrong way.' He paused. 'But she feels all the same.'

'But it's so extreme, so destructive and it's always been like that,' Pansy said despairingly. 'Drink. Drugs. Nothing's changed. Once she threw herself out of a window and broke both her legs.'

'Maybe she thought she could fly.'

'It's not funny.'

'I wasn't trying to be funny.'

'Sometimes I feel that our roles have been reversed in a weird sort of way – you know, like she's the child and I'm the mother.'

'I hardly knew who my mother was until I was about five.'

'Why?' Even in the dark she raised her head to look into his face as if she might see something she could read or understand.

'I had nannies, childminders or whatever you want to call them, one after the other. She could afford it, she was doing really well as an attorney. Still is.'

'What about your father?'

'They divorced when I was nine and he remarried. I see him about once a year, but he has another family now.' And Frank didn't fit in with that pretty picture. His father was almost white and his new wife from a prominent Irish American family; an exotic-looking black son had proved a bit of an embarrassment.

Shrouded by the darkness Frank allowed sadness to creep into his face; in many respects his mother and father were two of a kind. At twenty-eight he had almost become used to the cruelty and indifference he sometimes found in strangers, but he had yet to become hardened against the same treatment from his own parents.

'How come you don't have an accent – American, I mean?'

'My mother wanted me to have a traditional English education – public school and all that.'

'Well, she cared enough to want that for you.'

He said nothing.

'She did though, didn't she?' Pansy persisted.

'You don't understand.'

'Help me to, then.'

'It's late, and I'm tired.'

Pansy stiffened. 'You always close up against me.'

'Pansy,' he sucked in a breath. 'Don't.'

'It's true. When things get personal you just switch off. Unless it suits you to tell me otherwise – like your quaint philosophy on polygamy.'

'Oh, come on . . .'

'You could have told me before we slept together.'

'I didn't plan it that way,' he said gently.

'I mean, why did you wait until—' her voice wavered and she paused helplessly, 'by the time . . .'

He turned to her in the darkness, placed a finger over her lips.

'Stop torturing yourself, will you?' He kissed her lightly, began touching her body with deft, skilful fingers until he felt her tension seeping away.

'Frank?'

'What?'

'Nothing.'

After the sex and the loving she lay still, eyes open and staring into the night-time shadows, long after their talk had ceased and his breathing had evened out into sleep.

The Chinese lanterns had gone out one by one and now the lawn and the lake were almost indistinguishable in the darkness because the moon had gone, blanked out by a mass of cloud so there was little light, except from the house – and that only feeble.

Eve was drinking another coffee, sitting at the breakfast bar and looking out through the closed window, but after a time she got up and pulled the Venetian blinds shut, unable to bear the black unblinking stare of the glass any longer. She would have wished the skylight away, too; it was a vulnerable spot positioned directly over her head. What did she expect? A ghoul to emerge out of the night and press its face up against the glass, or the *tap-tap* of a skeletal hand at the window-pane?

A long time ago she had waited in this house, in her room upstairs, for a *tap-tap* on her door, and when it had come – and gone (not too soon, oh, no) – she had flung back the bedclothes and sat up with staring eyes and listening ears and keen nostrils, dreading and desiring and doubting.

A long time ago.

Her eyes narrowed and she remained transfixed for a few moments until her body relaxed and she brought one cold hand up against her aching forehead as her mind stole away from the memory. She started as the sound of Tony's snoring broke into her consciousness. He was lying on a sofa in the sitting-room and she realised that she was glad he had been forced to stay, glad that she was not alone in the house. Everyone seemed to leave so quickly once the ambulance had come and gone; she had only rediscovered Tony later and hadn't had the heart or the will to get rid of him.

Automatically her gaze drifted to the ceiling. Jack had not so much as murmured, but she would go up and see him, stand by his cot and look down on his little sleeping form. It was amazing that he had slept through all the chaos and more than fortuitous that he had not awoken at the wrong moment – which would have made matters so much more complicated. In her solitude she flushed with shame, still unable to come to terms with the unease she felt when holding her own child. And on those few occasions when she did take him in her arms, most times he would cry as if he knew better than she did.

Pansy, on the other hand, seemed to exude just the right amount of security and love that Jack required; but now she had her own troubles to contend with, her mother had seen to that.

Eve reluctantly played back that last scene on the lawn in her mind. Pansy had broken down again as Minty was laid, ever so gently, onto a stretcher. Andrew had reached out to comfort his daughter and in his haste had missed his footing, falling flat on his anxious face. His ex-wife, of course, had been oblivious to the mayhem she had caused and would, no doubt, go on causing.

There was that incongruous image of Minty's false eyelashes which had still been partially stuck to her eyelids, bobbing and quivering blackly like two curious insects as her body was lifted into the ambulance. And her jewellery – dull slabs of metal clinging to her wrists and neck, as if verdigris had already put paid to their lustre.

Eve walked out of the kitchen and down the narrow flagged passage to the hallway and paused on the threshold of the sitting-room to watch Tony as he slept. He was splayed across the sofa: mouth open, blankets kicked off revealing spindly brown legs and azure blue Y-Fronts. She closed her eyes for an instant, then climbed the stairs to Jack's room and watched him in much the same impassive way as she had done her guest.

And Tony had been a baby once, she thought abstractedly, a sweet innocent little thing like Jack, clean and soft and peachy, smelling of talc and warm milk. What happens to us as we grow up? What happens as we travel towards that distant, mysterious land called adulthood; what joys, fears, pains and distortions of truth and reality are endured and absorbed to make us what we are?

Eve stared sightlessly into space. What had happened to her?

She shook her head, shifted her eyes wearily to her shoes which were still lying beside the cot where she had left them hours earlier, when she had stood at the window and seen Minty at the end of the jetty like something plucked out of a dream.

And Minty had said that there was a man in the water.

The wooden landing stage was barely visible now, swallowed up by a depth of blackness that is found only in the country, never in towns or cities.

But Minty had been drunk, out of her head, and the dark can play tricks and shadows take on lives of their own.

She, Eve, really had known a man there – not Andrew, Andrew came later – but in that other time when she had been swamped by the subtle caress of seduction. She had lain with the other one in the long grass and in the lake and in the special place. Let him do terrible things to her.

In secret: the secret lovers. No one had ever found out.

Her face crumpled in puzzlement and she could feel her heart thudding too fast, too hard, as if in shock.

Had she?

The sound of a vehicle in the driveway made her turn and she saw the headlights of Andrew's car weave carefully around the side of the house. She swallowed slowly, deep in her throat, because there was a kind of sick excitement building up inside and she realised that she wanted her husband very much.

No. She wanted a man.

He was standing in the hall as she came down the stairs, shoulders drooping, staring through the study doorway at the prostrate Tony.

'If it was yesterday, or tomorrow,' he began tiredly, 'I would probably say that he's pathetic, but right now, I'm simply jealous that he's asleep and I'm not.'

Eve was standing very still, just looking at her husband and playing with a twist of her hair, the expression on her pale face flat and unreadable.

'Are you all right?'

She made no answer.

'Eve?' He took a step towards her and the movement seemed to snap her out of her thoughts and she blinked and smiled, all at once.

'Sorry,' she said. 'I was miles away.'

'On another planet would be nearer the mark.'

'How's Minty?'

'Not conscious, but they think she'll be okay.' He placed his hands on her shoulders. 'I told Pansy to go back to Fulham; it seemed the logical thing to do.'

Eve nodded.

'You don't mind?'

She shook her head. 'Let me make you a coffee.'

'No, thanks. All I want to do is sleep.'

'Sleep,' she said dully. 'Of course.'

His eyebrows came together in a deep frown. 'What is it?'

She thought how exhausted he looked and that she must be going a little crazy to expect sex from him now. Maybe her hormones were doing a few rollercoasters; or maybe it was simply being here, in this house.

She shook her head, 'Nothing,' rubbed her temples. 'Go to bed.'

'Aren't you coming too?'

'Well, yes.' She was smiling, almost regretfully, 'I'll be up in a bit . . .'

'It's gone four in the morning, Eve.'

'I'm okay.' She looked in the direction of the kitchen. 'I want a hot drink. That's all.'

He looked at her doubtfully. He was missing something, he knew he was, but he was simply too tired to argue, so he kissed her lightly on the lips before ascending the stairs. Eve waited at the bottom as Andrew climbed them, one hand on the bannister as if she might change her mind and follow him instead of listening to his footsteps fade and die as he made his way to their room. She turned then and switched her attention to the sitting-room and Tony's body, walked into the room and stood over him, scrutinising him sharply, except there was more than mere scrutiny in her unremitting gaze, there was speculation.

Like an empty shell with something working through.

Eve stood there a long time until the sound of a bird broke the moment; it began piping its song, the same note over and over as dawn crept across the sky. A breeze skimmed the surface of the lake, travelled up the lawn to slip sinuously under the door and through the cracks in the old wood, causing her to shiver.

She shifted her gaze to the window and the lake beyond, walked back into the hall and then outside, down to the water's edge. Darkness was stealing away, the colours and features of the landscape were lightening now to black-greens, black-browns, black-greys and a mist was ghosting up from the lake, turning the rim of the water milky-white.

She knelt down and looked expectantly into its lonely depths, her face transported, seeking, touched by some fleeting moment of comprehension, but there was nothing to be seen there except her own reflection mirrored in the water.

* * *

'Christ. I feel awful.'

Andrew swung round and stared at the wavering figure in the doorway. Tony did, indeed, look awful.

'Bacon and eggs?' he offered. 'Muesli?'

'God. No.' Tony staggered over to the breakfast bar and hoisted himself up on to one of the stools. 'I don't suppose you'd have anything resembling some health-salts – would you?'

'No idea, actually, but I can look.' Numerous cupboards were opened and closed and each slam seemed to pierce Tony's fragile skull like a pistol shot.

'Panadol, paracetamol, gripe water, TCP, milk of magnesia,' Andrew turned and found himself grinning, 'but unfortunately no health-salts.'

'Your sympathy is overwhelming,' Tony said flatly, fishing into one of his pockets for a half-crushed pack of cigarettes, pulling a gold lighter from the other. 'I'd like a coffee if that's not too much trouble.'

'Black?'

'Please.' He lit up one of the cigarettes and found his mind turning uncharacteristically to the previous evening, but it all seemed blurred and strangely unreal. Minty had disappeared after giving him a mouthful of abuse and then he had picked up that obligingly lewd girl, no, correction, she had picked him up. He realised that he could hardly remember her face, that in fact it was only her tongue which provoked recall: a wriggling, slithering, serpent-like thing which had succeeded in making his penis actually ache. That had never happened to him before. So much for innocence; she'd probably been around the block more times than he had.

'You don't really expect my sympathy, do you?'

Andrew's voice cut into his thoughts as he pushed a mug of coffee across the worksurface towards him. A tremulous ring of smoke emerged from Tony's mouth and floated to the ceiling.

'Why not?'

'For God's sake, Tony,' Andrew said impatiently, 'you were half out of your brains before you even arrived last night.'

'So?'

'So don't expect any sympathy from me.'

'So was your ex-wife.'

'Exactly. And look what happened.'

Tony looked blank. 'What did happen?'

Andrew gaped. 'You mean you don't know?'

Tony had the grace to blush, it showed even beneath his fake tan. He shrugged. 'Know what?'

'Minty nearly drowned.'

'Christ,' he said, raising his eyebrows and taking another deep drag on his cigarette. 'I must have fallen asleep. Is she all right?'

'I wondered when you were going to ask that.'

'But how?' Tony screwed his face up in perplexity. 'Where?'

'In the bloody lake, you cretin.'

'Okay, okay.' He held up a hand in mock-defence. 'But just cool it, will you?' A foggy image of Pansy's furious face formed in his head. 'I've already been abused by one member of your glorious family in the space of twenty-four hours – no two, if you count Minty. I don't need any more, thank you very much.' At least he knew why now, at least as far as Little Weed was concerned. Pansy was always Little Weed to Tony, always popping up when she wasn't wanted.

'Surprise, surprise.'

'What was she doing in the lake in the first place?'

'Going for a swim, apparently.'

'Silly bitch,' Tony muttered, shaking his head and rolling his eyes. 'Why the hell can't she settle for a drink and a smoke like everyone else.'

'Depends what you're intent on smoking, I suppose.' Andrew looked darkly at Tony. 'And what had she had? Or, more to the point – what had you given her?'

'Don't pull that one on me. Minty's hardly unworldly, she's a grown woman in case you hadn't noticed – and I can't tell her what to do. If she wants some of my stuff, I let her have it because (a) she'd get it from someone else if I didn't and (b) I can't stand the hassle.'

The last time he had made a half-hearted attempt at standing up to her she had taken her rage out on his precious wardrobe of clothes, throwing everything out of the window. The little cobbled courtyard outside his mews had been strewn with Lanvin shirts and silk underpants. One of his ties still hung limply from the topmost branch of a neighbour's plum tree; it seemed to wave spitefully at him every time he left the house, a horrible reminder of Minty's dark side. As if he needed one.

'Coke?'

'No, thanks.'

'I don't mean the bloody drink, you idiot, I mean cocaine. Did you give her any?'

40

Tony looked back at him warily.

'Some.'

'You mad shit. Letting her have that on top of everything else.'

'Oh, come on, Andrew. You lived with the woman, you know what she's like.' Tony stabbed out his cigarette in a nearby plant-pot, lit up another. 'She's bloody dangerous when she's had a couple.' Well, verbally, anyway. 'Sometimes I wouldn't even like to guess what's going on in her head.'

'Or what's going on in yours.'

'Actually,' Tony began dreamily, ignoring the implied barb, 'most of the time I'm making up extraordinarily amusing conversations, particularly between pompous, tight-arsed establishment types – you know, the boorish sort just waiting to be sent up. Sometimes it's so bloody hilarious that I burst out laughing.' He chortled and shook his head with mirth. 'People think I'm crazy.'

'That's not what I meant.'

'Really? How very silly of me.' Tony tried to look mystified. 'What did you mean, then?' He whined in parody and then pulled a face. 'Isn't that the response you wanted? I knew you'd tell me anyway, so I thought I'd save my breath.'

'How perceptive of you.'

'Been listening to gossip again, I suppose.'

'I don't have to. We worked for the same agency, remember? We even went to the same parties in the early days, we even shared a flat for a while. I know what you like to get up to.'

Tony regarded him steadily. 'We all have our own little preferences.'

'That must be the understatement of the year.'

'What the hell have you heard now? Look. I do what I do, but I don't force anything on anyone. I never hurt in the real sense of the word . . .' he shifted in his seat, 'Christ – I get bored, Andy – I am bored. I've been bored all my bloody life.'

'Am I supposed to feel sorry for you? You sound like a five-year-old.'

'This is all about Minty, isn't it? Otherwise you wouldn't bother with the lecture. Makes you a bit of a hypocrite, doesn't it?'

'So, I'm a hypocrite,' Andrew offered resignedly. And he was, because he had become used to Tony's less attractive habits a long time ago until Minty. Divorce failed to sever all the ties; he was still protective of her, even if he didn't want to be.

'Maybe if Claudia hadn't died . . .'

'Oh, give me a break – you were cheating on her well before the accident – cheating on each other if I remember correctly,' Andrew scoffed, exasperated at the way so many people, and not just Tony, could delude themselves quite happily when they felt like it. 'Then you inherited all her money which gave you an excuse not to work so hard . . .' He had spent most of his time languishing on so-called business lunches, long boozey things at the RAC Club or L'Escargot where he notched-up enormous expense accounts, ' . . . which gave the agency an excuse to give you the boot – with another fat cheque in your back pocket.'

'You can be very hard, Andy,' Tony said with thinly disguised sarcasm. He was trying not to smirk, like a little boy who has been caught turning the pages of a forbidden book.

'Bullshit.'

'But I do care about Minty.'

'Do you? I doubt it.'

'She makes me laugh.'

'And?'

'She's still an attractive woman.'

'Is that why you ended up with someone half your age last night?'

'Christ. You're becoming so self-righteous, Andy. It would make me puke, if it wasn't so tedious.' But, in truth, he was beginning to find youth a little tiresome. How could you possibly hope to find Nirvana with someone who'd never heard of Brian Jones? Yet he let the illusion drag on; it gave him an image and kept Minty on her toes.

Not forgetting the sex thing. Or lack of it. No way was he going to let on that he was finding it almost impossible to get, or keep, an erection these days. He really didn't want to think about that any more than he had to. It was the coke, probably, the late nights and the booze. He was burning himself up. More to the point, he was getting desperate.

His eyes strayed to his designer jacket. It was crumpled and the shoulders dusted with sand-sized specks of white. Dandruff. Christ, he was falling apart. He shot an envious glance at Andrew who was breaking an egg into a frying pan. Non-stick, no doubt. No dandruff either.

'And how's the pulchritudinous Eve?'

'Fine.'

'Still sleeping off last night, I suppose?'

'So would you be if you'd been up until dawn worrying about your husband's ex-wife.' He placed two strips of bacon under the grill. 'And it was her birthday party. Remember?'

'Minty certainly chooses her moments.'

'You could say that.'

Tony had a sneaking suspicion that Minty had planned to mess up the party somehow, perhaps not in quite the way it had turned out, but she'd managed pretty well all the same.

She would never admit it, of course. It was enough for him to know that she was intensely jealous of Eve, which was understandable he supposed, normal even; women were like that, but she was also deeply curious about her ex-husband's new wife and that puzzled him. What was there to be curious about? He watched Andrew potter at the stove as he smoked and finished his coffee. 'Minty said Eve had been depressed.'

Andrew stiffened just perceptibly and Tony sat up, interested despite himself. He had always wondered how someone as unforthcoming as Andrew had managed to hook a woman like lovely Eve. Okay, so she'd been his secretary, but a lot of crap was talked about bosses and their secretaries; most of the time you got a slapped wrist, or worse (amazingly, they could actually have you for harassment these days, just for patting a well-rounded bum). Besides, Eve had been known as the Ice-Maiden in the agency – off-limits, untouchable, frigid. Yet, Andrew had done it. He was quite a bit older, too, and not even good-looking, not in a real sense – he was, well, pleasantly ordinary, but he did have all his own hair, Tony admitted grudgingly: good teeth, good shoulders . . . Tony sighed. No paunch. And I bet he can still get it up.

'Post-natal stuff. Practically back to her old self now.'

'Her old self?' Tony repeated parrot-fashion, promising himself that he'd lay off the fags and the booze and the coke, pamper all his secret parts, become a vegetarian, go jogging . . . Get back in touch with his body. He visualised this last thought in graphic detail and it had the effect of restoring his flagging sense of humour. Narcissism with bells on.

'Yes.'

'What's that?'

'What's what?'

'Her old self?'

Andrew wheeled round. 'What the hell are you getting at?'

'Aren't we touchy.' Tony drained the last of his coffee and studied Andrew over the rim of his mug. 'Just a question.'

'She's fine, I told you.' Andrew turned back to his egg and his bacon. 'We're fine.'

'How lovely for you both,' Tony responded dryly.

Keeping his back to Tony, Andrew jerked one finger sharply heavenwards.

'Oooh, get you.' Tony belched, but it was the beginning of him knowing that things were not so fine, after all.

Minty opened her eyes.

For a long time she lay staring up at the ceiling and an odd thought came to her that the world held too much light, that the brightness might blind her.

It was a striplight, her confused brain told her as her mind opened and sharpened, something you have seen a thousand times before.

There were tubes protruding from her body, performing all the tasks she should have been able to do for herself. She grimaced when she became uncomfortably aware of the catheter, it skulked beneath the bedclothes and out the other side like a thief. Who had put it there? A trainee who needed the practice? And didn't they gag at the thought of sticking tubes into the uncharted nether regions of some stranger's backside? No, probably not. It merely became an unsavoury chore, routine, like everything else in life. You can get used to anything, given time.

It was hot in the room, a smothering, dehydrating sort of heat that is often found in hospitals. Minty grimaced. After all, she should know, she'd been in and out of them often enough.

A ragged sigh escaped her lips as she tried to think, tried to remember, but the only sensation she could muster was that of a dreamer who has awoken empty-handed, and she didn't like that. Minty's thin fingers began to pluck nervously at the white cotton sheet.

She could recall being in the water, swimming, and then she had gone under. Everything that followed seemed the stuff of illusion or dreaming – even enchantment. Yet there had been something purposeful about it, as if there was an obtuse or symbolic message in the madness of those last beautiful moments.

The water had closed over her head like a shroud and he had kept her there because he had wanted it. And because he had wanted it, she had not struggled; she had accepted his will like a child does an adult who has power over him.

44

Tears blurred Minty's vision. Even in the midst of the pain there had been pleasure.

I would die for you, pleasure. All she would ever want in this life.

They should have left her there, let her sink into that rich black creamy mud. Death amongst the pond weed.

Minty's pale brow buckled into a frown: but he hadn't wanted that. She didn't know how she knew, but she was as certain of this as she was certain that it was Eve he wanted, and not her.

Heartbroken, Minty closed her eyes.

Andrew was halfway out of the car when Pansy opened the door and stepped out of the Fulham house. Behind her stood a man, tall and black and stunning. Andrew froze for an instant, but recovered himself before his shock could become obvious.

'Who's this? he asked with forced jollity.

'Frank, Daddy.' She felt herself blush. 'A friend.' Why on earth did she say that?

'Oh, right.' Andrew held out his hand and Frank took it; they looked back at each other warily.

Eve, Jack in her arms, was watching them from the other side of the car. She smiled conspiratorily at Pansy, but her eyes drifted back to the tall young black man. He was laughing softly now, at some witty small-talk remark Andrew had made, but then he was turning his head, looking across at her and their gazes met.

'This is Eve,' Andrew's voice said from somewhere, 'my wife.'

She nodded in response, caught by the boy's profile. He was proud, she thought, and also dangerously good-looking. All at once she found herself trying to imagine him and Pansy together, in bed, but couldn't, was glad she couldn't and felt herself redden. Quite suddenly she realised that he reminded her of her brother, because he was tall like James, had the same sort of build, and there was something about the voice . . . Her brow wrinkled in puzzlement as old impressions passed and took shape across the screen of her mind. Strange how memory can play tricks.

Sometimes she could almost conjure her brother up, sometimes if she closed her eyes and opened and narrowed them she thought she could see him in the shadows, standing a pace behind her, amongst the trees at the lake house. He had loved the trees, loved to hide and tease and chase. And sometimes he had frightened her.

Eve felt disorientated suddenly, touched by an eerie feeling of *déjà vu.* Nature is cruel, she thought, dark and ruthless and cruel.

'Can I help?'

She blinked and found herself looking into the concerned face of the black boy. Frank.

'No,' she replied abruptly. 'No. Thank you.'

Frank stepped back and let her pass, watched Pansy as she took the baby from her father's wife. The woman had acted as if she were snapping out of some dream, and not a particularly nice one at that. His eyes followed her and she swung round as if she had sensed him looking at her and smiled a little. It was an apology, he realised, for that edge to her voice; she looked lovely when she smiled, different. Pansy's father was holding his hand out to her and she took it and went with him into the house.

Frank swallowed hard and made himself turn to Pansy who was standing there, waiting patiently, blissfully unaware of what had just occurred.

It could be said that Frank was a little in shock and if, at that moment, he had been asked to describe how he was feeling, he would have said that the sensation closely resembled that of being kicked very hard in the stomach.

Three

'This is a part of fatherhood I could do without.'

Eve smiled to herself. Andrew was speaking from the bathroom, in between cleaning his teeth and taking a shower.

'Calm down,' she said, 'he's a boyfriend. That's all.'

'A friend, she said. Some friend.' He finished wiping his face with a towel, half-threw it at the hook on the door, missed and swore.

'What is it, Andrew? You're not jealous, surely?'

'Of course not.' He walked into their bedroom and kicked off his slippers.

Eve watched him for a moment. 'Is it because he's black?'

He sighed heavily. 'I don't know. Maybe.' He shook his head. 'Which makes me a bit of a shit, doesn't it?'

'Pansy would say it's the generation gap showing . . .'

'And she'd probably be right.'

'He is rather gorgeous.'

He glared at her. 'Not you as well?'

She laughed. 'Don't be silly. I'm just admiring her good taste.'

His face buckled into a frown. 'I've never thought of myself as racist.'

'I suppose it's easy to spout platitudes when they don't affect you directly, we're all guilty of that.' She took off her robe. 'Anyway, black or white, you're always ludicrously suspicious of any boyfriend of Pansy's.'

'And probably rightly so.' He thought of Tony, and worse – that gauntlet of temptations and dangers young adults run without really knowing what horror they may finally embrace at the end.

'He's nice, Andrew.'

He paused. 'Yes. I know.'

'Didn't exactly outstay his welcome, either. Did he?'

'No. Which was probably my fault.' He sat down on the edge of the bed with a sigh.

'I don't think Pansy noticed.'

'He did.'

'You can't be sure of that, and even if he did, you can make it up to him next time.' She kissed the back of her husband's neck. 'Can't you?'

'I suppose so,' he said, then flicked his arm impatiently into the air. 'And he's in showbusiness. Do you know what that pathetic word conjures up for me? Seediness and exhibitionism. Why did she have to decide on acting, for heaven's sake, it's full of insecure, egotistical weirdos . . . why couldn't she want to be a barrister or a teacher or a doctor – something normal.'

'Because this is what she wants, what she's always wanted.'

'She's a very bright girl, it seems such a bloody waste.'

'Pansy's only twenty, Andrew, give her time.'

'What a boring old fart I must sound.'

'No.' Eve laughed. 'Just fatherly.'

'Maybe,' he replied unconvincingly.

'Anyway, now that we've been through all that,' Eve began patiently, 'perhaps we can get on to something more pleasant.' With great deliberation she commenced pushing his open pyjama-top down his arms so that it fell away, and then began running her open palms across his bare shoulders very slowly, back and forth, over and over.

'That feels good.'

Eve said nothing, her face impassive and still as she slipped out of her nightdress and pressed bare breasts against his back. Andrew turned his head and looked at her.

'Eve?' he asked softly. 'Do you want to . . . ?'

'Don't look so shocked.'

'I'm not shocked,' he said, 'it's just that . . . well, normally you . . .'

'I know,' she said. 'I know.' Normally she waited for him to make the first move; in fact Eve could hardly remember approaching him to satisfy her own needs and she didn't know why. Perhaps, somehow, she had changed and she hoped that was a good thing.

Andrew caught hold of her wrist, brought her round to face him.

'What is it?' she asked. 'Have I done something wrong?'

'Oh, no,' he said quickly, 'not at all, but I suppose there have been times

48

when I've wondered . . .' he broke off, exquisitely aware of her gaze on him.

She crouched in front of him. 'What?'

He let go of her wrist and lifted his hand to cup her face, let the hand slide into her heavy dark hair. 'Why you married me.'

She stared at him intently. 'You know why.'

He looked back at her without speaking; she had never told him that she loved him and, even now, he couldn't bring himself to ask.

'Andrew?' she pleaded.

'Are you happy?'

'Yes. Of course.'

'Sometimes I've thought that you don't laugh enough.' He smiled sheepishly. 'Sounds silly, doesn't it?'

She said nothing.

'Even when you smile . . .' he continued, 'it seems careful, controlled, as if you're not smiling as much as you could.'

'Stop this,' she said softly and for a few long seconds placed her fingertips over his lips. 'Don't.'

He shook his head. 'I'm a fool, that's all.'

'No.'

'I am,' he said with resignation. 'But nothing I've said makes any difference to the way I feel.' His young and lovely wife would probably never guess what he had felt when she agreed to actually marry him: a terrifying combination of disbelief and vulnerability.

'I care,' she said with a surge of despair. 'I care very much.'

Now it was his turn to place fingertips over her lips. 'I spoke out of turn. Forget it – please.'

She scrutinised him for a long moment, knowing what she should say, but unable to say it; concealment had fallen like a shutter. Instead, and as if in atonement, she began to make love to him just as she had planned.

Yet an expression of bewilderment weaved across her face because it suddenly seemed so very easy, so inexplicably part of her that, for a fleeting second, she was caught by unease and perplexity.

Even as this thought took shape and fled, her soft, seeking fingers were stealing across his skin, pressing and rubbing and caressing, and as each second of her seduction passed Andrew was telling himself that real love can be silent, too, that it does not need words or trite phrases to be heard. It can express itself through touch alone. It didn't matter, his mind ran on, that she still failed to confirm the one thing he needed so badly to know.

He looked into his wife's face. Her eyes were closed in anticipation, the lips slightly parted as if she were suddenly a little breathless. Then she stood up, as if inviting his scrutiny and his eyes roamed down and over the lavish contours of her body: all ovals and hollows and creamy softness, wondered if she could feel his warm breath against her almost-dusky skin, wondered about her. She was like fire or ice – his Eve – there was no in-between.

'I want to spend the rest of my life with you,' he whispered.

But her expression told him that Eve did not hear, she was busy dreaming elsewhere, just as her body was busy with him, and the skill and power she employed was totally new and unexpected. All his fantasies made real.

Andrew shuddered inside.

'Sorbet,' Frank said, uninterested, 'I'll just have sorbet.'

Pansy frowned. 'What flavour?'

'I don't know. You choose.'

She tightened her lips and switched her attention to the menu. 'Lemon, lime, mango?'

'Mango.'

'Are you all right?'

He looked warily back at her. 'Why do you ask?'

'You've been funny ever since we left the house.'

'I'm tired.'

'Didn't you like him?'

Frank smiled dryly. 'Do you think he liked me?'

Pansy blushed. 'Of course. Why shouldn't he?'

He placed both elbows on the table, rested his chin on his hands and looked directly at her. 'Because, my sweet child, I'm this amusing browny-black sort of colour which makes some creamy-white people see red.' He sat up and drained his glass of beer. 'Just in case you hadn't noticed.'

'My father isn't like that.'

'Isn't he?'

'No.'

'You didn't mention how I kept life and limb together, did you?' He laughed unkindly, 'Being "in showbusiness" – and for the record, I hate that phrase – could mean almost anything, but he'd really think you'd lost your marbles if he knew I was a transvestite as well.'

'You're not a transvestite!'

'I know, but he'd think I was.'

'Why? Because you're trying to earn a living in the only way you know how?'

'Pansy,' he said with exaggerated patience, 'he wouldn't see it that way, believe me. Besides –' he continued carelessly, 'I enjoy it, almost the next best thing to straight acting.' He was kidding himself, of course.

'You hardly know him.'

'I've spent my whole life knowing people like him.'

'That's not fair!' Her expression was flat, almost shocked. 'Why are you being so judgmental?'

Frank looked away and Pansy stared at his stony profile, her face a study in misery.

She watched him for a moment before adding, 'He was perfectly nice to you . . . you even seemed to enjoy yourself, and Eve liked you – I could tell.'

He shifted his gaze back to her face. 'Did she?'

'Yes, she did, as a matter of fact.' Pansy regarded him steadily. 'Eve's very good where my boyfriends and Daddy are concerned.'

'I see.'

She stiffened. 'What do you see exactly?'

'Well, right now,' his voice was heavy with sarcasm, 'she's probably busy persuading Daddy what a nice boy I am – even if I am black.' His face clouded over. And how would she do that, pray? Not with great difficulty, not someone like her. He realised, with curious bitterness, that Pansy's stepmother had touched him somehow; he could still see her face, hear her voice, feel that hollow sickness in his stomach.

'What on earth's wrong with you.' Pansy's eyes blazed. 'If anyone's got an attitude problem, it's you.' She had never seen him like this before and it scared her a little.

'And what the hell do you know, Pansy?' he said softly and the softness was filled with scorn. 'I mean, what do you really know?'

She looked back at him with alarm, saw out of the corner of her eye a waiter approach and inwardly gave thanks.

'Do you still want your sorbet?' She jerked her head in the direction of the waiter.

'No. Let's just go.'

'Okay. Fine,' she said tautly and began fishing in her bag for her purse.

'Don't,' he said. 'It's my shout.'

'No, it's mine.'

'Let's not argue about it. Okay? Besides, as I'm being such a shit, I deserve to pay.'

She stood up as he placed the money on the table. 'Why are you being such a shit?'

He sighed with exasperation. 'I don't know,' and looked at her half in apology. 'I really don't.'

The moon was up, hovering over Putney Bridge like a gigantic luminous balloon. They walked a little apart, hardly speaking, but stopped for a moment to peer into the Thames. The tide was in and the water seemed deceptively close; Pansy was instantly reminded of the lake house and her mother's accident. Taking everything into consideration, including this evening, the weekend had been pretty dreadful. Disastrous even.

'What did you mean in the restaurant when you said "what do I really know?" ' He had sounded almost cruel then, she thought, horrible. 'I mean,' she continued with reproach, 'do I understand you so little?'

'I shouldn't have said that.'

'But you did.'

'Pansy – I don't even understand myself.'

She was staring into the water, but she could feel his eyes on her and when she turned to look at him the darkness and the colour of his skin made his face almost invisible.

'You talk to me as if I'm a child – and a very naive one at that.'

He tilted his head back wearily and somehow the action irritated her more than words could have done.

'You don't have to walk me home,' she said abruptly, 'I'm quite capable of getting there by myself.'

'Don't be silly, Pansy.'

'How ironic – you sound just like my father.' She walked away from him, striding out, with angry little movements of shoulders and arms.

'For God's sake . . .'

He followed her from a distance, feeling sick at heart, caught her up at the traffic-lights and grasped her arm.

'What the hell do you think you're doing?'

'Walking home,' she snapped. 'What does it look like?'

'Not like this, Pansy,' he said haltingly.

'Not like what?'

'Like strangers – it's childish, stupid.'

'You started this.' Her eyes accused him. 'I was happy, actually, before you got yourself into this mood, but I don't suppose you even noticed. You might not realise it, but it's not unusual to be happy when you're with someone who matters to you.'

He said nothing.

She stared across the street, her eyes roaming sightlessly up the Fulham Road. 'I get on your nerves, don't I, Frank?'

'No. Of course not.'

'Well,' she said tightly, 'like you said, what do I know?'

'I told you, I shouldn't have said that.'

She began to walk across the road.

'Pansy . . .' He ran after her. 'This is dumb.'

'I want to go home, Frank,' she said quietly, all the anger suddenly gone and in its place only weary resignation. 'I want this horrible weekend over.'

'Look, I'm sorry.'

'It doesn't matter.'

'That's a stupid thing to say.'

'Probably.'

She quickened her pace and he fell into step beside her, glancing, now and then, at her set, carefully arranged face. He sighed inwardly because he liked Pansy, he really did. What was it then that had made him react so badly to that talk of her father? After all, he had often experienced that wary look in the eye, that style of behaviour which was at once polite and completely indifferent, and usually he didn't over-react, usually he ignored it.

'Come back to my place.'

She didn't reply.

'Pansy?'

'No.'

'Why not?'

'I'm not in the mood.' she said sharply, 'just like you've not been in the mood . . .'

'Oh, come on.'

'Why don't you phone one of your other friends – I thought that was what being polygamous was all about.'

He took a deep breath. 'I want you to stay with me tonight.'

'How very kind.' She shook her head and snorted softly with contempt. 'Strictly speaking, polygamy is about more than one partner, but you don't have any partners, Frank, you just use the word as an excuse to sleep around.' She wanted to hurt him, just as he had hurt her, and yet she wondered how it was possible to be so angry with someone and still care for them. Love them, even.

They drew up outside the house.

'Pansy . . .'

'Anyway,' she said quietly, 'we're both tired, aren't we? It would be a waste of time.'

'I wasn't necessarily thinking about sex.'

'Sorry. My mistake.'

He looked back at her in silent frustration, realising that it was useless to argue. 'I'll give you a call tomorrow.'

'If you like.'

'I am sorry, you know,' he said, 'about tonight.'

'Are you?'

'Yes.'

'Goodnight, Frank.'

He watched her walk up the path to the house, fumble for her key before opening the door and closing it behind her. He waited at the gate as the hall light went on and then off, lifted his eyes to the amber half-light evident on the upper floors where her father would be sleeping with his wife, the stepmother. Eve.

Despite the sun that had started the day, it was now a dull afternoon, the sky that white-grey colour which might or might not bring rain. Eve flicked her eyes briefly to the heavens before walking through the automatic doors and into the building.

She didn't want to do this, but she had promised Andrew and so she would go through the motions because of a burdensome and irritating sense of duty. She followed the endless arrows, down the endless corridors before she found herself standing outside the door behind which she would find Minty and for an instant she closed her eyes.

It was bizarre really, she thought, visiting her husband's ex-wife in hospital, a woman who clearly resented her and who only ever seemed capable of leaving chaos in her wake.

She gently tapped on the door and when there was no reply she opened it and gingerly went inside. Minty was lying flat and apparently sleeping. Eve breathed a soft sigh of relief as she approached the bed; perhaps she could escape before Minty awoke, then she could still tell Andrew that she had kept her promise, even if a word had not passed between them.

She placed the basket of fruit she had brought on the bedside table and waited, not wanting to take the armchair because her body would sink into the deep yielding cushions and her face would then be level with Minty's, inches away.

Instead she remained standing, studying the gaunt, closed features with curious fascination. Something had been done to her face, it looked unnatural somehow, odd, and then it dawned on Eve that the cheeks had been brushed with rouge, the mouth touched with lipstick. It seemed so out of place on Minty's waxen skin and beneath an incongruous cap of bandages. In fact, it was impossible to relate the person lying in the bed to the dazzling self-assured one who had come to the party sheathed in designer gold lamé.

It was three days since Minty had slipped into the water, yet it seemed longer, much longer, than that. Eve tried to press down the memory of those minutes by the water, but the images were creeping relentlessly back, especially that last one of Minty jerking herself upwards in that last half-second before . . . What? There was a subtle change in Eve's eyes, something that lingered there momentarily, and for an instant she felt confused and probed reluctantly for the cause, but could find none.

'Hello, Eve.'

The voice made Eve jump, sent a hand up to her throat; Minty's pale eyes were wide open and staring at her.

'Minty.'

'Who did you think it was?'

Eve shook her head. 'You surprised me. That's all.'

'I knew you'd come.'

'Did you . . .' Eve smiled uneasily. 'How do you feel?'

'All right.' She touched her head. 'They've shaved off my hair.'

'It'll grow back.'

'I suppose so.'

'You must have given your head a hell of a bang.'

'I don't remember.' Minty moistened her lips, 'But I do remember being in the water, swimming, and then – nothing.' Except the nothing had been everything.

They looked at each other and then Eve turned away, made herself focus on an innocuous picture hanging on the white hospital wall: poppies in a field of corn. It made her think of the lake house. There had always been one or two poppies growing among and swishing in time with the long grass – their big blood-red heads nodding heavily, that black central core a sightless unwelcoming eye.

And the memory made her think of other things, too.

She had to ask.

'Just before you went in you said . . .'

Difficult to get her tongue around the words.

'What?'

' . . . that there was a man in the water.'

'Did I?'

'Yes.'

'I don't remember.'

Eve was still looking at the picture. 'You called across to me.' Screamed.

'Did I?'

'Yes.'

Minty turned her head slowly, her eyes thoughtful and probing. 'You should have come in.'

Eve shook her head.

'It was beautiful,' Minty's voice continued silkily, 'the water – like a caress, only more so.'

'But cold,' Eve murmured vaguely and rubbed at her temples as if a headache was coming on.

'What's the matter?'

'Nothing.'

'You should see yourself, you look worse than I feel.' Minty caught her wrist and stared at her intently. 'What is it? Tell me.'

Eve whipped her head round as if the contact stung. Minty's steady gaze held a fugitive gleam, the seed of conspiracy, and Eve felt her arms gooseflesh. 'I'm all right, Minty,' she said stiffly.

Minty let go and watched her for a moment. 'You don't have a cigarette, I suppose?'

Eve shook her head.

'Christ,' Minty seethed, 'I hate this place.'

'It's hardly forever.' Eve found herself almost unable to look at the woman in the bed; she felt irritated, ill at ease and more than anything, she wanted to go. Escape.

'How's Andrew?' Minty asked with a hint of mockery. 'I must have given him quite a fright – hasn't his dear old ulcer reared its ugly head again in sympathy?'

'Would you really want that for him?' Eve said quietly. 'Would you?'

'Aren't we serious?' Minty retorted dryly. 'But don't worry, it's only my warped sense of humour.' She was amused. 'I always manage to shock you, Eve. Are you really so easily shocked?'

'Must be the boring life I've led.'

Minty regarded her steadily. 'I doubt that, somehow. I don't know why, but I do.'

Eve made no answer.

'I hardly know anything about you, really, do I?' Minty paused, her eyes gleaming with interest. 'I mean, where were you before Andrew? What were you doing?'

'You know what I was doing.'

'I don't just mean secretarial stuff, I mean friends, family – a past?'

'We hardly know each other, Minty – so why should you know anything about me?'

Minty shrugged. 'It just seems odd that I've heard nothing at all; except something about a mother you hardly see, and a brother you never see.'

'Well, you needn't concern yourself about me because there's nothing much to know. Besides, it's really none of your business. Is it?'

Yet sometimes when Eve lay in the dark, shards of memory would force their way out of her subconscious, curious and unsettling fragments rising inexorably into her mind: like pieces of blackened driftwood shooting to the surface of still water and breaking free. There would be that sour taste of doubt in her mouth and her heart would beat and beat, and then finally a question would come before she was allowed to fall into a fitful and wretched sleep, the one which asked what would happen if anyone ever found out.

'Lots of people are not what they seem.' Minty was scrutinising Eve's stony profile. 'Have you ever thought about that? There's the top layer, the one that everyone is allowed to see, and then there are the underneath layers, scores of them, some overlapping, some coupling . . .' She took hold of Eve's unwilling hand and continued dreamily, 'I suppose it's the essence of what we really are. Someone wrote about that once you know: "how strange we grow when we're alone, and how unlike the selves that meet and talk . . ." I forget the rest. It's one of the few things I can recall from my Godawful school days.'

'I shall really have to get back,' Eve said, looking with something close to wonder at the long white fingers wound around her own. Holding hands? Perhaps the accident had affected Minty's brain. 'It's getting late.'

'I hated school. Weren't you a convent girl, too? Didn't you hate being sent away whether you liked it or not?' Minty squeezed her eyes tight shut for an instant. 'All those bloody rules, all that stifling crap about good old Mother Church . . . I seemed to spend half my life on my knees. Repulsive.' She visibly shuddered.

'It wasn't that bad.'

'Yes. It was.'

They fell silent for a moment, before Minty spoke again.

'I came to despise my parents. I was in Amsterdam on a shoot when I heard the news that my father's plane had crashed. I opened a bottle of Krug to celebrate then hired a couple of pretty Indonesian boys to entertain me. My father would have gone berserk if he'd known.' She started to giggle. 'Maybe he did – if you see what I mean – observed me fucking the natives from on high.'

Eve glanced down at her hand which was still held in Minty's grasp and Minty saw, but did nothing. 'His body was unrecognisable apparently, burnt to a crisp.'

Eve closed her eyes for a second and said wearily, 'Do you have to, Minty?'

'What?' Minty frowned, but her lips tilted into a small smile which Eve recoiled from just a bit. 'You have that funny look on your face, like the one you wore before I went into the water – as if I'm crazy or something.'

'God, Minty,' Eve responded in exasperation, 'are you really surprised?'

'You sound like Andrew.'

Eve raised her eyes to heaven.

'Did he send the flowers?' Minty glanced in the direction of the handbasin where an unwrapped bouquet lay.

'No.' Eve stood up and at the same time extricated her hand. She walked across the room and read the card stapled to the glossy cellophane. 'Lilies – from Tony.'

Minty snorted with contempt. 'God. He's an inept bastard,' she said furiously. 'Trust him to get it wrong. Why not a bunch of red roses, for Christ's sake, even pink roses – or orchids? Orchids are lovely. Not lilies, for crying out loud. Aren't they rather funereal?' She glared at the ceiling, wrinkling her nose in disgust. 'I'm sure someone told me once that they foretell death, or bad luck or something equally grim. Perhaps he thinks I'm dead?'

'Oh, give it a rest, Minty.'

Her face crumpled just perceptibly. 'I suppose I have behaved rather badly.'

'Perhaps you feel you had cause.'

'But you don't think that.'

'I don't know what I think,' Eve said. 'It's Pansy you should be concerned about.'

Minty's fingers plucked at the sheet. 'I should never have divorced Andrew.'

Eve winced inwardly. He divorced you.

'I was a fool to let him go,' Minty's voice ran on.

'Minty,' Eve said, wondering at her control, 'don't.'

'Sorry. That was naughty of me.' She sighed heavily, suddenly feeling depressed, there seemed no fun in the game any longer. She was simply being a bitch and the novelty was beginning to wear a bit thin. 'Besides he'd never have me back even if he was free. He doesn't want me any more. I know that.' She sighed again. 'I was such a bloody fool – no, correction – I am a bloody fool.' She turned her face very slowly to the window. 'Tony says I'm a masochist. Of course, he would say that, but he's probably closer to the truth than I care to think about.'

'When you get out, you must take care of yourself.'

'Must I?'

Eve sighed in exasperation. 'Why do you have to make everything such hard work? If you need an excuse, think of Pansy, she's been worried sick about you.'

'Has she?'

There was longing and even disbelief in Minty's voice and Eve felt a surge of pity. She stared at her husband's ex-wife curiously, at the pale slender face, trying to understand the change. 'Of course she has. She's your daughter, Minty, she loves you.'

'The word love is a little over-used these days.'

'Not in this case.'

'No,' Minty said softly. 'Perhaps not.'

Silence fell between them, and much more besides.

'I must go,' Eve said at last.

'Will you come again?'

'I'll try.'

Minty looked back at her and their eyes met. 'Thank you for coming.'

Eve smiled. 'Get well, Minty.'

The woman in the bed smiled haltingly in return, her eyes following the other as she started away, paused to look back again and then opened and closed the door behind her.

The lines on Minty's forehead deepened sharply and she closed her eyes, listening to the fading footsteps and then the silence of the empty room; for a few moments she felt lonely then sick and afraid. She imagined she heard a low grating whisper and instantly her eyes flickered open and she found herself staring at the poppy picture Eve had studied with such peculiar interest. She lay transfixed as her fears began to recede, to be replaced by a remarkable sensation of calm.

The shadows would be lengthening at the lake house, she thought, and the air would be heavy and still. In the purplish light night insects would whir their little wings and later the water would whiten under the stars. Perhaps a wind would pick up and the world there would fill with gusts and floatings and blowings, and gnats would dance in the air.

Atop the white linen sheet, her fists clenched and unclenched in unconscious spasm, knees twitching, her body swept by a hot ripple of sexual desire. Minty's eyes were glassy and unseeing, but her face wore a weasel look, as she switched her gaze to the place where Eve had stood and smiled.

The sky was already darkening by the time Eve left the hospital. She caught a cab and sat crouched in the back, head leaning against the window staring, unseeing, at the people in the street. Her mind was on Minty and what she had said, or rather, failed to say.

Just before her accident she had said there was someone in the water. 'He's here', she had said, no shrieked. Eve's eyebrows drew together in a frown, but Minty had been drunk or high on something, or both. Perhaps it had only been moonshadow, even wishful thinking. Nothing more. Eve hated casting her mind back, picking over and over what had happened as if, like a sniffing animal, she were looking for something. In fact, thinking about it upset her and in a way she couldn't explain.

She asked the driver to drop her off at the gates of Bishop Park, so that she could walk the rest of the way home. It wasn't the view from the river path she was interested in, but the path leading through the churchyard and the church. Eve had avoided it many times – it was not a Catholic church, after all, but it would do now, she needed it to do now. There was something safe about a church, comforting, and she hadn't been inside one for a long time because she thought she had put all that away somewhere. Lost it. Lapsed. Yet you could deny yourself the sacraments for years and years and still only be 'lapsed', as if it was simply an oversight, or the result of mere forgetfulness.

Not many people were truly in disgrace or truly damned. Excommunicate. Not many.

The Roman Church hated losing any of its flock, and because initiation rites of immense solemnity began very young they left an indelible and ineradicable psychological mark. Clever, really, and so very simple.

But this was an Anglican church and empty, yet there were the familiar effigies and statues, and plaques carved in the names of people long-dead. Eve sat at the back in one of the wooden pews, supping up the silence and coolness like a shy child, before looking up at the altar and the stained glass rising above and behind it. A pretty church.

The church attached to her old school had been larger and much more grand than this. The altar had been adorned with silver on white linen, the doors of the tabernacle beaten gold and illuminated by great wax candles, the kneeling pads covered in plush red velvet, and the carved and ornamented wood polished and pampered like a babe. Every alcove had been inhabited by a sainted statue, and in one of the transepts there was a gilded shrine dedicated to the Virgin, her blue-draped head crowned, the pale vacuous face blank and unwavering. One of her delicate porcelain hands, entwined with a rosary, had been raised as if in blessing, yet on dark days Eve had thought the hand was not blessing but warning – of sin, both mortal and venial. Mortal sins, which 'kill' the soul. For an unguarded moment her heart yearned for the dark embrace of a confessional box and the priest's voice.

Gold and wax and light and secrets.

She had once thought that saying 'shit' had been a mortal sin, and confessed as much to a world-weary priest, but it had not been so, of course. Later, she came to discover that there were far worse things to stain one's soul with than mere excrement.

Eve squeezed her eyes tight-shut and sank to her knees, pushing the padded cushion away, felt cold stone come up hard against her flesh. It hurt for a few minutes, but then the pain faded and numbed as memory took over. How long ago? Ten years? No, twelve. Twelve years since school, but things had begun to happen before then, big ugly misshapen things that no longer seemed real.

When Eve eventually stood up the skin of her knees was red and sore, the joints stiff and she sat back in the pew until she felt able to walk normally again, like other people.

'Where on earth have you been?' Andrew asked. 'I've only been in ten minutes myself, I was beginning to get worried.'

Eve smiled with an effort. 'I found Minty a little exhausting, so I took a walk through the park to clear my head.'

'It's nearly eight o'clock.'

'Sorry,' she said. 'I forgot the time.'

'Was she that bad?'

'I was keyed up before I went.' Eve sat down at the kitchen table. 'Silly, really.'

'I shouldn't have made you go.'

'I'm okay, Andrew.'

'Coffee? A drink?'

'A G and T would be lovely.'

'How is she?' He opened the fridge door and pulled out a bottle of gin, and tonic.

'As well as can be expected I suppose.' Eve sighed a little. 'Feeling sorry for herself, I think. She looked awful.'

'Was she civil?'

'Oddly enough, yes.'

'Nearly drowning probably concentrates the mind wonderfully, but Minty's had near misses in the past and it hasn't made an iota of difference in the long-run – she's always seemed set on self-destruction.' Andrew walked across the kitchen, two gins in hand, and sat down beside her. 'I doubt this time anything's changed.'

'I don't know . . .' Eve said quietly .

'She must have been very convincing,' he said, his curiosity aroused.

'Not convincing, exactly.'

'What then?'

'Different.'

'She's just had a knock on the head, Eve, it's hardly surprising.' He sipped at his gin, watching his wife over the rim of his glass. 'And she's sober, remember. Give her time, my love, and she'll return to the old Minty.'

'Am I supposed to be reassured?'

He shook his head. 'I don't know – maybe "better the devil you know"?'

She smiled. 'Perhaps.' She slipped off her shoes. 'I take it Jack's in bed? I meant to be here – Pansy must think me horribly remiss.'

'No she doesn't,' Andrew said. 'Besides, she seems a bit preoccupied. I think she and Frank have had a row.'

'Oh, dear.'

'Ssssh . . . here she comes now.'

Pansy clumped into the kitchen, Doc Martens resounding on the varnished floorboards; she wore black tights, a red leather mini-skirt and a black tee-shirt baring her midriff. Andrew suppressed a smile and then looked into his daughter's mutinous face.

'Hi, Eve,' she said and marched into the kitchen area.

'Hi.' Eve replied. 'Jack all right?'

'Fine.'

'I'm sorry I was so late back.'

'Doesn't matter.' Pansy brought out a can of Coke from the fridge as her father exchanged glances with her stepmother.

'How's Frank?' he ventured.

She shrugged. 'Okay, I suppose.'

'From the look on your face, I would say otherwise.'

'Would you?' she said sullenly.

'Come on – what's up?'

She stared into space and shook her head with barely suppressed frustration. 'He was in such an unbelievably rotten mood yesterday.'

'After you left here?'

She nodded.

Andrew's face reddened. 'That might be something to do with me.'

'You were very nice to him,' Pansy said defensively.

'A little cool perhaps?'

She turned around and looked at her father. 'Were you?'

He nodded.

'Why?'

He said nothing.

'Your father is always touchy about your boyfriends, Pansy.' Eve said, hoping to steer the conversation away to a safer area.

Pansy met her father's eyes. 'Is it because he's black?'

He took a deep breath. 'Well, I suppose I'd be lying if I said no – but it was more of a surprise really.' He looked shame-faced. 'I'm sorry.'

'Frank was right, then.'

'Was he?' Andrew's mouth fell open. 'I never meant . . .'

'I thought you, of all people, Daddy, would at least be fair.'

'I didn't mean . . .'

'No,' she said accusingly. 'I don't suppose you did.'

'Pansy . . .'

'I'll be in my room if you want me.'

'For heaven's sake,' he pleaded as she strode past him, 'can't we discuss this?' But Pansy had gone and Andrew only caught the elephant sound of her Doc Martens as they thumped up the stairs.

'Oh, God,' he exclaimed wearily and cupped his forehead in one hand as a door slammed above his head. 'How do I get out of this one?'

'Give her a few minutes to cool down,' Eve said gently. 'Finish your drink, then go and speak to her.'

'What on earth do I say?' He threw back his head and gazed bleakly heavenwards. 'That I can't help it if I'm racist, it's something to do with my age?'

'You're not racist.'

'Just the armchair variety – is that what you're trying to say?'

'No,' she said patiently. 'But you probably would have reacted the same way if Frank had been Japanese.'

He said nothing.

'Finish your drink,' Eve said again and pushed the glass so that it touched his hand. He began shifting it from side to side with one dejected finger.

'Minty wouldn't have reacted the way I did, you know.' He shook his head, 'That's a brownie point to her.'

'Maybe, but by now Minty would have been halfway to seducing him.'

Andrew gave her a grudging smile and picked up his glass. 'I'd better speak to her now. I can't relax knowing she's up there thinking evil thoughts about me.'

'Go on then. I'll prepare some supper, you must be starving.'

'Just a bit.'

She watched him trudge wearily across the room to the open door and blew him a kiss of encouragement when he turned round, because there was an expression of comical desperation on his face.

'Hope I get back all in one piece . . . daughters can be very emasculating, you know.'

She smiled. 'Don't worry.' But he would, she thought, as he disappeared from view; Pansy's respect mattered very much to him. With a sigh Eve switched her mind to food and her eyes swept across the kitchen and came to rest on the massive pasta jar sitting in a corner of the marble worksurface. Spaghetti with a chilli sauce and green salad. Easy and quick. She pushed her chair back and stood up just as the doorbell rang.

When she opened the front door, Frank was standing there and, inexplicably, she found herself blushing.

'Is Pansy in?' he asked.

'No . . . Yes.' Eve was looking up into his face. 'I'm sorry, let me rephrase that – she is in, but right now she's upstairs having a talk with her father.'

Frank opened his mouth to speak then closed it again.

'But please come in. I don't suppose she'll be long.'

He stepped passed her into the brightly lit hallway and stood there a moment. There was a crash-helmet in his hand and he laid it on a chair, and when he straightened he flexed his shoulders a little beneath the padded leather jacket. He seemed to fill the narrow passageway and she found herself watching him, stung by memory, felt it seize her and force her back through the years. The sensation swept over her so quickly that she stayed where she was, rooted to the spot, and when she did not follow him immediately, Frank looked round and saw her staring at him.

'Is there something wrong?'

'Oh, no,' she said, lying. 'Nothing. A noise outside, I think.'

He looked back at her. Her eyes were wide and the pupils dilated. What was the matter with her? 'Do I go this way?' he asked to break the moment, and gestured towards the open door of the kitchen.

She nodded in a vague sort of way before a smile suddenly bloomed on her lovely mouth and he wondered if he had imagined everything.

In the kitchen she offered him a drink, but he refused. His Harley was outside and besides, he didn't want alcohol blurring his senses when it came to rationalising things with Pansy. He wondered what heavy discussion she was having with her father. About her dubious choice of boyfriend?

Eve was walking across to him, bearing a steaming mug of coffee and he watched her, unable not to, really. She was wearing black jeans and a deep green blouse, silk of course. Did she know about herself? Did she know how her breasts moved beneath the thin fragile material? Or how her hips swung so innocently as she drew close to him, her hair falling forward as the mug was placed on the table. He could smell her: sweet, clean, succulent smell and some famished part of him seemed to wake and cry out. For an instant Frank thought he was going mad.

'Sugar?'

'No, thanks.'

She moved away from him and began pulling saucepans out of a cupboard. 'We're having supper soon,' she said, 'would you like to stay?'

'Maybe I'd better wait until I've spoken to Pansy.' Eve had her back to him now, filling one of the saucepans with water and placing it on the stove.

'I'm sure Pansy would like you to stay,' she said over her shoulder.

'We had a disagreement of sorts. She might not be too keen.'

'As bad as that?'

He shrugged. 'I don't know. I wasn't exactly at my best last night.' She was laying onions and tomatoes on a chopping-board, pushing her hair back from her face as she reached for a knife. He looked away, only to be confronted by her reflection in the glass of the French doors.

'Well,' Eve began, 'I don't think meeting us, or families in general come to that, is ever easy,' she said carefully, 'so I'm not surprised your evening didn't entirely run smoothly.'

'Perhaps,' he said. 'But I was definitely out of order.'

'Really?' She turned her head and glanced at him. 'And Pansy wasn't?'

'No.'

She smiled. 'You're being very honest.'

'There's not a lot of point being anything else.' And he had really believed that until yesterday.

She was pouring olive oil into a frying-pan, scattering dried herbs and garlic across the surface, and he was watching her every move, motionless in his chair.

'How is Pansy's mother, by the way?'

'I saw her today. I think she'll be fine.'

'Pansy worries about her a lot.'

'I know.' Eve fetched up a deep breath. 'I think it's called role reversal . . .'

He smiled and she must have sensed this because she turned and looked back at him, and for an unwary moment their eyes met and held, but then, startled, Eve shot a glance at the open door as Andrew and Pansy approached.

Frank stood up as they walked into the room, saw Pansy's eyes grow round and large, and her father stop in his tracks. The man blushed, too; so they had been discussing him.

'Eve,' Pansy began, 'you should have told me.'

'Frank's only been here a few minutes, and I didn't think you'd be long . . . I've asked Frank to supper by the way, unless you had something else in mind?'

Pansy shot a glance at him and her stomach did a quick somersault. 'Can we go out?'

'Anything you say.'

'There's a bistro round the corner – it's supposed to be good.'

'Okay.'

She was yielding already and she realised with a wisdom beyond her years that it was pointless to argue with her feelings; she was giving in because she just couldn't help herself. Whatever the rights and wrongs of their relationship, she would just have to let it run its course because there was nothing else she could do.

Sometimes it is impossible to be sensible, she thought, sometimes we know what we do is wrong for us even before we do it.

'They'll be back soon . . .'

'No, they won't,' Eve said. 'It's only nine-thirty.'

'Let's go upstairs.'

'Why not here, Andrew?' She looked hurt and he wondered why he was being such a prude.

He gazed at their empty coffee cups and their unfinished brandy, at the rich redness of the rug they had bought together in Egypt on their honeymoon and on which she now wanted to lie with him. He smiled at her uncertainly. 'I don't know.' He felt such a prat somehow, so irrationally uncomfortable and then added clumsily, 'I wasn't expecting it – you – like this.'

'Aren't you glad?' She took his face in her hands and kissed him long, long. 'Don't you want me?'

'Of course I want you.' Who wouldn't? Who wouldn't want his lovely wife? He looked at her for a long moment, struggling to find the words. 'Perhaps I'm just not used to this, the "new" you – and new is just what it feels like.'

'Does it?'

'Oh, yes,' he said very softly.

'Don't think about it then.'

Her voice had a salving quality, silky, soothing and as he studied her she ran her tongue along the edges of her upper teeth as if her mind were relishing something censored, or forbidden, and he felt lust and the lust made him hard and needful. So he didn't resist when she began unbuckling his belt and sliding the zip of his trousers down, but she paused before proceeding any further and very slowly slipped off her blouse. She was naked underneath, and as she moved up against him her gaze was holding his, but in an unnervingly speculative way.

She seemed frantic, her face filled with disconcerting excitement. Hot swollen breasts pressed and splayed across the sweat-dampened cotton of his shirt as if his wife would force herself inside him; yet all the time she was looking back at him and he was looking back at her and he had that feeling again, of things running out of control.

She sank to the floor and leaned back on her haunches, throwing her head back and thrusting her breasts forward. He was remotely aware that his mouth had gone dry, that she was rolling to one side and kicking off her jeans, that she was lying on the rug with her arms outstretched and smiling at him, a small slanting smile full of sensual promise.

'Eve,' he whispered in a funny, squeezed voice. 'Eve.'

She opened her legs and began stroking herself, eyes half-closed in a kind of rapture.

And he felt an eclipse creeping across his heart, something hopeless and beyond him, but he still crouched down and lay beside her, still ran his hand across her skin. And she reached for that hand, brought it to her mouth and slaked the yielding dewy flesh of his palm greedily with her tongue. He watched her, half fascinated, half repelled; there was a part of him whispering that there was something unnatural in her urgency, something not right. And then she was lifting her head and giving him that smiling look again and he felt himself go cold.

'Eve . . .'

But she only closed her eyes, releasing his hand at the same time before moving her head down.

'Eve?'

An insect buzzed through the warm air as his miserable gaze came to rest on the top of her head. He laid a gentle hand on her hair, tried to distract her and bring her away because his erection was collapsing and there would be no getting it back; not here, not now and he didn't know why. Even as this thought took shape and fled, she was staring at him and then backing off, and he was filled with shame.

'Go to bed, Andrew,' she said dully.

'It's not that I don't . . .' He was filled with shame.

'It's okay.'

'I didn't mean . . .' She lay there, breasts still rising and falling.

'I said it's okay.'

He winced at the edge to her voice. 'Come upstairs.'

She shook her head and he watched her helplessly for a few unbearable moments. She drew her knees up to her chin and gazed mutely into the empty fireplace.

'Please, Eve.' His trousers were pooled around his ankles and, blushing, he began to pull them up.

'I'll come up when I'm ready.' She paused for a second, waiting for him to finish, 'And I don't feel ready yet.'

'Are you all right?'

'Yes, I'm all right.'

'You don't sound it.'

'I'm sorry.'

'You don't need to be sorry – this is my fault.'

'It's no one's fault,' she said quietly and he knew she was thinking of something else.

'I don't know what happened,' he said, and longed to add, 'to you, or to me'.

She smiled in a sad sort of way and said in a low, meditative voice, 'Perhaps I don't either.'

'We'll talk about it,' he began hopelessly.

'No.'

'Not right now,' he said, 'later maybe.'

She made no answer.

He apologised once more, but she kept her back to him so he could not read her expression and humiliation swept through him again; yet he remained where he was, standing over her like an impotent buffoon, unable to stay, but unable to go.

'Will you come up?' he asked.

She said nothing, then – 'Give me a few minutes. Will you?'

'Okay.' He sighed inwardly with relief. 'I'll run you a bath. Would you like that?'

Eve shrugged and nodded absently.

'Right,' he said and with more conviction than he felt. 'I'll go on up then . . .'

'Right,' she repeated softly.

He hovered for a few more moments, his hand above her shoulders, but unable to touch her, and then walked slowly out of the room. He was reminded of the night at the lake house when he returned from the hospital and Eve had waited up for him. Hadn't he gone to bed alone then? But for different reasons, he told himself. Different reasons.

'We're doing a new number on Saturday night,' Frank said. 'Will you come?'

'If you want me to.' Pansy cast a sidelong glance at him as they walked along the street. His arm was slung around her shoulders and on the pavement their shadows joined and stretched ahead of them.

'I wouldn't ask if I didn't want you to.' He toussled her hair. 'Stop being so defensive.'

'What is this new number?'

'It's not so much a number, actually, as a playlet.'

Pansy guffawed. 'And how, exactly, would you describe this playlet?'

'Lurid, my sweet,' he said dryly. 'Very lurid. A Victorian melodrama with your proverbial wicked villain ravishing your proverbial comely maiden. It's hilarious, but quite obscene, of course.'

'What part do you play?'

'The heroine. Well, one of them.'

'Oh, Frank,' she said with a trace of despair. 'Don't you mind?'

'Not really. I'm used to it in a depressing sort of way. I think it's called character-building. Besides,' he added, 'the money's not bad.'

'I suppose I could say the same . . .' She sighed heavily. 'But as much as I adore my gorgeous little half-brother, I don't want to spend the rest of my life playing nanny to him.'

'Something will turn up, sooner or later.'

'I need an Equity card.'

'Do cabaret then.' He saw her grimace. 'Why not? It is a way.'

'Because I want to act.'

'There are other ways. Don't be so precious.'

'I can't help it.'

'Try.'

'I can't sing, or pull rabbits out of hats, or juggle.'

'How about stripping?'

'Not funny, Frank.'

'You could, you've got a nice body.'

'It's hardly voluptuous.'

'You have a lovely bum, my dear.' Frank began drawing her in the air with his hand. 'I can just see you in one of those gilded cages, wriggling your delectable little ass about.'

'Stop it,' she chided gently.

'It would only be for six months and then eureka – one Equity card.'

'I couldn't. I'm not brave like you.'

'I'm not brave, just practical. I close my eyes and think of England – well, something like that.'

'My father wouldn't approve,' she said feebly.

'He needn't know.'

'He'd know.'

A picture of Pansy's father formed in Frank's mind, that careful searching of eyes. Oh, yes, he'd know.

They were drawing up outside the house and he turned to her, hands on her shoulders. 'Sure you won't come back?'

She shook her head. 'Not tonight.' But she wanted to, yet something stayed her and she supposed it was that she still didn't trust him.

Frank scrutinised her sharply and almost guessed what she was thinking. 'Maybe Saturday then?'

'Maybe Saturday.'

They walked up the narrow path and Pansy slipped her key in the door. 'Coffee?'

'No. I need some sleep.'

'You'll be all right driving home?' Without thinking she cupped his cheek with one hand and then withdrew it almost instantly; the gesture seemed to say so much, so many things.

He smiled. 'Yes. I'll be all right. I'm a big boy, or hadn't you noticed?'

Pansy blushed and he laughed. She moved away from him then, to the Harley, and swung a leg over the seat and sat down.

'I wish I had a camera,' he said.

She looked back at him beneath half-closed lids and wondered at how happy she felt, but it couldn't last, she thought, wistfully; happiness came in fits and starts, if it came at all. It never stayed.

He was staring at her and grinning when he remembered his crash-helmet, it was still sitting on the chair, just inside the door. 'I'd better get my helmet,' he jerked his thumb in the direction of the house and she nodded.

The door was unlocked, of course, Pansy had just done that, so it was easy to push it open and step into the hall. There was no light coming from the kitchen, but the drawing-room door was slightly ajar and a lamp still on. Despite the silence he knew someone was there and he found himself peering through the crack where the door met the hinges, and what he saw made part of him wish that he had not indulged his curiosity with such ease.

Eve was there, Eve stark naked lying on a beautiful rug touching herself. Eve arching her pelvis and thighs as her climax peaked and mushroomed, hot open mouth stretched wide in a gasp of pure pleasure.

The most erotic thing Frank had ever seen.

His throat constricted as he fought to suppress a deep sob of desire and silently brought his hand up to the door, so that his long dark fingers lay flat against it.

After a moment he turned his face away, but he would remember every move, every sound, every posture.

Somewhere far away a car's engine stalled and a dog barked, like sounds heard in a dream.

Four

When Pansy heard the front door click shut, she looked up from her seat on the bike and wondered at the strange expression on Frank's face. She had been humming to herself, 'Lavender's Blue', an old nursery rhyme her mother used to sing, and she found herself smiling. Minty had seemed different then, but the tune died on her lips as she stared back at him.

'What's the matter?'

He had difficulty in speaking. 'Nothing.'

She frowned and got off the bike and his stomach did a quick flip.

'I bumped my head as I picked up the helmet,' he said quickly, 'on the stairs.'

'Is that all?' she asked. 'You look as if you've seen a ghost – or did you happen to collide with my father in the process?'

'I bumped my head, Pansy,' he repeated patiently and to emphasise the point, began rubbing it, vigorously. 'That's all.'

'Oh,' she said doubtfully.

'But I did hear someone coming down the stairs,' he lied, 'so I got out quickly.'

'They won't bite, you know,' she said gently.

He averted his eyes and thought of what he had seen.

'Your hand's shaking,' she remarked as he brought it away from his head.

He surveyed it for a moment and forced a smile. 'Must be the thought of bumping into your dear old Dad.'

'Ha ha . . .'

He tweaked her nose and her mouth corners turned up a little and, relieved, he said, 'Now let's talk about something else – like what time will you be over at the weekend?'

— 'In time for the show.'

'Okay.' He swung one of his long legs over the Harley and watched her as he strapped on his helmet. Pansy seemed very innocent, very young as she stood there, and he found himself pulling her into his arms with no calculation at all. He closed his eyes for an instant and felt her mouth move on his. Pansy's pretty mouth. 'Little Flower,' he murmured.

But then the thought came creeping out of nowhere, rising up to poison the moment, as he wondered what it would be like to have *her* mouth move on him. Have *her*.

If the clouds cleared a little more it could develop into a nice day, she thought. Eve was standing in the kitchen looking at their bit of garden through the French windows. Already wasps were hovering over the climbing ivy, anxious to have their fill of the purple berries which grew plump and juicy amongst deep green leaves. And the wasps were strangely big things this year, greedy and intrusive, coming into the house when it suited them, making Pansy yelp in surprise and run from the kitchen.

Eve sipped at the coffee mug held in her hands and felt a little better. She hadn't slept very well and had awoken with that anxious feeling deep in her chest, a feeling akin to slow, sludgey panic, so she had quietly slipped out of bed not long after dawn and made herself a cup of hot, sweet tea. Andrew had stayed sleeping which was something of a relief; he would only worry and she was a little tired of being the cause, particularly after last night. And she couldn't explain it, not the way she had been with him – brazen. Like a whore. Her forehead buckled into a frown because she knew there was a part of her twisting away from some fact, or fear, some wisp of suspicion she could not yet bring herself to identify.

Her eyes shot to the ceiling as she heard someone moving about upstairs and she took a gulp of tea. Last night was over, she told herself, gone, and there was no need to go on raking over it as if she had done something shameful, something really wrong. That was silly. Besides Andrew had a big meeting today, some sort of prestigious presentation which would mean a great deal of money for the agency if things went well, so she didn't want him concerned about her on top of everything else.

She took a deep breath. When he came down she would tell him that she was fine, that it had been the brandy or something. Something. She tilted her head to one side and stared sightlessly into the garden for a few moments, before the sound of feet on the stairs brought her attention back to the morning and preparations for breakfast.

'You're up early,' Pansy said, coming into the kitchen, Jack in her arms. Eve nodded. 'The birds woke me.'

'I think the birds woke your son, too,' Pansy said wryly.

'Oh, I'm sorry. I didn't hear a thing.'

'It's okay. That's what I'm here for.' Pansy looked into her stepmother's stricken face. 'Hey, it's all right – he was fine once I took him into bed with me. Look, you hold him while I prepare his breakfast.'

Eve took her child into her arms and waited for him to cry. She had almost got used to his disquiet when she held him, presuming that her anxiety conveyed itself to him in invisible, but nevertheless clearly discernible, waves.

For a long moment Jack seemed to survey his mother with eyes, she judged, that would probably become the same colour as his father's. One of his small plump hands entwined itself in her hair and she smiled, catching the smell of him, a milky, buttery sort of smell full of sweetness. On top and to the back of his head the hair made a cowlick, a soft silky comb of fluff that she wound around one finger as his little mouth began to twitch uncertainly, as if he were trying to decide whether he would smile or frown. But finally Jack frowned, and then Jack cried.

Every time this happened something inside Eve seemed to tighten and pull just a little more out of shape. 'What is it?' she whispered helplessly. 'What do I do?'

'You don't hold him enough . . . that's all,' Pansy said softly over her shoulder.

'Is it really that simple?'

'Well, I'm no expert, but it's probably something do with it,' she smiled and added, 'besides, he's hungry. So sit him in his high-chair and feed him, that's bound to put you in his good books.'

Eve did as she was told. 'You must think me rather pathetic.'

'No, I don't,' Pansy said, passing her stepmother a shallow dish filled with an unappetising mush of baby cereal. 'You've had a difficult time, but things will straighten out.' She tilted her pretty head on one side, 'And you're still not sleeping, are you?'

'Some days are better than others,' Eve responded evasively. What could she say? That a doting husband, a lovely baby, a wonderful nanny, money, security – good God, she was even beautiful apparently – that all these things were not enough to give her the one thing she craved, peace of mind?

The doorbell rang and she jumped. 'Who on earth can that be?'

Pansy ceased buttering some toast and looked up. 'I'll go, it's probably only the postman.'

But it was not the postman, it was Tony, looking for Minty.

Eve looked back at him, wide-eyed. 'Isn't she still in hospital?'

He shook his head. 'They let her out today, and I was supposed to pick her up – she gave me very strict instructions, you know – even about this bloody wig . . .' he pulled what looked like a tiny cap of blonde hair from his back pocket, 'but she'd already left by the time I got there.' He sighed heavily and sat down at the kitchen table. 'I thought she might be with you.'

'Why?'

'Oh, something she said . . .' he said vaguely. 'God knows, I can't remember.' Tony glanced at his watch and pulled a face. 'And no wonder; look at the bloody time. When I think of all the trouble I've put myself to – practically got up with the bloody lark this morning.'

'That must have been a bit of a shock to the system,' Pansy smirked.

Tony looked at her sourly. 'Pour me a coffee, would you, sweetie?' he said. 'Black, please.'

Pansy scowled and picked up the coffee percolator with barely concealed irritation.

'But where could she be?' Eve scooped up another spoonful of breakfast cereal destined for her baby son's gaping mouth. 'You called the house I suppose?'

'Of course.' He brought out his cigarettes and planted one between his pallid lips. 'Mind you, she's been behaving very strangely. Quite weird.'

'What do you mean?'

Pansy slopped a mug of coffee in front of him and focused on Tony's, as yet, unlit fag. 'Don't smoke in front of Jack, please. It's bad for his health – and yours, come to that.'

'I didn't know you cared.'

'I don't.'

'Oh, come on, you two,' Eve said tiredly. 'Can't we call a truce for a while?'

Tony gave another dramatic sigh and, gazing longingly at the offending cigarette, reluctantly put it away. 'Anything for a peaceful life.'

'I asked you what you meant by "weird"?'

He shrugged. 'Well, not the same somehow – different.'

'Did you mention this at the hospital?' It was Pansy now.

'Did you?' he parried.

'My mother was fine when I saw her,' she snapped. 'It's you who always manages to make her weird; it's the effect you have on people, and her in particular. Maybe she's finally woken up to that fact, which would explain why she left the hospital without you.'

'Oh, give it a rest, will you, sweetie. We live together, remember – she even leaves the door open when she has a pee. Don't you think I'd notice if she'd changed or not?'

'God you're disgusting.'

'It's called a sense of humour, something you might appreciate – if you had one.' He chortled into his coffee and slapped his knee with mirth.

'Oddly enough, every time I look at you I want to burst out laughing.'

'Ooooh – nasty,' he mocked, 'and did anyone ever tell you that you have no respect for your elders and betters?'

'Now that really is funny – coming from you.'

'Aren't we on good form this morning.'

'Can we stop this please,' Eve broke in, 'it really isn't very helpful.'

'I didn't start it,' Tony protested. 'She's always got it in for me.'

'Oh, grow up,' Pansy sneered.

'What's going on?' Andrew stood in the doorway. 'And what the hell are you doing here, Tony?'

'Thanks for the welcome, I must say.'

'You know what I mean.'

'Minty's disappeared.'

Andrew looked over Tony's head at Eve and she raised her eyes heavenward. 'Tony went to the hospital to pick her up as they'd arranged,' she explained, 'but Minty had already left.'

'She's probably at home.'

'I phoned,' Tony said.

'Maybe she was still on her way.'

'An hour later? Come on.'

'She could have gone to a friend's – anywhere, for heaven's sake. Why the dramatics?'

'She's not herself, I'm worried about her,' Tony said a little sheepishly.

'Do me a favour, Tony,' Andrew said in disbelief, determined not to be dragged in again. 'And I don't have time for this. I've a big presentation this morning.' He darted a glance at the kitchen clock. 'And if I don't get held up or have any unnecessary distractions, I might just get there.'

'Do you want breakfast?' Eve asked.

'Toast and tea would be fine.'

She got up, but Pansy gestured for her to sit down. 'I'll do it – Jack's mouth is still hanging open.'

'And how is my favourite boy this morning?' Andrew sat down on the other side of the high-chair and looked at his wife, inordinately pleased to see her feeding their son. Things would be all right, given time, he thought. And last night, well last night had just been unfortunate; Eve would see that.

'You'll get a cab tonight?' He was regarding her steadily, as if he might read her mind, understand.

Eve switched her attention from her son to her husband and felt a flutter of relief at his look of pleasant inquiry. He didn't look bruised or regretful; she hated it when she did that to him. She nodded. 'Will eight be all right?'

'Perfect.'

'What's this then?' Tony piped-up.

'The Elektra bash – no expense spared according to Bill. And we earned it. So why not? The agency did brilliantly to win such a massive account, or should I say Bill Streiber – the man you love to hate.'

Tony gave a disgruntled shrug. 'Someone had to.'

'Do I detect a trace of the green-eyed monster?'

'No,' Tony shot back. 'I just find Bill a bit of a pain in the ass, that's all. He's always so bloody smug, so bloody full of himself.'

'He's an ad man, what do you expect? Don't be such an old woman.'

Tony's eyes flared; he hated the word 'old'. 'I suppose he's still shagging that secretary of his with the wonderful knockers . . .'

Andrew winced and darted a glance at Pansy who was out of earshot. 'For God's sake,' he hissed. 'Are you on something?'

'No.'

'Well, do you think you could exert a little self-control and spare us the gory details?'

'Sorreee,' Tony said with obvious insincerity and began drumming his fingertips on the table, his eyes roving around the room until they came to rest on Eve. 'You know, Bill always had a thing about Eve.'

'Shut up, Tony,' Andrew said.

'He did.'

Eve turned her face to the window, the sky was low with grey cloud now, as if it was closing in. It made her think of the winter to come, which she hated, all those long black nights and dark wet dawns.

'So what if he did,' Andrew's irritated voice continued behind her.

'He's a good-looking bastard, a bit oafish perhaps, but nevertheless good-looking.'

'What are you getting at?'

'Nothing.'

'You're bored, Tony, that's your trouble – bored stupid. Now can we talk about something else until you decide when you're going to leave us?'

'Okay, okay – just finishing my coffee.'

Andrew turned to Jack, saw that his wife had put the baby spoon down and was gazing out of the window, that funny blank look on her face. He frowned in exasperation and picked the spoon up himself.

'You always have been the fatherly type, haven't you, Andrew?' Tony observed dryly, lounging back in his chair and sighing.

'What's that supposed to mean?'

'Just an observation.' He crossed his legs, began beating the air with his foot. 'Christ, I could do with a smoke.'

'Why don't you stand in the garden?' Pansy said as she brought her father tea and toast.

'It's starting to rain.'

'I know.'

'Ha, ha. Very funny.'

The doorbell rang.

Eve seemed to snap out of her reverie and turned to Pansy who nodded. 'I'll get it.'

Tony followed her with his eyes as she left the room, an expectant look on his face.

'You don't think . . .' Andrew began.

'Yes, I do think.' Tony responded.

Andrew groaned.

'What?' Eve asked, but then heard her own answer as the sound of Minty's voice floated into the kitchen. 'Oh.'

Andrew stood up. 'I'll forget the toast.' He took a gulp of tea and switched his attention to his wife. 'I'll see you about eight, at the

Dorchester – we're meeting there for a couple of drinks before moving on to the club.'

'Let me walk you to the door.' She wanted to wave him off, be alone with him, if that were possible, just for a moment, just to apologise and reassure.

'There's no need.'

'I want to.'

They smiled at each other over Tony's head, and he was unable to resist watching, stung by a combination of nausea and envy. 'How very touching.'

'Bye, Tony.' Andrew nodded in the direction of the hallway and grinned maliciously. 'Looks like your worries are over.'

'Just beginning, you mean,' Tony muttered, all his good intentions fading with the sound of Minty's dulcet tones. And he had wanted to see her, had missed her, even. He didn't understand it. People are weird, he thought, bloody weird, then he closed his eyes for a long moment as Minty strode into the kitchen.

'Can't you stay for a quick coffee?' she was shouting after Andrew.

'Sorry,' came the instant response.

'Sorry,' Tony repeated parrot-fashion and slowly shook his head, then, through gritted teeth said, 'hello, my love.'

'Don't give me that crap, Tony,' Minty said tartly. 'It's too early.'

'Where did you get to?'

'I didn't want to wait.'

'Why not? We agreed that I'd pick you up.'

'I changed my mind.'

He was peering at her, a funny look on his face; she was wearing a navy-blue baseball cap, pulled very low down on her bald head. 'I thought you'd at least want to wait for this . . .' He retrieved her wig from his pocket and dangled it in the air.

Minty snatched it out of his hand and shoved it into her handbag.

'Coffee, Mum?' Pansy interjected and gave her a hug. 'Are you okay?'

'Thanks, darling. And yes, of course I'm okay. I hope Tony hasn't been worrying you; his imagination has a tendency to be over-fertile,' she smiled unkindly, 'which is more than I can say for another part of his anatomy . . .'

'You bitch,' he seethed, reddening.

'Now, now,' she said condescendingly, 'not in front of the child.'

His mouth curled into a thin smile, the sort that promised revenge later. 'Anyway,' he continued resentfully, 'getting back to your strange disappearance, it was bloody thoughtless not to let me know. You could have called at least.'

'I forgot.'

Tony shook his head in resigned disbelief. 'And why here?' he asked, bemused.

'What do you mean, "why here"? Why *not* here, for heaven's sake?' She drew an impatient breath as if she were dealing with an imbecile. 'Isn't this where my daughter currently lives? Aren't I allowed to see her when I wish, or do I need your permission?'

'Don't be ridiculous.'

Minty raised her eyebrows and then switched her attention to the doorway as Eve walked back into the room.

'You're looking a little tired, my dear.'

My dear? Eve smiled with an effort. 'Am I?'

'Yes,' Minty replied firmly. 'Isn't Andrew taking care of you?'

'Andrew always takes care of me,' Eve said quietly. 'Would you like some breakfast?'

'Just coffee, and Pansy's doing the honours.' Minty sat down. 'I hope you don't mind me popping in like this, but I wanted to see my Little Flower,' Minty waved a hand at her daughter.

'I wish you wouldn't call me that,' Pansy said stiffly and thought of Frank.

'And you, of course, Eve . . .' Minty ran on, ignoring the request.

'Me?'

'Yes,' Minty said. 'I wanted to thank you for your kindness.'

Eve's eyebrows drew together in a frown. 'I haven't done anything.'

'Your visit – last week,' Minty prompted. 'It meant a lot to me.'

Tony rolled his eyes. 'I told you she was different.'

'Shut up,' Minty retorted, her pale skin refusing to blush.

'Yes, my love,' he replied with mock deference.

'It was sweet of you, Eve,' she continued easily, 'and I thought a great deal about our conversation after you left.'

'Really?' Eve said flatly.

'Oh, yes.'

'I don't remember much about it.'

'We discussed my accident, didn't we? What I saw.'

'Saw?'

'Well, thought I saw.' She shrugged lightly. 'I've been thinking that it might be a good idea for me to go back there – to the lake house – you know, just to clear my mind about the whole thing; get it out of my system, as it were.'

'Jesus Christ,' Tony blurted out, 'you were out of your depth and got a knock on the head – you probably saw stars for God's sake. What's all the fuss? A good shit would get it out of your system.'

'I said shut up, and we can do without your lavatorial humour, thank you.'

'Mum nearly drowned,' Pansy said, 'she could have died.'

'All right,' he replied in exasperation. 'But I can't believe you'd want to go back to that godforsaken place again . . .' he looked sheepishly at Eve, 'no offence.'

'It's none of your business,' Minty snapped.

'I just prefer civilisation, that's all – you know, street-lights, taxi-cabs, that sort of thing . . .'

'Tony.' Her voice began to rise.

'Okay, okay.' He lifted up his hands as if to ward her off.

'You wouldn't mind, would you, Eve?' Minty's voice was all softness now, coaxing.

'Go if you wish.'

'We could all go.'

Eve met Minty's eyes, felt a flicker of panic, tried to repress it, to relax. 'No, I don't think so.'

'Why not?' she pressed. 'We could make a weekend of it – have a glorious dinner party and wipe all the bad memories away.'

Tony visibly cringed. 'I don't believe I'm hearing this.'

'I told you to shut up.'

'Have it your own way.'

'What do you say, Eve?' Minty seemed excessively pleased with her suggestion, so much so that she could scarcely keep the excitement out of her voice. There were two hectic blotches of colour on her white skin, high on the cheekbones. She seemed like someone who was working towards the fulfilment of some dream, some dangerous devotion.

'Is this why you came?'

'Of course not,' Minty said too quickly.

But it was.

Jack began to grizzle and Eve moved towards him, to pick him up. Anything to avoid Minty's searching gaze, but Jack's grizzle changed to a whine and then into a full-blown tantrum as she lifted him from his chair and held him against her like a shield. His face reddened, the cheeks swelling angrily with engorged blood as he fought his mother's arms and his sticky, cereal-coated fingers found their way into her hair, to pull and tangle and add to her anguish and bewilderment.

Once Frank had called his women 'screwing-friends', but he didn't any longer, it seemed inappropriate somehow, particularly after recent events. Now he didn't know if it was Pansy, or Eve, who had really got under his skin. Even as their faces took it in turns to take shape in his mind he was guiding Victoria's eager mouth to his erection, and any emotion he felt he put away, to think of later. After all, he hadn't planned it like this; it had happened, as they say, on impulse.

Victoria had been there for him when he got back from the club; she had her own key and had let herself in and waited – for sex – it was as simple as that. She was a friend, she had been a colleague, now they found each other mutually convenient, at least in a physical way.

There was no real feeling involved, of course, that was something outside the unspoken guidelines of their 'relationship', and something that would not fit in with either of their plans, but lately things had turned around a trace. Victoria had been arriving more often, too often, and it was beginning to grate a little because he realised he didn't want her in the same way any more.

This was another new and troubling feature in his life, and he felt vaguely oppressed by a sensation that something was not right.

Frank tried again to put his thoughts aside as Victoria moved to straddle him, her favourite position. She was one of the few girls he had known who really liked to be in control and her skilful manipulations usually made it easy for him to forget, everything. Not today.

Frank was remembering.

His mind was stealing back to the other night and he was swept by a sudden hot lust which was much more than Victoria, much more than anything he had ever felt before. The memory inflamed him, he seemed to see and hear and smell Eve all over again. It made him feel shaky and out of control.

Frank closed his eyes for a moment, then pushed Victoria away, flipped her over and pulled her up on to her knees so that his front pressed against her back.

'What are you . . . ?'

He didn't answer her. He was intent on blanking Victoria from his mind.

But Victoria murmured something more, laughed a little, and her laughter irritated him. Frank squeezed his eyes tight shut and swore between gritted teeth. 'Don't speak. Don't say a bloody word.'

'I hear and obey, oh master . . .' She chuckled throatily and he was shocked by an urge to slap her – punish her? His mouth was dry, heart thumping nastily in his chest as he made her lean over. She was on all fours, big round bottom trembling just a little and then he did slap her, hard, with both hands, one after the other, and the creamy flesh bounced and jiggled and Frank leaned his head back in a gesture of frustration, as if he were vainly trying to make sense out of his feelings.

'Do it again.' Victoria had turned her head, was looking at him through a curtain of yellow hair.

He blinked and looked back, felt a flicker of distaste.

'Go on then . . .' She was pushing against him, it was like being crushed by a plump cushion, but it did the trick, just as Victoria knew it would, because his penis regained its momentum, jerking to attention like a clenched fist salute.

Frank stared, then very slowly, very carefully placed his open palms on her rump. His face wore a peculiar expression, an odd waiting sort of expression, as if he half-wanted to go on and half-wanted to stop.

'Frank?'

He moved his hands in sure circular motions, let the dampness of her sweat lubricate his lingering fingertips, felt his control begin to fray around the edges as that image unspooled in his head again. She had arched her back at the end; then she – Eve – had sunk down against that extravagant red rug and dug her fingertips into and through the thick pile. Frank looked down at his own hands.

'Frank?'

At the sound of Victoria's voice consciousness reasserted itself with unnatural clarity, so that the matter at hand, namely sex, became immediate and he drove himself forward, plunging into Victoria abruptly. She yelped with pain and surprise, and as his body closed up against hers the wet sound of their flesh clashing made him flinch a little inside himself.

'Oh, yes . . . I like that,' she said greedily, 'I do, Frank.'

Frank grimaced and then placed a hand over her mouth.

When they had finished they lay beside each other, not touching; she, wanting to sleep, and Frank wondering how he would tell her that he wanted her to go. He glanced at the clock on the wall and sighed softly; it was almost three, too late.

'Cheer up – it might never happen.'

Victoria was propped up on one elbow, watching him.

'I thought you were tired?'

'I am. What's the matter?'

'Leave it out, Vicki.'

She studied him for a long moment. 'There's someone else, isn't there?'

'There's always someone else. You know that.'

'I mean a real someone.'

'You're real, aren't you?' he said and prodded her thigh with a half-hearted smile.

'You know what I mean.'

'No.'

She sank back into the pillows and stared at the ceiling. 'You're not the same somehow.'

'Wasn't my performance up to par?'

'That's just it . . .' she said a little sadly, and he was surprised to hear that in her voice.

'What?'

'It was a touch too good. You were angry.'

'I've had a bad day.'

'So have I.'

'Sorry.'

'It's okay.' She sighed with resignation. 'I mean, it's your business after all, and you know me, I like to snoop.' She pushed back the bed covers and got out of bed.

'What are you doing?'

'I'm going home.'

'It's three in the morning.'

'My car's outside.'

'You usually stay.'

85

'I know, but usually it's fun, and usually you like me being here.'

'I still do.' He sat up, not knowing whether he was speaking the truth or not.

'Uh, uh . . .' Vicki wagged a finger at him. 'I don't think you know what you want, but it isn't me, which is a shame because I've enjoyed our little liaison.'

'What's that supposed to mean?'

'I'm telling you, before you tell me.' She began pulling on a pair of black leggings.

'Vicki . . .' he protested.

'It's for the best.' She was hopping about on one foot. 'You can call me when you feel better.'

'Thanks,' he said dryly.

For a moment her upper body was swallowed by a voluminous pink tee-shirt and as her face reappeared she grinned. 'Besides, I was getting greedy – hadn't you noticed?'

He didn't argue, there was nothing to say.

'Anyway, it's about time you got into a decent relationship.' Vicki had her back to him now, looking for her shoes.

'You kicked them under the bed,' Frank said flatly.

'Don't go sulky on me, Frank, it doesn't suit you.'

'The trouble is, I don't know what I'm getting into . . .'

'Oooh,' she said gleefully, 'sounds exciting.'

'It isn't.'

She stopped what she was doing and looked back at him with careful scrutiny. He was very still and in the lamplight his body could have been honed out of some dark mellow wood, but more than that, his face was pensive and sort of wounded-looking, elements in him she had not seen before. The funny thing was, they made her want him all over again; perhaps it was as well to put an end to things for the time being. She was beginning to like him just a little too much. 'Got it bad then, have we?'

'I wish I knew.'

But it was bad, he thought, very bad.

Light danced on the ceiling, laser strobes turned the sea of faces white, a beautiful girl blew coloured smoke into the air as if she'd been touched by magic.

Eve was standing above the crowd, in a gallery overlooking the dance floor. She wore the red dress, low-cut, clinging, the one that Andrew liked so much, but now she wasn't sure; she felt exposed somehow, lurid even, a scarlet exclamation mark studding the shadows. She glanced over her shoulder and saw him returning with their drinks and she found herself smiling. The smile seemed to break through her nervous feelings so that she wondered about herself and the way she reacted to simple, even innocent things.

Over the last few months she had been jumping at shadows and reading nonsense into everyday happenings – all those little fears without foundation. She had even probed for the cause, some offending event, but could not really find one to explain the feeling of helplessness which would sweep over her when she least expected it. She had even tried to probe the past but, to her vague discomfort, found herself withdrawing from it. What there was remained strangely isolated, odd little fragments set against a hazy canvas, and a part of her was glad of that. Besides, people who dwelled on the past never grew or blossomed or learned from their mistakes, someone had told her that once. Her mother? Her brother?

The past is a dead place, she thought, full of ghosts, and there is no going back, no return. The thought warmed her in a curious way, made her feel safe. Eve's smile broadened, glowed even, as her husband drew close.

'You look pleased with yourself.' Andrew gave Eve her wine and slipped an arm around her waist.

'I hoped I was looking happy.'

'Are you?'

'Yes.' She kissed him lightly. 'Yes, of course.'

'There's no "of course" in it.' He touched her mouth with one finger. 'You know that.'

'I know, but it happens to be true.'

'You looked worried this morning.'

'Well,' she rolled her eyes, 'having Tony and Minty for breakfast wasn't the most auspicious start to the day.'

'When did they go?'

'Jack had a tantrum,' Eve averted her gaze, 'quite a big one, as a matter of fact. They didn't stay long after that.'

Andrew's eyebrows drew together in a frown. 'He was fine when I left. Of course, there's no telling what sort of vibes are floating about when Minty and Tony are around and children pick up more things than we realise. It's uncanny sometimes.'

Eve reddened. 'He calmed down after a while.' Once she had given him back to Pansy. But she wouldn't think about that, not the screaming, the fingers caught in and tearing her hair.

Andrew sighed softly. 'Why don't we forget about this morning – and Minty and Tony and tantrums? Drink your drink and let's dance.'

She interlocked her fingers with his and felt unaccustomed gaiety seep through her like some excellent drug. It would be all right, she thought, everything would be all right.

The next hour was the happiest Eve could remember. They danced almost continually and when they did meet up with friends or colleagues, Andrew made sure to keep them at a discreet distance. They wanted this time together, a time that seemed right for once and without complications.

'I should feel old,' he said with obvious amusement. The music had finally slowed and when he glanced around them, it was to discover that they were surrounded, indeed swamped, by dozens of perspiring young things in mini-skirts and crotch-hugging jeans, 'but I don't.'

Eve laughed softly.

'Happy?' he asked. 'I mean *really* happy?'

'Oh, yes,' she replied with unexpected ease, wishing that she could preserve the moment, save it, stop everything at this point in their lives and not walk on into an uncertain future.

The speeches had been said, congratulations awarded and the party was busy reaching its peak when they returned to the gallery. If, at that moment, Andrew had not left Eve to fetch more drinks, or if he hadn't been caught at the bar by a colleague, things may have turned out very differently that night. In fact what occurred later may never have happened at all.

Eve stood to one side, away from the main crush, looking down on to the heaving dance floor. The mood had changed; the DJ had taken the music back in time to the early eighties. She had still been away at school then, in the sixth form and at night some of the girls would play music into the small hours and the sisters never knew, or if they did they turned a blind eye. Maybe they didn't care. After all, music wasn't sinful like sex, music was only sinful when it aroused feelings it was perilous even to try to understand.

And it had done that to her – reawakened all those things done secretly, in the dark, in the light, and in the long grass where she had pleaded lustily, guiltily, to the god of love.

Her face was very still, inflexible as the memory came creeping back, a memory she thought she had buried too deep for recall. For a long, timeless moment she stood there, gaze lingering sightlessly on the dance floor, but suddenly the hairs on the back of her neck began to tingle and her eyes widened in shock and fright. An expression of disbelief rippled across her face. 'No,' she whispered. It wasn't true.

Down there. *He* was.

She tried to pull her gaze away, but could not. Both hands clutched a rail as if she might fall, and a voice from the deeper ranges of her mind told her it was not possible. Yet she was exquisitely aware of his eyes: dark, vital eyes gleaming possessively, and the old blackness crawled over her even amongst that crowd and that music and the innocent sound of chinking glasses.

His look moving over her breasts, her waist, her legs and where the wandering lights picked out strands of her hair; the pearl choker, Andrew's gift, clasped around her neck.

But the music changed and the gyrating bodies were no longer freeze-framed by strobes of white light and the face had gone. Her eyes had tricked her, of course, that was it – some cruel figment of her imagination had easily made of him an illusion amidst those frenzied dancers, some moving darker shadow that had swum before her eyes for an instant. She bowed her head and stared at the carpeted floor on which she stood, as it was brightened suddenly by a small mosaic of artificial light, a stray strobe from the dance floor that managed to shame everything for a second or two. There were stains, you see: drink stains, shoe stains, dust and stickiness.

Eve shook her head gently, feeling sick and stupid. She pressed her fingers to her cheeks, but they were strangely hot and the heat seemed to steal down her neck, then into her breasts and further, cruising down her body in smooth, perfect lines. She was a little alarmed, yet vaguely thrilled by the warmth building. She thought someone spoke her name, whispered into her ear, and the sound made her shudder with both fear and desire. There was an odd feeling of caressing fingers stroking her spine, the backs of her arms; lips tracing that special place at the back of her neck as if he knew where to touch, as if this man had been there before. And it wasn't Andrew. Andrew was too gentle, too considerate, over-cautious because she frightened him. But every lover left a mark. Didn't they? Their imprint, some little sensuous quirk that was peculiar to them – a kiss, an embrace that was theirs and theirs alone; even brief, brutal lovers.

And then he did speak her name, over and over, like an incantation and there was no mistaking that deep melting voice, she recognised it at once, as if she had been waiting to hear it for years and she strained forward, yearning for it. His name came to her like a drowned thing, and she shuddered again because he would laugh at that, at the hideous irony.

'Little Evey,' the voice murmured. 'Evey. Evey. Evey.'

On and on. The only one who had ever called her that.

And she thought she would die, fade, from the pain of it. She was afraid to move, afraid to turn around and see. Even when he stepped in front of her she still couldn't see, not who it really was, and when the man took her hand and guided her into a darkened alcove she went with him like someone hypnotised, as if she had no will of her own, which was the way it had been in that other time – despite the disgust and the self-loathing she had been drawn irresistibly to him like a fragile moth to a burning flame. Shame had been banished, and only he could do that. It was, if you like, a gift he had had.

Dirty treasure in a dusty box.

The man was squeezing her breasts, pinching the nut-hard nipples so that she whimpered with the pain-pleasure; he was forcing his tongue into her mouth, lifting her dress and pushing his fingers up, between her legs. She pressed against him, heedless of reality, encouraging, asking, swept away on a wave of wonder.

Even when he pushed her thighs apart and pinned her against the wall, she was still encouraging, still giving way.

His beautiful mouth on her sex.

And then he was inside, and everything was so easy.

No one could do it the way he could. Cruel. Rough. Overwhelming. She clutched feverishly at his head, the delicious weight of it, felt the shape of his skull beneath her fingers, ran her hands through his thick black hair. Breathed in *his* smell.

Her head went back in silent agony. Whom had she ever loved as she had loved him?

And then he moaned and her eyes did see.

Eve froze. It was like a veil lifting, a nasty stained veil peeled back to reveal some horror, because she found herself staring into the face of her husband's boss.

She drew in a breath to scream, yet nothing came out, but her eyes blazed so brightly that Bill snapped his head back and not only lost his erection, but also his balance.

'How?' He was steadying himself against the wall, looking confused and even afraid.

She said nothing, only twisted her face away, the back of her hand to her mouth and he could see her long nails, red and glistening, picked out and favoured by the insipid light. She had used them on him, digging into his flesh, through his shirt.

He shook his head in a dazed fashion, stared down at his open flies and limp penis. 'But how . . . ?' he said once more in a choked voice, and looked frantically around as if he hoped someone might tell him. There had been a weird half-second when he saw felt . . . What? A feeling of being someone else. Having thoughts that were not his own. Bill glanced again at the gaping hole of his trousers and nervously strove to push his genitals back into the safe confines of his underpants.

'I don't know . . . I mean . . .' he began clumsily. She was still looking away from him, hair hiding her face so that he couldn't read her expression. The thin straps of her dress still hung halfway down her arms and tentatively he reached for them, intent on placing them back on her shoulders, hiding the evidence.

'Don't touch me,' she said suddenly and in a mad fearful croak so that Bill jerked his hand away as if he had been stung.

'Look, Eve . . .' he began again.

'Go away.'

'Eve,' he tried once more, 'I don't know what happened, one minute I was . . .'

She laughed a little wildly and turned to him at last, and he was shocked by the expression on her face. He took a step back, there was a sort of fuzziness in his head and then a sensation of panic.

'Look. We have to talk.' Anxiously he pushed a lock of thin, pale hair back from his forehead. 'We've got to work out what happened here.'

'Nothing happened.'

'I'd love to believe you, but . . .'

'Nothing.' She was lifting the straps of her dress, placing them carefully back on her shoulders, then smoothing down the skirt as if there was a film of dust clinging to the material. 'We bumped into each other, that's all.'

'Eve,' he said uneasily. 'This is crazy.'

'I don't know what you mean.' She closed her eyes for a moment and rubbed at her temples. 'We bumped into each other,' she said again.

He shook his head. 'No.'

'Would you fetch my bag for me please, I left it by that pillar . . .'

Bill glanced over his shoulder, saw it lying there, and for an instant it seemed like a little animal, curled up and watchful, the gleam of the narrow clasp two fugitive eyes looking out. He was distantly aware that his mouth had gone dry, but he still walked across, his gaze fastened on the object with peculiar distaste, and yet when he drew close the bag was just a bag and he wondered what was wrong with him.

And when he looked back Eve had gone. Of course she had gone, that's why she had asked him to fetch her bag so she could make easy her escape. He stared at the dark spot where he had left her, the offending alcove where the unbelievable had happened. Hadn't it? He squeezed his eyes tight shut for a moment and pinched the top of his nose, unable to comprehend.

That haunted look on her face, as if she saw things he had never dreamed.

'Bill?'

He wheeled around, his heart knocking unpleasantly against his ribcage, and found himself staring into Andrew's puzzled face. 'Andy.' He took a deep breath and clapped his managing director on the shoulder with irritating bonhomie. 'How're you doin'?'

'That's Eve's bag.'

Bill glanced down. His hands were nursing the soft leather pouch, a gold chain trickled between his fingers. 'I thought it must be.'

'Why?'

'We bumped into each other.' His eyes flinched a little and Andrew looked back at him warily.

'You bumped into each other?'

'Yeah. As simple as that.' Bill grinned broadly, his upper lip pulled back to reveal perfectly capped teeth, but his voice wavered unconvincingly and he found himself wondering whether, if he said it often enough, he might actually come to believe it. Just as Eve had.

That odd waking image of the little animal swam back into his memory and Bill shivered inside himself.

* * *

92

'I'm going to have a bath,' Eve said and Andrew screwed up his face in astonishment.

'Now?'

'Yes. Now.'

'But it's gone two . . .'

'I want a bath, Andrew.' She walked away from him and into their bathroom. 'I feel dirty.'

'Are you okay?'

'Why wouldn't I be, for heaven's sake? I've had a wonderful evening.'

'Up to a point,' he said, 'I would agree with you.'

She swung round and looked at him. 'What do you mean – "up to a point"?'

'Hey . . .' he held up his hands, 'I didn't mean anything. Halfway through the evening your mood seemed to change, that's all.' She had been happy, he knew she had, and then she had just been different. Not unhappy, nothing so simple as that, in fact she had hardly stopped smiling.

'You married a moody woman, or hadn't you noticed?' She spoke a little ruefully, but smiled nevertheless and was relieved to see his face relax in response. 'I'm sorry. I don't know how you put up with me.'

He looked at her for a long moment and said very slowly, 'That's easy.'

Eve felt a dull species of shame, and guilt and fear, but she still smiled and the smile stayed fixed on her face until she was able to close the bathroom door behind her.

The water was very warm and she sank into it up to her lovely, creamy neck and stared aimlessly at the ceramic tiles on the opposite wall. She began to scrub herself, hard, even strokes of the cedar brush which came faster and faster as despair gave way to disbelief, and disbelief to the unthinkable. Then she stopped and so abruptly that the sudden silence frightened her.

On the stand beside the bath sat a large palm plant and beside the plant were Andrew's shaving things; for some reason he always left them there: all the usual paraphernalia – soap, brush, razor blades; he wouldn't use an electric shaver, said it didn't do a good enough job.

Eve reached for one of the razor blades with no calculation at all. It was wrapped in a thin film of waxy paper, delicate really, light as air. She peeled the paper away and scrutinised the perfectly formed sliver of metal which now lay in the palm of her hand; she stared at it for a long time.

It didn't hurt when she drew it across the white shadow where her watchstrap normally was, and the blood seeped out in a little bubbly line, so she drew another line parallel to the first, a long clean line, but still within the confines of the watchstrap shadow where it wouldn't show. Then she dropped her arm gently into the water and saw how the blood began staining the water in an inky-red cloud. The hurt came slowly, a sort of soreness stealing out of the wounds, and graduating into a series of dull rhythmic throbs.

She could feel her heart pumping in unison and the echo of it beating back in her ears. It was like the steady, relentless sound of his voice calling her name. It was like the sum of all the things she should never have and never want.

Five

'We could have spent the morning in bed.' Frank rested his hand on Pansy's knee, saw the edges of her mouth twitch into a smile, but she kept her eyes on the road.

'I wanted some country air,' she said.

'We could have gone to the heath, or Primrose Hill. Why drive all the way out here when I'm still half-asleep?'

'Go to sleep then,' she grinned, 'but you seemed lively enough before we left.'

'That's different.'

'There are beds at the lake house and sofas, come to that, there's even a nice inviting green lawn sweeping down to the water. It's a lovely day, you can pass out there – if you want – and you won't be breathing in lung-fulls of exhaust fumes.'

'My lungs are used to exhaust fumes, they'll probably develop an allergic reaction to your country air.'

'Oh, stop whingeing,' she said good-humouredly. 'We're nearly there, anyway.' She took a hand off the steering wheel and gave his thigh a firm squeeze. 'A dip in the water might wake you up.'

'Naked, naturally.'

'Apart from sleep, you seem to have only one other thing on your mind.'

'What – more than usual?'

'Definitely.'

Looking vaguely puzzled, Frank slouched down into his seat and stared out of the car window.

The road began to narrow and Pansy scanned the high hedgerows

95

carefully, before seeming to make up her mind and turning the car into a driveway overhung by trees on either side.

'I would have missed it . . .' Frank said and sat up.

'I nearly did,' she replied. 'It's only the second time I've been here.'

'The party was the other?'

She nodded.

'What about your mother?'

'What about her?'

'Well, she nearly drowned here.'

'If you'd seen her that night, you'd hardly be surprised. It wasn't the fault of this place, it was her own fault. She has a habit of getting herself into deep water – if you'll excuse the pun.'

'I'll have to meet her.'

'She'd eat you alive.'

Frank's eyebrows shot skywards and for an instant he looked so comical that Pansy burst out laughing. 'Don't worry,' she said, 'I think she's trying to turn over a new leaf.'

'That's reassuring.'

She brought the car to a halt at the side of the house, so that it was facing the lake and they sat there a moment, caught by the beauty and the silence.

'I didn't think it would be like this,' he said softly.

'It's the water,' she said, 'that's what makes it so special.'

'Is it deep?' he asked.

'In odd places, apparently.'

'It looks old.'

'The lake, or the house?'

He shrugged. 'Everything, but the water looks as if it's been there forever.' A lone bird wheeled and cried, skimming across the surface to disappear amongst the reed beds and wild irises.

'Maybe it has.'

'Those trees, some of them are really big, even the shorter ones are gnarled and swollen with age.' He pointed. 'See that one leaning over the water, it's been bit by lightning or something.' The massive trunk had been split open and the dark wound had made what was left grow forked and twisted, so that the main body of the tree tilted at an almost impossible angle over the bank, two or three disconcerted branches trailing their tips in the water. 'We should know the names of trees – and birds come to that – it seems almost sacrilegious that we don't.'

'You're getting very heavy all of a sudden.'

'Maybe it's the country air . . .' He gave Pansy a dry smile.

'Why don't you take a look around while I put the kettle on?'

'Yeah, I'd like that – something cold, though. I don't know how you can drink tea on a day like this.' He opened the car door and paused for a second. 'This place belongs to Eve, doesn't it?'

'More her family, or rather her brother. I think Eve's mother signed it over to him when she went to live in the States.'

'Where is he?'

'Abroad, somewhere. He's sort of nomadic and not a great believer in keeping in touch; at least, that's what my father told me. I think he sends the odd postcard, but Eve hasn't seen him in years.'

He turned his attention back to the water. There was a dream-like quality about the place, and he fancied that if he gazed at the lake long enough it might exert some curious mesmerism on his mind, yield up some sweet mystery.

'Mind you don't trip over the molehills,' she said with a laugh.

'I have twenty-twenty vision, my dear,' he said, affecting an effeminate voice and swinging his hips ever so slightly.

'Maybe you have – but don't forget to look down – mere mortals like myself are much closer to the ground.'

She watched him wander off, pleased at his obvious interest because the lake house had lost none of its charm for her; she had wanted to return ever since that disastrous weekend. And it was funny, really, how her mother wanted the same thing; but perhaps she should stop being surprised at anything Minty said or did.

Pansy climbed out of the car and reached into her jacket for the key to the house; she had taken it without asking and she wasn't quite sure why. She looked up and squinted into the sun, looking for Frank, but he was disappearing into the trees. She found her thoughts switching to Eve and her obvious reluctance to come here and how her mother was trying to push the issue. It seemed to make no difference to Minty that her ex-husband's new wife had no love for this place, but her mother would have her own way in the end. Eve's quiet obstinacy would be no match for the bulldozer effect of her mother, and Minty enjoyed stirring things up, particularly where her father's marriage was concerned. It was impossible to blame him for divorcing her; it was probably the best thing he had ever done which, in the general scheme of things, was a pretty sad statement of fact.

Pansy looked hurt for a second and then angry; her mother could be an incredibly stupid woman, an incredibly stupid bitchy woman, and yet. And yet. Pansy smiled and shook her head slowly, there was something oddly endearing about her. One does not choose to love, she thought, it just is. Her gaze wandered away from the house and across the lush green lawn to the spot where she had last seen Frank. And sometimes one expects too much.

The trees linked hands above his head, almost completely blocking out the light in some places and then creating sun-dappled pools where it found a way through, and when Frank stepped into them he would look up, tracing the line of the tall trees to a sky which seemed unusually far away.

The grass was high, well above his ankles and stippled with late summer flowers. He began following a trail that must have been a well-worn path once. Now it was only a ragged and overgrown ribbon of ground, looping and twisting its way through the verdant undergrowth with the lake running parallel on one side, glinting at him between gaps in the scrub like some wise and knowing walking companion.

In shady hollows rich green moss carpeted stones and dead wood beneath trees spiked with brackets of yellow fungus. Once Frank paused to touch and was delighted by their perfection and cushion softness.

The air was amazing – all earthy smells and whisps of flower heads and so still, hardly disturbed by the gentle whir of insect wings. It all seemed very English somehow, and almost unnaturally perfect: a fairytale wood born of wishful imagination when knights were bold and people believed in magic and folklore and enchantment. He smiled to himself; he wasn't just getting heavy, he was getting poetic.

He stepped back, his foot jarring on something hard and metallic. A thin rusting bar lay at his feet, half-hidden by tree root and weed, and when he reached down for a closer look he saw the spikes, three in a row and a tiny skeleton still impaled there. He drew back in disgust, but even as he did so his eyes were focusing on a ragged piece of silky black fur stubbornly clinging to a minute bone. A mole. A very dead mole in a very nasty trap.

Frank stood up and looked around. It was like finding a maggot in a beautiful, shiny apple. He supposed he was thinking like a 'towny' – in ignorance. Nature always provided apparent pests: foxes, rabbits, badgers, moles; and man always managed to find ways of getting rid of them, and usually unpleasant ways. It was a dog eat dog world, hadn't his mother told him enough times?

Even in fairytale woods.

A breeze stroked his cheek like a sigh and he lifted his head to better appreciate the sensation, moving away from the spot that had offended him and when, a few moments later, he thought he heard something, a gentle sound of humming, it did not seem strange at all – perhaps a girl, sweet moist lips pressed together tight so that the sound emanating from the chords in her young throat was deeper, more serene. He stood still and listened, but the strains were drifting away from him, to where some trees clustered against the bank and the wood straggled to an end. He didn't want to lose the sound. There was something enticing about it, whether it was a clever mix of the breeze combining with the sough of the grass and rustle of leaves, he didn't know, but it was marvellously seductive.

He increased his pace as he approached and only realised he had entered a grove after forcing his way through some thorny undergrowth, where the sound faded and was lost and his head cleared. He gazed around at the scrubby open space and ring of pale trees. Ash? He had no idea, but he became aware of the silence now, heavy and thick, followed by an irrational feeling of being watched. He peered into the shadows, but there was nothing, no one, except his imagination, and then he looked down and saw water, a fine trickle just visible in the swathe of long grass, running outwards from the centre of the grove. He traced it to the edge where the ground sloped into the main body of water and bulging roots of trees sprouted from the bank, making excellent handholds for any would-be swimmer. And someone had swum here, it was obvious; he could see no other place, apart from the jetty, which would lend itself so favourably (and so secretly?) as an access point into the lake. Eve had come here, often. Frank couldn't explain how he knew, but he was as certain of this as he was that she had not been alone.

He glanced at the placid sheet of water and began stripping off his clothes.

Pansy unfolded two garden chairs and placed them on the lawn, there was a matching table somewhere, so she went back into the house to find it. By the time she had set it up and arranged tea and iced coffee on a tray, Frank had been gone almost half an hour. She sat down, poured herself a drink and waited.

The water was extraordinarily still, dozing beneath a cloudless sky which had a hazy cast, promising that the day would stay warm and drowsy. The sun hung almost directly overhead now and she closed her eyes for a few seconds, let the heat beat down on her eyelids and then, startled, she snapped them open. There was an anxious feeling in her chest, a timid puzzlement about the eyes. Something was wrong. A crow called, its harsh cry abruptly searing the stillness. Pansy frowned; that was not it.

She stood up and for a long moment stared into the distance, her gaze finally locking on a far bank where some willows trailed their leaves in the water, where shadows moved.

'Frank?' she said uncertainly and walked quickly to the edge of the lake and shaded her eyes. There was someone there. 'Frank?' she repeated again, but loudly so that her voice would carry, and it did, echoing eerily across the water.

A bleak silence followed and she felt a shiver, a slight wateriness of the stomach. An unsettling image slid into her mind of pondweed and black water.

She started running, keeping as close to the bank as she could, heedless of the briars and spikey shrubs which snagged her loose skirt. Twice she stumbled over bared roots, once she tasted earth.

Someone was in the water. Struggling.

Her father had warned her not to go into the lake, the mud was as deep as the water; she should have warned Frank. What had she been thinking of? And after her mother . . . Out of the corner of her eye she saw arms flailing, the tip of a head as it went under and came up again. She could feel his fear. Oh, God, yes, coming off him in waves, and a sort of outrage that made her cringe a little inside herself, as if the force of his personality, his thoughts, had sprung out of his body.

A vagrant branch blew into her face, obscuring her vision for a moment and when it cleared she stopped dead, a look of shocked surprise making her mouth gape; Frank was walking towards her, his jacket slung leisurely over his shoulder.

He grinned at her expression. 'What's the matter with you? You're as white as a sheet.'

She shook her head very slowly, confused and out of breath.

'You were in the water . . .'

'No.'

'I saw you.'

'I intended to, but it's freezing in there and I didn't like the way the mud and weed oozed up and around my legs. When it got as far as my knees I decided to come out.'

Pansy said nothing, but switched her gaze to the lake and moved wordlessly past Frank to the water's edge.

'There was someone,' she said softly, almost to herself. 'I saw . . .'

'When?'

'A moment ago.'

'Where?'

'Up a bit. Behind you.'

'I've just come from there.' He stared fixedly at her and then took her hand, and together they walked back to the place where he had been.

Glancing only cursorily at the grove she let go of his hand and walked across the grassy space to the point where the ground fell away into the lake. She gazed across the expanse of water to the house, to the place where she had stood, trying to gauge the spot she was searching for. A few feet away were the willows, there were no more until the bank curved round to meet the lawn; it was here, it had to be. She examined the sloping ground beneath her, was oddly chilled by the footprints left in the soft dark mud and then the water beyond, choked by an abundance of luxurious green weed.

'You must have seen me.' Frank had come up behind her.

'How could I?' she protested. 'I saw someone only seconds before I bumped into you. He was going under . . .'

'Here?' he asked. 'Are you sure?'

She sighed heavily, anxiously. 'Yes. Well, I'm as sure as I can be. He was further out, though, not close to the bank.'

'Perhaps it was a trick of the light – maybe a fish or something?'

She shook her head. 'No. And there are no fish, the weed eats up all the oxygen, nothing very large can survive in there.'

'A bird – having a quick dip?'

'It was a man, Frank.'

He held up his hands. 'Okay, okay. But I was here all the time and I didn't see anything. Come to that, I didn't hear anything, either, and if someone's drowning I would have thought they'd make quite a lot of noise. Don't you think?' He gestured at the mud. 'And there's only one set of footprints down there – mine.'

She didn't respond immediately, but Pansy's eyebrows drew together in a frown and then she said vaguely. 'You're right. I didn't . . .'

'What?'

'Hear anything.'

'Not even a splash?'

There was a worried look on her face. 'No.' And the more she thought about it, the more the quality of her experience seemed illusory and dream-like. It had the insubstantial feeling only dreams have, of strange fleeting visions that cannot be sustained by memory.

'Weird,' Frank said.

Pansy nodded, but still stared at the water; she felt weak and a little nauseated from her scare.

'May be it was a mirage, Flower?' He was trying to make her smile.

'Don't call me Flower, Frank,' she said absently. 'I hate it.'

He looked taken aback. 'Okay.'

They fell silent.

'He was white.'

White hands, white arms waxen with water. She squeezed her eyes shut and blinked them open again.

'What?'

'He was white, so it couldn't have been you.'

'You don't know what you saw.'

'I know it wasn't you.'

'But you thought it was, didn't you? That's why you looked so stunned when you saw me walking towards you.'

'I jumped to a natural conclusion.'

'This is crazy, Pansy,' he said, with a trace of impatience. 'Who was it, then? We didn't see anyone when we arrived. I didn't see anyone when I was here. Neither of us heard a thing – not a scream or a shout, or even a bit of splashing.' He waved his hand in the air with exasperation. 'What the hell are we talking about here?'

'I don't know.'

'Do you want me to jump in and take a look around – would that help?' He was getting irritated. 'I mean, I might drown in the process, but if it makes you happy . . .'

'Don't be stupid.'

'Look,' he said firmly, 'if you really think there's someone in there we'd better call the police.'

All at once her shoulders seemed to slump. 'No.' She drew a deep breath. 'I know what you're saying makes sense . . . it just didn't seem like a mirage, that's all, or a trick of the light.'

'I was here, Pansy – there was no one.'

'Perhaps it was a bird, then . . .' she said dully, her voice trailing away unconvincingly, but the certainty she had felt was fading now, by slow degrees.

'Once I thought I saw a UFO in broad daylight,' he said, 'it turned out to be a hot-air balloon.'

She tried to smile, but the expression on her face was both wary and puzzled.

'Let's go and have that tea,' Frank said gently, 'my throat's parched.'

She nodded and then looked back at him, one eyebrow cocked. 'You don't like tea.'

'I know,' he said with a slanted little smile, 'but right now, what does that have to do with anything?'

Pansy shrugged. 'Nothing I suppose.'

'Actually, I'd say anything to snap you out of your present state of mind.' He kissed her mouth lightly, slipped his tongue a fraction between her parted lips. 'Do anything . . .'

'Would you?' she asked softly.

'Oh, yes,' he said. 'Here, even . . .' Frank glanced down at the rough circle of grass. 'This place has a pagan air, sort of primitive, don't you think?'

'No,' she said abruptly and drew her face back. 'Let's go back to the house.'

He studied her for a moment, thought he saw both bewilderment and a little fear. 'Anything you say.' He put out his hand for hers and she took it.

As they walked away Pansy was unable to resist a look back, a look destined for that patch of water which had caused her such anxiety. It appeared so peaceful now, hard to imagine that that placid surface had ever been disturbed by anything but the soft sough of the wind.

'Don't tell anyone,' she said.

'Why not?'

'Because I don't want you to.'

'Okay.'

'Not my father,' Pansy persisted. 'Or Eve.'

'I said – okay.' He darted a glance at her tense profile; they were coming to the place where he had found the remains of the mole, but that was something else, he decided, that would be better kept to himself. 'I won't tell a soul.'

Pansy said nothing. She could see the lake winking at her from behind a lacework of trees, the sunlight falling in a broad jagged blade, brilliant and intense, turning the water white. Like the man's skin.

'I don't want to come.'

Minty glared at Tony. 'You will. It's a very healthy and positive way to start the week.'

'Healthy!' he exclaimed. 'She gives me the creeps.' He was smoking a cigarette, sitting in an old seventies cane chair which hung suspended from the ceiling by a long chain. Every few minutes he would make it spin with a jerk of his foot, but he always seemed to end up facing Minty.

'Immaculata is a clairvoyant, naturally you would find that creepy.'

'Oh, yes?'

'Yes.'

'Why?'

'Because you're a man,' she scoffed. 'Well, something that passes for a man.'

'Very funny.'

'By the way, have you been to see the quack about your problem, yet?'

'What problem?'

'Your dick problem.'

'There's nothing wrong with my . . . me,' Tony protested feebly, his face flushing.

'Except that it seems to have taken an extended vacation.'

'I've been busy. It's tiring being freelance.'

'Busy? You?' She threw back her head and let out a peal of laughter.

'Piss off, Minty.' He squirmed.

'Now, now . . .' she said, turning to a mirror and considering her reflection. She looked better, much better than the etiolated hag that had lain half-comatose in a hospital bed like a dead leaf. 'Besides, erect or otherwise, your dick holds no thrills for me, not any more.' Her skin was better, too, maybe it was staying off the booze. With great delicacy she touched her white-blonde hair which was growing back nicely. She looked a bit like Annie Lennox.

'Bully for you.'

'You haven't cleaned Harry out, either, have you?' She wrinkled her nose. 'It smells in here.'

'Yes, I bloody did.' Tony shot a glance across the room at his hamster's cage, but the little rodent was nowhere to be seen; he'd be snuggled-up in his house, of course, straw stuffed in his ears to keep out Minty's harping. 'Yesterday, as a matter of fact. I always do him on Sundays.'

Minty scrutinised her some-time lover from the mirror. Tony's face had softened, which frequently happened when he was discussing his pet. Curious, really, coming from a hardened old roué like him, but she liked him for it, although she would never say so.

'Actually, I might pop him over to the vet's, he seems a bit down in the dumps,' Tony's eyebrows drew together in a frown. 'I don't think I've seen him on his wheel for a couple of days.'

'Harry can wait.'

'Stop trying to organise my life.'

'Get your jacket.'

'No.'

'You're coming to Immaculata's.'

'You can't make me.'

'Oh, yes I can,' she snapped back and defiantly folded her arms. 'You owe me.'

'You can have it at the end of the month.'

'Now. Or I kick you out.'

'This is my bloody house,' he said, outraged.

'I don't care whose house it is.'

'You should listen to yourself, you sound like some crazy woman.'

'Put it this way, if you want a peaceful life, you'd better come with me.'

Tony sighed dramatically. 'Why, for God's sake?'

'Because I hate driving.'

'Get a cab.'

'I – want – you – to – come – with – me.' Her voice was beginning to rise.

'You want me in tow because you can't bear being alone.'

'Shut up.'

'Touch a raw nerve, did I?' he observed cruelly.

'What's a few Tarot cards to you, anyway?' she said grudgingly. 'They won't bite.'

'It's that woman,' he whined. 'Something about her – apart from the obvious: those repulsive, unappetising hands for a start.' He screwed up his face in disgust. 'I mean, have you really looked at them? The knuckles seem as though they've all been broken at one time, and the thumbs . . . they're bloody huge, like someone's squashed them flat with the heel of a navvy's boot.' A reluctant picture of Immaculata's doughy fingers took shape in his mind, splayed across the gaudy star-cards like some pallid amoeba. But worst of all she smelt old, and he hated that.

'Aren't we squeamish all of a sudden? I thought you liked a bit of blood and gore, a bit of pain . . .'

He ignored her remark. 'You must have noticed.'

'Of course I have, I'm not blind. Perhaps she was in an accident, who knows? Anyway, I think it gives her a lovely touch of authenticity. She's a real Romany, you know, spent half her life in a caravan . . .'

'So she says, and what does that prove?' Tony shook his head in exasperation. 'I had an aunt who lived in Mabelthorpe in a caravan; she was as mad as a hatter.'

'That would explain it.'

'What?'

'Your behaviour.' She picked a piece of fluff from her lapel. 'Is there a gene defect?'

'Don't be bloody stupid.'

'Just a thought.'

'I don't need your twisted little thoughts – and I don't need Immaculata,' he seethed, 'and I bet that's not her real name. If you did a bit of digging you'd probably discover she's really called Doreen. Anyway, you only saw her a month ago. Why so soon?'

'Things change. People change,' she said mysteriously, but there was deliberation in her voice, a sort of eagerness.

And Immaculata told her things, things that weren't bullshit, things that had meaning. Once she had seen Immaculata she was always left with a lovely feeling of sureness and direction, but this time there was an edge – it would be different somehow. Minty returned her gaze to her reflection, certain that this difference went hand in hand with the new and puzzling, yet delicious, sense of anticipation which had been growing steadily since her discharge from hospital.

Tony spun away from her and, using his foot as a brake, stopped the cane chair so that he was looking out of the window. Across the street the plum tree grew, the one from which one of his silk ties had bloomed.

'Please, Tony.' Minty's voice was suddenly diminutive and coy, like a little girl's.

He swung round and gaped at her. 'Oh, Christ, you're not using that one on me – we're both a bit long in the tooth for role-playing, aren't we?'

'I want you with me, Tony.'

'Balls.'

'I do,' she said softly and began moving towards him with a slow, undulating walk.

'Don't start, Minty.' She was wearing a little black suit with white piping; the skirt was too short really, but Minty had good legs, in fact they were the first thing that had attracted him to her, and today they were enclosed in black designer stockings. She never wore tights and she knew he knew.

Tony swallowed slowly. He didn't want to look, or imagine, or fantasise, but he just couldn't help himself. What was it about sex that made all, or any, good intentions fly straight out of the window? Yet it was one of the few things in his life that had never let him down, at least until now, but now nothing was working as it should. He was fifty and fraying around the edges.

'Start what?'

'Whatever you've got in mind.' He watched in glum trepidation as she drew close.

'Why don't you let me help you?' There was a funny little smile on her face.

'Help me what?'

Minty placed a hand on his crotch.

'No.'

'Why not?'

'You're playing games.'

She got on her knees before him. 'I can make it better for you.'

'Why are you doing this?' He felt his face going uncomfortably hot.

'Because I need you, Tony.'

'No, you don't.' His eyes gave her an uncertain, suspicious look.

She was opening his zip and then she had him, massaging his flaccid organ between her silky palms. She raised her eyes and saw him looking, smiled. Tony sighed and took a long, trembling drag on his cigarette.

'It won't work, you know.'

'Oh, I think it will.'

'You've been at my stuff , haven't you?' he accused her weakly. 'You're bloody stoned.'

'I haven't touched anything.'

'I don't believe you.'

She stopped what she was doing and looked at him long, full in the eyes, before he was forced to drop his gaze. 'You said I was different – and I am.'

'It's your dip in the water,' he offered lamely, 'that bump on the head.' She was kissing him there, so lushly, lapping him up, and it shocked him somehow. How long had it been? How long since she had touched (wooed?) him like this?

'Perhaps,' she murmured, 'perhaps not.' Actually, there was something in what Tony said, although he couldn't know exactly what it was except that she no longer felt obliged to please him as readily as she had done. In fact, she was the one more in control now, as if, somehow, their roles had been subtly reversed. And when she went over all that had happened in her mind she hardly knew why, or how, herself.

Something in the water. Something wonderful.

Her hands were beginning to ache with her careful ministrations, but Tony was hardening at last. Not long now. He moaned a little, a trickle of saliva escaping from the corner of his mouth.

'We must arrange a visit to the lake house . . .' she said firmly. 'It's become quite a passion with me.'

He nodded obediently, hardly aware of what she was saying.

'. . . once we've seen Immaculata.'

There was a glazed expression on Tony's face as Minty's smile broadened. 'I'll call Andrew and arrange something, after I've finished with you.' She took him in her mouth and he whimpered, his breath becoming ragged and uneven as the pleasure peeked and crashed out. It was over in a matter of seconds. Minty grasped the tail of his shirt and wiped her lips. 'You see,' she said. 'I told you I could do it.'

Andrew was slipping on his jacket as the telephone rang.

'Minty . . .' he made a face at Eve. 'How are you?'

Eve mouthed a 'no' at him from the doorway and made exit signs with her hand.

He watched her grab the sports bag sitting in the hall and open, and then close, the front door behind her.

'No, sorry,' he said into the phone. 'You've just missed her, she's off to the gym.'

'I didn't know she was a fitness fanatic.'

'She's not. It simply makes her feel good.' He sighed patiently. 'Perhaps you should try it.'

'Oh, God, no.' Minty sounded aghast. 'I hate enforced exercise.'

'What can I do for you?' Andrew glanced at his watch. 'And can it be quick, I'm just on my way out . . .'

'I wondered if we could arrange a weekend at the lake house?'

'Why? I would have thought it's the last place you'd want to go?'

'Look upon it as therapy – you know, after the accident,' she continued obstinately. 'Eve didn't say anything, then?'

'Say what?'

'About my suggestion – about going to the lake house.'

'No, she didn't.'

'How strange.'

'Not strange, Minty.' He felt irritated. 'Maybe she just doesn't want to go.'

'But that's silly,' she said sweetly, 'it's so beautiful, so peaceful. It would do her good.'

'She lived there most of her life, perhaps the novelty's worn off.'

'Nonsense.'

'Not nonsense, Minty, fact.' He raised his eyes to heaven and then placed a hand on his midriff, suddenly aware of a dull ache. His ulcer. Andrew cursed softly, his mind painting an unlovely image of an inflamed stomach lining.

'What did you say?'

'Nothing, nothing,' he said wearily and then added, 'besides, she might think you're going to take another dubious dip into that rather chilly water, which is enough to put anyone off.'

'I've learned my lesson.'

He thought she was feigning meekness and he scoffed.

'Really, I have, Andrew.'

'Save your breath, Minty, it's not working.'

'I haven't drunk a drop since I came out of hospital.'

'That's the best news I've heard in years.'

'Don't mock,' there was that meekness again, 'I'm really trying.'

'Are you?'

'Yes, Andy, I am.'

There was an awkward silence as he wondered despairingly whether she were telling the truth.

'So,' Minty said brightly, impatiently. 'Can we go?'

'Go?' She'd lost him.

'To the lake house.'

'I'm sure we can let you have the keys, if you really want. Eve won't mind.'

'But I want us all to go.'

'Look,' he said. 'You do what you want, but don't drag us into it.'

'But you will ask Eve, at least, won't you, Andy?' she pleaded. 'Give it a shot for me?'

'I thought she'd already given you her answer? Why can't you accept it?'

'Please, Andy.'

'What is this?'

'Please, Andy.'

'All right, for heaven's sake.' He heard her deep sigh of relief and felt distinctly uneasy. 'If this is one of your games, Minty . . .'

'It isn't,' she protested. 'I swear.'

He hesitated, pausing for a long moment. 'I'll ask once, and that's as far as I'm prepared to go.'

'Fine, fine,' she said quickly. 'That's all I wanted – such a little thing, really.'

Andrew frowned, confused by the excitement in her voice and the unaccustomed deference.

'You won't regret this, Andy.'

'I hope not.'

'Speak to you soon.'

Not if I can help it.

He listened to the click of the telephone as she rang off. There was an apprehensive look on his face as he replaced the receiver and stared blankly across the kitchen to the garden outside, the tall redbrick backs of houses beyond. He had no intention of asking Eve about a weekend at the lake house; if she had wanted to go she would have told him so by now. Minty would have to wait. Besides, what was all this so-called concern for Eve? Even Bill Streiber, his boss, kept asking after her in a nervous kind of way and it was beginning to annoy him.

Noises filtered down from upstairs, the comforting voices of Jack with Pansy, the *clip-clop*, *clip-clop* of his son's wood-block train as it was pushed around the floor.

His wife was elsewhere, of course, relaxing at the gym. Please God. Maybe then she would sleep and not dream, maybe then he wouldn't be pitched out of his own sleep and dragged into a waking nightmare.

He had awoken at some dark hour of the morning, to an Eve shuddering and convulsing, bathed in sweat, and when he had touched her she had simply opened her mouth and screamed, a reedy shriek of pure fear that had chilled his blood. The shrieking had ceased abruptly on a raw sob, an exhausted and lonely remnant from her night-time terrors. He had caught her against his chest and she had buried her face in his pyjamas, crying into the pale blue material until she had fallen asleep.

In the morning, when he had looked back at his tired self in the bathroom mirror, there had been a saucer-shaped stain on his pyjamas, still damp from her tears.

They had not talked about it; they never talked about it. Once, when he had tentatively broached the subject, she had shrugged it off and hidden behind a curtain of flippancy, blaming Jack's difficult birth. But the nightmares had been part of Eve before Jack, and probably before that.

Andrew made a soft, despairing sound. What, then, had actually happened before? What something in her past made her dream such horrors? He could ask again, and again, but he knew she would never tell him.

She swam and swam until her limbs ached. No weights today, no step-ups or knee-bends or sit-ups, no sweat trickling down skin and burning muscles. Swimming soothed Eve like nothing else and she needed to be soothed, taken out of herself and away from the shadows hounding her. And they were shadows, weren't they, jumbled up with memory and imagination? She needed to believe this because any other alternative was unthinkable.

Perhaps she was going crazy.

Last night had been a bad one. Lying against Andrew in the fretful silence, pretending to fall into sleep, not opening her eyes once so that there would be no questions and no sex, comforting or otherwise. And he had a right to ask. Sweet, lovely man pulled into his wife's nightmares, and a wife who clamped her mouth shut on secrets so secret she was unable to acknowledge them.

But they were beginning to peep out (oh God, not peep, leer). Whom had she seen the other evening? What had she done? Yet, at the time, some intervening darkness seemed to thin and she had known, had seen, and although the recognition faded some sensation stayed with her afterwards, lingering lushly in the air like incense. Eve licked her lips, aware that her mouth had gone dry. A part of her had wanted to cleave to it, had ached towards it.

Fill me up again. Oh please. Do it again.

She moaned aloud and rubbed at her wrist. Beneath the sticking plaster the wounds were beginning to itch. She darted a glance around her. There was only one woman, old, at the other end of the pool, swimming doggedly to ease the stiffness in her arthritic joints. Two or three women wallowed in the jacuzzi, swirling jets massaging soft, placid flesh whilst their mouths talked.

They were all naked and used to seeing each other's bodies, their beauties and imperfections, and probably much less shy than when with their men. They were different people here, she supposed, more free, released for a few hours from their duties and the probing and critical eye of any partner.

For a few moments her eyes were wondering and sad. She had striven to belong here, had behaved as though she did belong, but she had never sat in the jacuzzi gossiping and giggling with anyone, never chewed over a medical problem, the state of her marriage or discussed the result of her last smear.

Eve climbed out of the pool and padded over to a shower unit, let the water cascade down hot, hotter, until her body burned so that she made a suppressed groan, a little mewling sound like a hurt kitten before she switched it off, because she wasn't that brave.

She was a coward and she was a whore.

The door of the steam room wheezed as she opened it, wheezed when she closed it behind her; it had wheezed since she joined the club, like some old gent with a persistent chest complaint.

Eve stretched out on a ceramic bench, on the little square tiles dripping with water and other people's juices, settled her body horizontally along the highest point where the steam was warmest: face on hands, belly to tiles. There was the scent of lemon verbena, a touch of eucalyptus and something else she couldn't name, but it didn't matter because she was closing her eyes and drifting away.

Someone had told her once that memory can be awakened by fragrance, that the memories smells can trigger are somehow more intense than those dredged up by conscious effort : . .

She thought she heard the steam room door wheeze open and then close again.

That same someone had told her that smell provides a short-cut to our deepest memories and can bring them back, complete with the emotions and sensations we had at the time.

Eve shifted her position, felt the smooth flesh of another brush her calf. She moved her leg.

The lesson had gone on . . . that the most potent perfumes are derived from ancient animal scents, from bestiality, which eventually provided the deep and lingering base notes of exclusive fragrances.

A touch of anal sac behind the ears, madam?

He had laughed, then, and she could remember the laughing.

Who? Who had given her the lesson? Who had laughed?

A tickling sensation on the sole of her foot made her jump and she leaned up on one elbow and looked through the steam. Someone had come in, she had heard the door, but apart from the low thrum of the water filter there was nothing to hear and no one to see and even the steam, after a while, gave way to shapes and bits of bodies: the curve of a thigh, the rounded arch of a back, a bowed head.

But there was only steam.

She lay down again and closed her eyes, dozed, dreamed a little, tried to make herself keep awake, but knew it was useless and didn't really care. The muscles in her face slowly relaxed, the frown lines on her forehead decreasing, her mouth half-open in the helpless, dewy way of a child when it is touched deeply by sleep. Eve took on the look of a young girl, perhaps the girl she had been, on the brink of womanhood and ripe for seduction.

In her dream, she was that girl, and in her dream she was in water, black water clotted with weed, and the man was behind her and the man was doing things to her with his hands.

But the hand that glided up her leg, thigh and over her haunches, seemed much more than just a dream. The hand that wrote his name in the steamy sweat lying on her naked back was not really a dream at all.

* * *

Eve decided to walk home after the gym; her skin still tingled from the steam room. She wondered what would have happened if that woman hadn't woken her, an attractive middle-aged woman with yellow hair peeping from a plastic bath cap. She had helped her up with surprisingly strong arms and then out into the cool of the shower area, where she waited to make sure that Eve was all right. There was a vague, physical resemblance to Eve's mother, although Diana wouldn't be seen dead wearing a plastic bath cap, or walking around stark naked, either. She realised that she had never seen her mother with her clothes off. Eve's face buckled into a puzzled frown.

Diana had always worn beautiful, but such sensible clothes: blouses with high neck-lines, delicately embroidered cardigans with hand-made buttons, calf-length skirts, loafers and blazers and cashmere jackets with silk scarves draped across the shoulders. She had kept most of them sheathed in plastic in her wardrobe and draped on velvet hangers, and when she intended to dress, or change, she would select an outfit and matching accessories and take them into the little windowless room off her bedroom, where there was a long oval mirror. It always smelt of lavender in there, lavender and rosewater, the scent of her skin.

When Eve had been quite small she had walked in while her mother had been dressing and Diana had yelped in surprise and irritation, scooting her out imperiously like a very large and bothersome fly.

Once she had walked in on her mother with James.

Diana had only been dressed in a slip, a creamy satiny thing and one of the lacy straps had fallen down her arm; across the shoulder a row of angry fingerprints burned red.

Eve had been drawn by her brother's laughter, and the laughter had been thick with mockery and disdain and it didn't stop when his much younger sibling came into view, despite their mother's obvious discomfiture. And when Diana had tried to cover herself, he had caught her hand and held it so tightly that the knuckles had turned white.

James seemed to find their mother – her clothes, her manner, her little daily rituals, her beliefs – darkly hilarious. And sometimes Eve found herself wondering if that had been all.

He had developed a deep irreverence for Catholicism and Catholics, particularly English Catholics although Eve had never really understood why. He had stopped going to church as soon as he was old enough to defy their parents, had started smoking as soon as he looked old enough to buy cigarettes. And Diana never chastised him, not in a real way, but after being expelled from school for the second time he had been sent to Salzburg to study music, and then he had hardly come home at all.

There was such a large age-gap between them that Eve could barely remember him in the early years, except for the sharp brittle laughter that was usually saved for their mother. And Diana had soaked up that laughter like a greedy sponge, and sometimes she had actually laughed with him, as if she shared the joke, which had made him laugh even louder. She adored James, you see, adored him. He had never been able to do any wrong where their mother was concerned.

Eve stopped to stare into the glass of a shop window, shifted the sports bag on to her shoulder and looked back at herself. She had been twelve and away at school when her father died. Three years later Diana had remarried an American and gone to live in California. Her mother with a golden glow, sporting a tan. Wearing shorts?

She had never seen her mother's thighs.

It was, she supposed, rather odd to be speculating on the body of her absent and now ageing mother, but as she turned away from the glass and approached the crossing on the Fulham Road she felt a little breathless, her heart pounding as if at an escape, but then, mercifully, she found herself wanting to laugh.

A motorbike had stopped on the other side of the road and the man sitting on it began removing his helmet. She was about to walk past him when he took her arm.

'Eve,' he said. 'I thought it was you.'

She looked down at the dark hand on her sleeve and then switched her eyes to his face. 'Frank?'

'I would have missed you if the traffic hadn't been so slow. Are you on your way home?'

'Yes.'

'Hop on. I'm on my way to see Pansy – I'll give you a lift.'

She looked startled. 'I don't think so.'

'Why not?'

'I've never been on a motorbike in my life.'

'It's a Harley, dear lady, not just a motorbike – and an experience not to be missed.'

'I couldn't.'

'Oh, come on. You only live once,' he pressed. 'And I'll be super-careful and go very slowly.'

'There's only one crash-helmet.'

'You do have me there,' he said wryly, 'but you can borrow mine.'

'You won't have one – isn't that against the law?'

He threw his head back in exasperation, almost laughing in disbelief. 'Look, I'll take off along the back-streets and if we get nicked I'll take full responsibility. Okay?'

She regarded the bike doubtfully for a moment and then slowly took the crash-helmet from his waiting hands.

'Good girl.'

'You're patronising me.'

'Just a little,' he said. 'Now swing your leg over, get comfortable and hold on to me.'

She did exactly as she was told and as he gunned the machine into life and drew away from the kerb she felt vaguely thrilled by the power building and then the brief sensation of speed as they turned off the main road, so much so that she was almost tempted to tell him to go faster and not just faster – to go – somewhere. Be reckless. Not care. Lose it all.

She had seen a film once, about two young men travelling across the States on souped-up motorbikes – great chrome things they had been, two-wheeled monsters with chin-high handlebars. As far as she could remember, the travellers had had no pattern or route or even faint idea where they were headed: they had ridden where they wanted, when they wanted on long, long dusty roads with no ending. Oh, God, and how she had envied them – their freedom, their wild bikes, their random future.

Eve closed her eyes and leaned her head just a touch closer and the warm leather smell of his jacket filled her nostrils. She felt the gaiety come back, the same sort of breathless gaiety that had claimed her for such a painfully short span of time at the party.

She almost groaned aloud when they arrived back at the house; it was too quick, too soon. And the house was empty, she knew it as soon as she stepped into the hall. Eve opened the cupboard built into the stairs and immediately realised Jack's pushchair was missing.

'Pansy's probably taken him to the park,' she said and then glanced down and saw that she still held Frank's crash-helmet in her hand. 'Yours, I think.'

He took it from her and hung it on the hatstand. 'You enjoyed your little trip, didn't you?'

Eve looked back at him steadily. 'Yes.'

'I knew you would.'

'How did you know?'

'Because . . .'

'What?'

'Because sometimes there's a look about you,' he felt his throat tighten up a little, 'like there's a bit of wildness inside somewhere . . .'

She said slowly, strangely, 'Someone else said that to me once.'

Frank stared fixedly at her, unable not to as her eyes focused unhesitatingly on his. There was a remote look on her face, a sort of withdrawn expression as if her eyes saw something else, something or someone beyond the narrow confines of the hallway in which they stood.

'Are you okay?' he asked, and laid a hand on her shoulder.

Eve turned and for a long moment gazed down at his hand and then gently tilted her head, so that it came to rest on his fingertips, rubbed her cheek against them.

Numbly, as if from a distance, he whispered: 'Eve?'

She looked back at him without speaking, but in an odd, yearning kind of a way. Their eyes met and held and during the silence that pulsed between them he watched her mouth move and part and her tongue lick his warm salty skin.

'Please,' she murmured.

'Eve . . .'

'Please.'

The softly uttered word seemed to oscillate in his mind and he fought to control his breath, but he knew what he would do, he had known all the time. There was no question.

She was staring at him, making his head spin, but her gaze began moving restlessly over his face and upper body before she stretched out and touched him, as if she were reassuring herself that he was real.

'Yes,' he said.

He looked down as her hands reached for the buttons of her blouse and watched with scared lust, as she unbuttoned every one and pulled back the thin material so that he saw. And the seeing made his heart pound in his chest, in his ears, dried up all the saliva in his mouth. She moved closer, rested her shifting hands lightly on his neck, let them steal down and across his torso where they paused for a moment, before the creamy, supple fingers began pushing aside his tee shirt and the hands slid inside. He felt a little unsteady, and panicky, as if everything was drawing away.

She reined him to her, embracing him with shameless intimacy: pressed her mouth against his, her flesh against his flesh, brought her tongue to his nipples and rolled them into her mouth. The sensation was so exquisite, Frank thought he would die.

With a low moan he buried his fingers in her hair, caught the rich heaviness in his fists and leaned his head back against the wall. His eyes were only half-open in a kind of rapture, but his gaze drifted to the window above the door, a translucent pane of glass which allowed the sun to shine through. His mind was suddenly full of the lake house and the wood where he had walked, the spaces in that shadow-lace of trees where the light had shone down the colour of butter.

Frank was back in the grove and she was there, Eve, in a pink gingham dress. She was running and he was running after her, his arm reaching out to grasp and take, and when he caught her (and there was no doubting that, although he couldn't have said why), he would force her against a tree and lift her skirt and have her there, with the thick fissured bark pressing into her back and buttocks and into the palms of his hands.

And then he saw the hands and the hands were white.

Frank recoiled, his odd daydreaming sensation abruptly supplanted by a shudder.

The sun dimmed as a thin wrack of cloud passed across its face and the little scene in the hall was bathed in a dull light – jaundiced and sepia toned.

It seemed to him that his desire, his fascination and need for Eve was sapped by that greyness, sucked away by something outside himself. Not now, a voice seemed to say.

Not yet.

Outside the gate clanged shut and he heard Pansy's soothing voice talking to the baby.

'Eve,' he stroked her hair gently, then urgently, 'Eve.'

She looked up, a puzzled, almost innocent expression on her face.

'They're back,' he said and nodded towards the door. Her hands were still on him and he lifted them away, confronted again by the nakedness of her breasts. He squeezed his eyes shut for a second before covering them, his hands fumbling for the buttons. And all the time Eve stood mutely, waiting for him to finish and staring up at him, child-like, as he smoothed down her hair. He took her hand and led her into the kitchen. 'I'll make some coffee.'

He sat her down and quickly walked away, over to the other side of the kitchen, to the kettle and the mugs and the safety of everyday things.

'I don't know what you must think of me,' she said all at once. 'I was miles away.'

He turned and looked at her quizzically. To what exactly did she refer? Him? Their episode in the hall? But then she smiled, a curious yet radiant smile that made his stomach lurch.

Frank reached for the kettle, saw that his hand was shaking and his palms clammy with sweat. He wiped them on his jeans and took a deep breath. He could hear Pansy in the hall, Pansy picking up the baby from his pushchair, Pansy laughing and walking into the room; Pansy's pretty face lighting up at the sight of him.

Six

'**H**ello, Pansy,' Eve said.

Frank watched her carefully, caught by that smile again, but caught, too, by momentary dread. Yet Eve's expression, her demeanour, gave nothing away. In fact, it was almost possible to believe that nothing had happened between them at all.

'Eve. Hi!' Pansy turned to her stepmother with a grin. 'I didn't see you sitting there. Everything okay?'

'Everything's fine,' Eve said calmly. 'I had a wonderful time at the gym and then I met Frank in the high street and he gave me a lift home.'

'On the bike?' Pansy's eyes grew round.

'Yes.'

'Wait 'til Dad hears about this!' She threw back her head and laughed. 'You obviously missed the rain, then . . . it's just starting to drizzle.' She switched her attention to Jack who had stiffened in her arms and was staring very hard at Frank. 'Your Mummy's been very naughty, she took a lift on a strange man's big bad motorbike.'

'And I don't think he likes the strange man, either . . .' Frank said ruefully, 'not by the look on his face.'

'It's probably the colour of your skin,' Eve said, playing with a twist of her hair.

There was a moment's odd little silence as the remark was inwardly digested. Frank looked hard at her and felt the blood soar into his face, but neither she, nor Pansy, would notice and for exactly the reason Eve had just stated. By George and strike a light, how very fucking perceptive . . .

An expression of hurt surprise came and went on Pansy's face and she studied her stepmother for a long moment.

121

'I mean that Jack has never met anyone black before,' Eve continued as artlessly as if she were talking about a change in the weather, 'he would probably react in the same way to someone wearing glasses, or a turban or a top-hat.'

'In that case it's just as well I wasn't wearing my crash-helmet or he might have thought he was meeting a Martian . . .' There was an edge to Frank's voice, and reproach, as if his words were also asking why she wanted to say such a thing. Let her, or anyone, think it, but not say out loud, no matter how well meant.

It's called tact, a funny old-fashioned word in these dying days of the twentieth century.

But especially not her, not after what we did, what we were to each other. And what was that, his mind said, what exactly was that? A quick grope in the hall to be precise.

'I haven't embarrassed you, have I, Frank?' She gave him a slow, delicious smile and he felt himself harden just by looking at her. She was teasing him. Yes, she was. Behind her grave dark eyes she was laughing and he had not thought her capable of that.

A tease. A prick-tease.

He didn't understand and he had a sudden urge to shake her, or yell at her, but instead moved a little sideways so that the breakfast bar might hide the evidence of her effect on him, and away from Pansy's sharp eyes. It wouldn't do for his girlfriend to see what was happening to him . . . and it was Pansy he was concerned about, wasn't it?

'I mean,' Eve continued smoothly and went on in that same smooth voice, 'I was just making a point, and children are so sensitive, particularly at this tender stage of their little lives. Pansy's always telling me that.' She turned to her stepdaughter, 'Aren't you, Pansy?'

Pansy nodded slowly, obscurely aware that there was much more than just a conversation going on here, but unable to grasp what it was. She shifted Jack in her arms and made to put him in his high-chair when she felt the letter which she had tucked between herself and her half-brother begin to slip.

'Oh, I forgot,' she said, 'this was lying in the hall when I came in, you must have missed it. It's for you.'

'Me?' Eve looked startled, all her disarming calm abruptly gone.

'Yes.' Pansy handed it to her. 'It's from the States.'

Eve took it from her outstretched hand and dropped it quickly on the table, as if it were something diseased and contagious.

'Aren't you going to open it?'

'Of course,' Eve said rapidly, 'but I've a few things to do upstairs, I'll take it with me.' She stood up as if to go.

'Have you had any lunch?' Pansy asked, eyeing her stepmother carefully.

'No, I'm not hungry. I'll have something later.'

'Would you like me to make you a sandwich?'

'That's sweet of you, but no thanks.' She looked at her son, who was still sitting placidly in Pansy's arms, and then gingerly lifted her hand to cup his round plump cheek. 'He's beautiful,' Eve said the words almost wistfully, 'but he looks at me the way he looked at Frank. Doesn't he?'

Pansy gazed at her, troubled. 'Not always.'

Eve caught her glance and smiled, laid a hand on her sleeve and said mildly, 'it's all right – really.'

Pansy tried to smile back, but failed dismally. 'Your letter,' she said, 'it's still lying on the table.'

'Oh, yes. I almost forgot it, didn't I?' She took it in her hand and folded it in two before sliding it into the pocket of her jeans. 'I'll see you later.'

Frank followed her with his eyes, waiting for her to turn and smile, or look – something, anything – but she just walked out of the kitchen as if he didn't exist, and he was shocked to realise how deeply she had wounded him.

'Do you think she's okay?' Pansy said quietly. 'She seems well . . . odd.'

'Does she?'

'Didn't you notice?'

'I don't know her that well. How would I know whether her behaviour was odd or not?' He shifted his attention back to the sink and the kettle which was sitting, empty and lidless, just as he had left it only minutes before. Minutes? It seemed more like hours.

'What's the matter with you?'

'I'm fine.' He felt a dull species of shame and started fiddling with the lid of the kettle unnecessarily, as if it wouldn't, or couldn't, fit.

'Shouldn't you fill it first?'

He closed his eyes for a second and rubbed at his temples.

'I'm tired,' he said.

'Why did you come over?'

'Why do you think?'

'If you came to see me, you don't seem very thrilled about it.'

'Sorry.'

Pansy strapped Jack into his high-chair and then walked over to the breakfast bar. 'I have to make his lunch.'

She stood there watching him and Frank met her steady gaze with unease, battling against a desire to look away from her. 'It was a beautiful day, I rode over on impulse because I knew you'd be here . . .'

'Did you?' she said expressionlessly.

'Yes.'

'How sweet.'

'Stop it.'

Her mouth parted in a slight smile as if she had just extracted from him what she wanted. 'Kiss me.'

He leaned across the divide that separated them and she met him halfway, and all the time he was wondering what he would feel when her lips touched his and knowing it could never be the same. Not after Eve.

He couldn't tell Pansy, of course, couldn't finish it between them because that would be the end – of everything. After all, if he stopped seeing her he would stop seeing Eve and he couldn't do that, not now, not while this longing possessed him. He felt a surge of self-contempt; he was not good at deceit and took no pleasure in betrayal, particularly with someone like Pansy whom, despite everything, he respected and liked, perhaps more than liked – he really didn't know any more.

Yet he hadn't planned it this way, he told himself with surly defensiveness, he just couldn't help it. It was down to her, the good stepmother. Quite simply, he had never wanted a woman the way he wanted her now, and nothing else seemed important; he had become, as they say, totally focused. And it hurt.

Perhaps this was the love that poets wrote of, he thought miserably.

And she's married, man, he screamed inwardly, she has a husband – your girlfriend's father.

With great deliberation Frank placed a hand either side of Pansy's upturned face and kissed her hard and long, as if to exorcise the feeling that was beginning to haunt his days, and his nights.

She had taken the letter out of her pocket and placed it on the dressing table, the one she had bought with Andrew from a dealer off the Portobello

Road. Eve counted on her fingers – only eighteen months ago. They had bought the wallpaper together, too; it was amber silk imprinted with gorgeously plumed birds and fat smiling Buddhas. Not at all restful, she realised wearily, and quite wrong for a bedroom.

She sat down on the bed and looked at the letter for a long time, then finally lifted her eyes to the ceiling. Their bedroom was built into a part of the house that had once been a large attic. It sloped steeply on one side, incorporating three dormer windows which allowed a great deal of light into the room, even on grey days like this one had become, but now the middle window stood open and rain was coming into the room. She stared at the wet patch of carpet where the rain had got in; it was spreading and darkening like an old tea stain. She stood up and closed it with a slam and then walked into the bathroom.

The cleaner had been. Everything was pristine, shining and neat, but especially the taps – they positively glowed.

Eve looked back at herself in the mirror over the basin and the only word that came to mind was tired: dog-tired, bone-weary, drained. Perhaps she had done too much at the gym. She turned on the cold tap (excuse my fingerprints please) and began splashing her face with water, over and over, and she felt better.

The sky had darkened outside and a throb of thunder rumbled away somewhere in the distance. As she patted her skin dry with a towel she leaned across to the window, saw sheet lightning blanket the horizon. It wouldn't last, she thought, it was a late summer shower and afterwards everything would smell clean and fresh and good.

When she was a child the water at the lake house had often flooded the surrounding grass after heavy rain, and from a distance the invaded banks had shone green, emerald green, like magical paths circling the edge of a secret underworld. She had thought there was a holiness about it somehow, something sacred, like an enchantment, or a spell.

With disturbing ease, Eve's mind returned to Minty. Minty in the lake that night, staring up at her, lips drawn back in that odd beatific parody of a smile. Minty in the hospital grasping her hand.

Minty and the man.

Eve bit her lip and closed her eyes for an instant and then began slipping off her clothes. She wanted, no needed, to sleep. There were sleeping tablets somewhere in the medicine cabinet and she rummaged through until she found the small brown bottle and tipped one out into her palm;

except one would be too much in the middle of the day, wouldn't it? She split it carefully down the middle with a fingernail and swallowed the half-tablet dry.

Had it been the same man at the party? The one watching her, the one whispering her name? She cupped her aching forehead with the palm of her hand and wondered.

And Frank . . . in the hall . . . something. A confusion of feelings played across Eve's face; but he was like him.

She moved to the doorway and surveyed the empty room; the dormer window had blown open again, the catch had to be loose. She put her hand through the gap and the rain blew down on it, wetting her fingers. She closed it again, walked slowly over to the bed and lowered herself on to it, then lay on her back and stared blankly at the wallpaper, trying to empty her mind.

That is a hard thing, perhaps the hardest thing of all. Easy to stop the body moving, but not the mind: the mind is never still, not really, not even in sleep; it continues working, rolling ever-onward under its own power.

The mind is the spirit and the spirit is pure energy, a priest had once told her, when he had been trying to convince her of the reality of life after death.

And energy never dies, he had said.

She lay quietly, listening to the sounds in the room, heard a board creak and felt a vagrant breeze creep up her naked skin, each change in the moving air like a caress. She raised her head just slightly and realised that the window had fallen open again, but she remained where she was, not caring any longer.

A pleasant, drowsy sort of haze washed over her and she squirmed a little against the coverlet, placed the flat of her hand on her stomach: pressed, rubbed and gathered the flesh with the tips of her fingers. She ran her hands slowly down her body, from breasts to hips, felt hot suddenly, damp all over and a little out of control, as if her senses had been heightened in some way. Yet the tiredness was on her again like a weight; it was the pill she had taken, she pondered dreamily, working like magic. Oh, God but her eyelids felt heavy.

Even as she was drifting into the dark her fingers were alive to the day, moving with a sureness and direction that belied the sleeping body to which they belonged. There was something stealthy in the way they crept across her lower belly and into the rich fur of her pubic hair, something unnatural, then further, until they found that wet warm place and the core at its centre. Eve twitched in her sleep, whimpered.

Half-wanting what had begun to stop, half-wanting it to go on.

Through half-closed lids she thought she saw him grinning, lushly, from the wallpaper but when she looked again it was only one of the Buddhas, its thick and heavy mouth seeming to move into a sly conspiratorial smile, and then the light changed and the smile had gone. A trick, that was all, of shadow or imagination; a childish thing that makes a monster out of a piece of furniture in a darkened room.

It reminded her of those early days after her mother had left and the nightmares had begun, and how he had come and laughed the bogeyman of her dreams away, stroking her hair. Stroking her. The image rose out of the years, complete with all its colours and bitter-sweet sensations. Except the bogeyman hadn't been in her dreams, or on the wallpaper: the bogeyman had been real.

He had told her stories, exotic tales of wonder and mystery, weaving seduction into words and dreams, all the while pretending to ignore what he was doing to her, just as she pretended to ignore everything.

He had been so difficult to resist; a wild card, enigmatic, amoral. Enticing and depraved.

He had corrupted her. And sometimes she had liked it.

She heard a small inarticulate sound which must have come from her own throat, then, 'Oh, God . . .' in a fainting little voice, her head shaking helplessly from side to side.

Stroking, touching.

On and on.

Eve shuddered and turned her face into the pillow as her climax peaked. The exquisite sensation mushroomed, sending vast widening rings through her body, impaling her against the soft downy coverlet. Her eyes flew open: huge, floating saucers in a stunned white face.

Tony sat on a chair in the corner, desperate for a cigarette. Minty was on the other side of the room, sitting at a small table covered with green baize, her arm outstretched as Immaculata finished examining the lines etched into her right hand.

'The cards now,' Immaculata said, 'but perhaps you would like a break first for some tea?'

'I'd like a break for a cigarette,' Tony said resentfully.

'You can't smoke in here, I'm afraid,' Immaculata said firmly, 'but please go outside if you wish.'

Minty swung round and glared at him. 'You're not going anywhere.'

He glared back, gripping the sides of his chair in an effort at controlling his voice. 'Well, in that case, perhaps you'll just get on with it. You're wasting time.'

Minty seemed to hesitate then pointed her chin at him in that silly, snobby way he detested before looking back at Immaculata. 'If you wouldn't mind . . .' she said sweetly.

'Of course.'

Tony watched Immaculata pick up the pack of cards which had been stacked neatly by her elbow from the beginning. They were ebony and gold, but in the centre of each card an eye had been painted, a great blood red thing with a dilated and staring black pupil – as if the cardboard image had just indulged in a massive snort of unbelievably good coke. The thought made Tony shift restlessly in his seat.

'We'll try the pyramid spread today,' he heard the clairvoyant's deep plummy voice say, and realised all at once how masculine she sounded. Tony darted a glance at her bulky figure hunched over the table and wondered whether she swung both ways, although, to be brutally frank, she looked long past it.

He found himself examining her sharply – well, he had nothing better to do and she was an interesting, if unappetising, target for his scrutiny. Besides, he was bored and she irritated him intensely.

Immaculata's salt and pepper hair was piled high on her large round head in a deranged mass and held together by three hairpins the size of meat skewers. She wore a huge baggy dress that looked like silk, but was probably polyester; he could see the outline of her underwear where the thin material had been drawn tight beneath her seated bottom. A vision of an enormous pair of knickers took shape in his mind and he had to clamp his mouth shut to stop himself from sniggering out loud. Every time she moved things clanged and dangled: beads, bracelets, earrings, and wasn't that a stud in her nose? Hideous. Inevitably his gaze came to rest on her unfortunate hands and he pulled a disgusted face behind her back.

'I could do a reading for you, too, Mr Sweeney . . .'

Tony jumped, like a schoolboy who has been caught turning the pages of a dirty book. She couldn't have seen him, he protested silently, but there was something in her dark brown voice that seemed to say that she had –

as if she had eyes in the back of that haystack of a head. He frowned, trying to comprehend this mystery and swallowed hard before answering. 'No. Thank you.'

'What a pity,' she said, turning round to look at him. 'I'm sure it would prove an interesting exercise.'

He quickly averted his gaze, peering nervously down at his Gucci loafers.

'I think he's afraid,' Minty piped up.

'Well,' Immaculata said, 'if I was Mr Sweeney I'd be afraid, too.'

Tony's eyes shot up. 'What the hell do you mean?'

'Most people who refuse to recognise their own psychic gifts are afraid.'

He snorted loudly. 'I'm not bloody psychic. In fact I don't believe any of this moronic mumbo-jumbo – I'm only here because she forced me into it.'

Minty shook her head in feigned despair. 'Do try and be a little gracious, Tony.'

'It's all right, Araminta,' Immaculata patted her hand, 'I quite understand.

Tony raised his eyes heavenward and stood up. 'I've just about had enough of this.'

'I wish I could reassure you on that point, Mr Sweeney,' Immaculata continued unsparingly, 'but sadly, one has no power over events that are already ordained.'

'Bullshit.'

'Tony!' Minty shrilled.

'I'll wait outside,' he said with barely suppressed fury.

'You're a Pisces, aren't you?' Immaculata's voice ran on.

'What if I am?'

'It's here, in the cards.'

'Minty told you.'

'No, she didn't.'

He couldn't resist a move towards the table, just a peep over her big plump shoulder and later, oh much later, he would wish that he hadn't.

The cards were laid, or spread, in the shape of a triangle – 'the pyramid' – and one of Immaculata's pasty fingers had honed in on a card portraying his zodiac sign.

'It could be anyone.'

'It's a man and it's you.'

He said nothing, but his face had grown pale beneath the artificial tan.

'There's another man here, too, but you don't – and won't know him.'

'Where?' Minty asked eagerly.

'I can't tell you that.'

Minty frowned in puzzlement.

'Would you like me to go on?'

'No. I wouldn't,' Tony snapped.

'Do you mind,' Minty protested, 'it's hardly your decision to make!'

'I don't care,' he said with a finality that discouraged further discourse. 'I'm leaving.'

'You're such a bloody killjoy,' Minty seethed.

'I don't agree with throwing good money away on this hokus pokus crap, that's all. I'll see you outside.' He stalked away, fishing into his pocket for his cigarettes at the same time.

'He does have a gift, you know,' Immaculata said quietly, 'I could feel it.' And his distaste, it had emanated from him like a bad smell. He had been wrong about the sex thing, though – she wasn't past it, she still yearned for the closeness of another human being as much as she ever had. Age had withered everything else, but not that. I am young inside, she thought. Inside this big fat body I am young, but no one knows.

'Tony – psychic? It hardly seems possible . . .' Minty shook her head in amazement.

'Perhaps we could finish now, if you don't mind,' Immaculata said abruptly.

'Oh, really?' Minty said with obvious disappointment, 'perhaps I could persuade him to cool down and come back.'

'I don't think so. Besides, the atmosphere has been ruined and I'm no longer in the right frame of mind to continue. I won't charge, of course.'

'If you insist,' Minty said reluctantly, 'but I'll call you soon and make another appointment, if that's all right.' Yet she felt cheated. Yes, definitely cheated, as if Tony had deliberately forestalled whatever Immaculata had been about to say next. And wasn't that why she had come?

Immaculata nodded in response and raised her hand to her lips where a small smile was fixed; her lipstick had smudged, some of it melting into the corners of her mouth. She waited patiently as her client smoothed down her skirt, picked up her dainty black handbag and left the room. For a long time the clairvoyant looked at the closed door and then turned her gaze back to the cards and began turning them over one by one.

The man she had seen there was not unlike her – alone – and he was coming, had come perhaps, and he was growing desperate.

'Don't ever,' Tony began angrily, wagging his finger close to Minty's face, 'drag me there again. Do you understand?!'

'You're so pathetic,' Minty retaliated, 'pathetic. You behaved like an infant, what's more a deeply unattractive infant – I've never been so embarrassed.' She stomped into the house, almost shutting the door in his face.

Tony stood on the threshold, not sure whether to go or stay, but he had no plans, no people to see, and everyone else he knew was working, or travelling, or doing something nauseatingly worthwhile. He followed Minty upstairs to their sitting-room and was slightly comforted by the sun shining brilliantly through the window, bathing the room with light. It had stopped raining and he hadn't even noticed. And Harry was running on his exercise wheel.

'Shall I make coffee?' he ventured.

'Don't start sucking up to me,' Minty said harshly, 'I can't stand it.'

'I'm not sucking up to you. I want a cup of coffee.'

'I don't know why I bothered taking you.'

His mouth fell open in disbelief. 'I didn't want to go. Remember! You practically pulled me by the hair to get me there. Remember! And I was proved right, wasn't I, but you just can't accept that. Oh, no, not you, you're always bloody right and if you're not right, you twist everything around to suit your warped version of events.'

'If you say so.'

'Christ,' his voice ran on furiously. 'And that woman . . . how can you swallow all that stuff? It's absolute cobblers.'

'No. It's not actually,' she said. 'And if you hadn't broken up my sitting in such spectacular and cowardly style Immaculata and I would have proved it to you.'

'Garbage.'

'You did it on purpose, didn't you?'

'Don't be ridiculous.'

'It was almost as if you knew what she was going to say,' she continued accusingly and then paused for an instant, head on one side, before adding:

'I bet she was right about you, wasn't she?'

He began jabbing his thumb repeatedly against his chest. 'Me? Psychic?' He was astonished that he could form the words without choking. 'You actually believe her?'

'Maybe I do,' Minty said reasonably. 'After all, she was spot on about your star sign.'

'Big deal. It was a good guess. Besides, she could have found out easily enough, probably does it all the time.'

'Unlikely,' Minty said. 'But you should have seen your face. For a moment back there I thought you believed her, let alone me.'

'On, no.' He shook his head vigorously. 'Not me.' Yet he could feel his certainty slowly draining away and that uncomfortable nervousness creeping back. It was that last look he had made over her shoulder, of course. Stupid thing to do. He had had an uneasy impression of something there, something unspecifiable (someone?) and he hadn't liked it. In fact, he hadn't been able to get out of that claustrophobic little room fast enough.

So much for the future.

'Not you?' Minty guffawed. 'You look scared witless.'

'Just shut up, can't you? I've had about as much of this as I can stand.'

'Tell me what you saw.'

Tony's eyes bulged. 'Are you nuts?'

'I want to know.' Correction – need to know.

'You're talking out of your backside.'

'Don't be coarse,' she said mildly. 'And calm down, you're going all red in the face. You'll give yourself a heart attack if you're not careful.'

'Oh, brilliant. Great. Thanks very much.' He had a sudden desire to weep hot tears of frustration, but instead whirled round and stormed into the kitchen.

Minty remained where she was. It was better to let him go and take his mood out on the cutlery; she could hear him banging things about as he made the coffee. Tony didn't lose his cool very often and when he did it blew over very quickly; not like her, of course, or at least not like she had been. Had he realised yet that she hadn't touched a drop for almost two weeks now? Good God, she could hardly believe it herself. And no coke, either, not even a whiff of grass. She couldn't explain exactly why this sea-change had happened, but it seemed to be the result of her accident.

In truth, the memory of those few minutes in the lake had never left her, they reverberated on and on like a poignant echo. It was as if she had left a part of herself there, as if all the beautiful things she imagined in those few feverish moments in the water had really happened. As if that man had actually been real.

Minty turned round and moved to the spot on the floor where the sun made a shining path. She would prise out of Tony whatever it was she needed to know, sooner or later. And, for his sake, she hoped that it would be sooner.

The air in the room seemed hot and dusty and over-used. She leaned across and opened the window, pushed the shutters back and let an insipid breeze waft its way into the room.

'How are you?' Pansy asked as Eve walked into the kitchen.

'Much better, thanks.'

'You looked, well – ill, earlier.' And she still didn't look right, there were two hectic bolts of crimson high on her cheekbones, as if she had a temperature.

Eve smiled. 'I was tired, that's all. Shall I make us some tea?'

'Please.'

'Is Jack having his nap?'

'Yes.'

'Where's Frank?

'He's just popped out to the off-license to get a couple of bottles of wine. I said he could stay to supper.' She darted a glance at Eve as she pulled two mugs from a cupboard. 'You don't mind?'

'Of course not,' she replied. 'I like Frank.'

'Does Daddy?'

'I think so. He hasn't said anything to the contrary, anyway. Why?'

'I don't know really.' Pansy looked at her half-bitten nails with a trace of despair. 'Frank just seems nervous, or something, when he's here. You know, not entirely himself.'

'Well, he doesn't know us terribly well. Perhaps that's what it is.'

'Yes.' Pansy sighed. 'I thought you'd probably say that.'

'I don't see what else it could be. Do you?'

'No. I suppose not.'

'You are getting on, aren't you?'

'Yes. We are.' She gazed out of the window, then qualified her answer. 'I think.'

'He obviously likes you a great deal; otherwise he wouldn't be here.' Eve began pouring their tea, 'And he made a special trip to see you today . . .'

'I know, I know.'

'Well, then.'

'I just feel out of my depth with him sometimes.'

'How old is he?'

'Twenty-eight,' she said a little bleakly, 'but sometimes it seems a lot more than that. He makes me feel so juvenile. And I don't think he's ever really been involved with anyone properly. I also think he likes to play the field – which scares me.'

'Sometimes playing the field can mean a fear of real intimacy.'

'Does it? How do you know?'

Eve shrugged and laughed. 'I read it somewhere.'

'When I was a little girl I thought things got simpler when you grew up, but they just get more complicated. I remember thinking that I would handle life a whole lot better than my parents – you know, that my relationships wouldn't be a series of disasters, for instance, that I'd never land myself with someone selfish or inconsiderate or cruel.'

'Sometimes they're not your choices to make.'

'What do you mean?'

Eve reddened just perceptibly. 'Sometimes things just happen, you get swept along by forces beyond your control. Not everything is subject to reason or commonsense, Pansy. Especially not love.'

There was a subtle change in her eyes, something indefinable, and Pansy wondered what was going through her mind. 'What were your parents like?'

'Highly conventional. Very Catholic – at least my mother.' In all the time Eve could remember her mother attending Mass Diana had never missed receiving Communion, and since it is sacrilegious to accept the sacred host with a mortal sin on one's soul, Diana must have confessed everything to the parish priest. Everything. Except Eve couldn't believe that. She looked dully into her cup, took a sip of tea. 'Very boring.'

'And your brother?'

She regarded Pansy steadily over the rim of her mug. 'A bit of a rebel, a tease, a great practical joker and last, but by no means least, a rabidly enthusiastic atheist. I used to wonder how my parents had ever come to have a son like him, but they worshipped the ground he walked on – my mother still does. I was an afterthought, or rather a mistake, born when my mother was halfway through the menopause. It must have been quite a shock. James was always the favourite.'

'That doesn't seem fair.'

'You wouldn't say that if you'd ever met him. He has the sort of charm you only ever read about in books.'

'How much older is he than you?'

'Almost sixteen years.'

'Wow.'

'I was five when we first met,' Eve said, 'and fifteen when he came home for good.'

Pansy's eyebrows drew together in a frown. 'I thought he left again?'

'Oh, yes,' Eve said slowly, 'but that was later.'

'Don't you miss him?'

Eve smiled and said softly. 'I have my own life now. And he has his.'

'But where, exactly, is he?'

The front door slammed and Pansy's question was put away, to think of later; Frank was walking down the hall and somehow talk of Eve's past no longer seemed of interest. He stood in the doorway for a second, taken off guard by Eve's presence, but then he was looking back at Pansy and she felt her heart skip a beat.

'Your father's just arrived. He's parking . . .'

'Andrew's early,' Eve said, glancing at the kitchen clock, 'that's not like him.'

Frank looked at her, then looked away, afraid the eagerness he felt would be in his eyes. He walked over to the breakfast bar with the wine. 'A bit of a workaholic, is he?'

'To a certain extent, I suppose,' Eve said and found herself staring at him, at the black leather jacket over the long lean back.

'I hope that doesn't mean he neglects you,' Frank retorted, and tried to make his voice sound light and mocking.

'I'm very lucky; Andrew is one of the most thoughtful men I've ever met.'

Well, bully for you. Frank put the wine down and reached for Pansy. It was a calculated move and made partly out of affection, but mostly out of revenge. He wanted Eve to see him kiss her stepdaughter, wanted her to believe that he didn't care about her or her perfect husband or her cosy middle-class existence. If she wanted to play games, he could play them too – and as she had pointed out, he was black, and weren't some women (white, of course) curious and excited by the thought of having one between the sheets? Something different, like a new toy, or a life-size sex aid to titillate themselves with when they got bored with their white husbands.

'We've been invited for some drinks . . .' Andrew said, striding into the kitchen, 'sorry it's short notice, but I only knew myself half an hour ago.' He paused for a second when he saw his daughter in the arms of Frank and, blushing furiously, immediately switched his attention to his wife. 'It's a pretty big client,' his voice ran on, 'American – he and his wife are only here for a few days,' he continued as smoothly as he could, 'you don't mind too much, do you?'

Eve shook her head and smiled, kissed her husband lightly on the mouth. 'I'll go up and get ready.'

'While you're doing that, I'll get some cigars from the corner shop. Apparently, Ed Ruben can't live without them, I even know his favourite brand . . .' He followed Eve into the hall, but couldn't stop himself from looking uneasily over his shoulder at Pansy, who was still locked in Frank's embrace. I shouldn't be feeling like this, he thought, I should be happy for her.

Eve went through her wardrobe very quickly, already decided on what she would wear, a plain black dress: long sleeves, gold buttons. As she hastily refreshed her face and hair, she could hear Pansy on the floor below, waking Jack for his feed, and Frank too. Frank. Something rolled over in her mind and she became very still for a second, even as her hands reached up to take the dress from its hanger.

And he was there, in the doorway.

'Where's Pansy?' she said a little breathlessly.

'Downstairs.'

'What do you want?'

'You know . . . you must know.'

'No.' She smiled faintly, shook her head. 'I don't.'

'In the hall,' he said, 'you were . . .'

'What?'

'Stop this,' he said, 'pretending – it's not funny.'

'I don't know what you're talking about, Frank.' But she did, didn't she? Deep down where things really matter, she knew.

'Oh, but you do,' he said and took a step towards her and she didn't shrink away, she just stood there looking into his face and wondering.

He took her hand and she interlocked her fingers with his and they stared at each other in silence.

'You'd better go,' she said.

'Yes.'

'And this must stop . . .'

'Yes,' he said, but it was a hopeless lie.

She watched him leave, moving backwards until he had to turn round and walk away. Eve's vision dimmed slightly with sudden realisation; it wasn't him that she was drawn to, it was someone like him. But she wouldn't think about that now, she just wouldn't let herself. And that wasn't so hard, was it? After all, she told herself, you've had plenty of practise, no need to pluck something ugly out of the quicksand of your memory. Leave it there.

Besides, she had Andrew to consider; this meeting was important to him and she mustn't mess it up. No funny blanks this evening, no echoes. She bit her lip, brow furrowing a little, knowing that, in the end, it would make no difference at all.

Outside, the sun was beginning to set and bruised clouds, gilded by the dying light, were massing along the horizon. A wind picked up, slipping through the window cracks and bringing a chill to the room, causing Eve to shiver.

Tony wished Minty had closed the shutters, they were banging like the clappers and he had no desire to get out of his nice warm bed and do something about them. The temperature must have dropped, he realised, because one of his feet was poking out from under the bedcovers and it was bloody freezing. Blearily he looked at the clock and groaned, in seven minutes it would be three in the morning.

Beside him, Minty snored softly. She was lying on her back, mouth hanging open, blissfully asleep, and he wondered resignedly why he was the one who had to wake up and feel obliged to do something about the damned shutters. He didn't know why, but it rather reminded him of the sinking feeling one gets on a half-filled tube train, when the proverbial loony staggers on and takes the seat right next to you . . .

Tony was shaken out of his musings by a huge cracking sound followed by a pause and then something smashing to the ground. He sat up in bed with a jerk.

'Jesus Christ,' he swore, 'what the hell was that?' He pushed back the covers and got out of bed with visions of shattered shutters littering the room beyond, and probably the precious little cobbled mews as well. Which would, no doubt, yield another letter from that old fart of a retired colonel next door . . .

Tony padded down the hall and stood on the threshold of the small sitting-room. The shutters were very much intact and still banging away in the wind, but far from broken. The same, however, could not be said of the seventies cane chair, his favourite; it lay prostrate on the kilim rug like a beached whale, and directly above it the ceiling dripped plaster.

'Shit.'

The shutters swung inward, blocking out the light from the street lamp and the room was plunged into darkness. Somewhere nearby a rusty hinge squeaked and there was the soft sigh of timbers creaking, as if someone was treading lightly upon them.

Tony shuddered suddenly, he had nothing on.

His hand reached for the light-switch, but nothing happened. He assumed the wiring had been damaged by the wrenching of the cane chair's anchor-plate from the ceiling.

There was something in the room.

The shutters swung outwards again and everything was touched by a dark light, like that of a crypt, Tony thought, with uneasy humour as his eyes scanned the gloom, and then he felt his throat contract at the sight of a low lean shape crouching next to Harry's cage.

'Oh, God . . .' he croaked. 'A rat.' His voice sank to a horrified whisper. Or something like a rat. For a strange, unreal moment he just stood there, paralysed, appalled that a rodent of such a size – any size – could be found doing walkabout in Belgravia, let alone in their very private, secluded little mews. Did the council know? Suddenly his addled brain registered a movement as the thing squirmed upwards and slithered to a stop on top of the cage. God, it was huge! A stoat maybe, or a ferret. No, a weasel, that's what it was he felt with certainty, although he had never seen one in his life, but something told him he was right. It was looking at him, head on one side, its slitty eyes gleaming with moonlight. And weasels had sharp teeth. Like needles.

It began to rattle the cage.

Almost without thinking, Tony was propelled into action. He pulled a pair of leather bellows from their place on the wall and hurled them at the offending mammal. They missed. Of course they missed, he couldn't see straight without his contact lenses and it was dark, wasn't it, horribly dark.

He heard a squeal and visions of Harry being eaten alive made him dash forward yelling and jumping up and down as if that might distract or frighten the creature. It did pause for an instant, turning its busy twitching head just enough to wonder if the jumping man might pose a threat, but by now the cage door was in its teeth, and it had no intention of letting go.

'Bastard,' Tony shrieked and slapped his hand down on top of the cage, but the weasel-thing only glanced up at him with something closely resembling disdain, opening its mouth with a feral grin. Tony wrinkled his nose with disgust; it smelt awful, as if it suffered from bad breath, some galloping form of halitosis.

He took a step back, trying to think fast, and logically, something he found hard at the best of times, but then turned around abruptly and ran out of the room. A broom, a broom! He flung open the cupboard in the kitchen and pulled out the mop as well as the broom, ran back along the hall and heard the heart-stopping sound of Harry's cage crash to the floor.

'Harry,' he wept, 'oh, God, Harry . . .'

He hovered for a moment in the doorway, trying to adjust his eyes to the darkness, saw a lumpy square-like mass lying by the table and a furious busy shape nosing its way underneath. Tony let the mop fall from his hands. It hit the wooden boards with such a clatter that his heart seemed to leap wildly somewhere in the region of his throat. He lifted the broom with shaking hands and wobbly legs and brought it down hard, but only heard the sound of brush-head meeting cold solid floor. Yet when he pulled it back and up, somehow the weasel-thing was clinging to it, its body whipping back and forth in the air like a snake. It was gripping the bristles with its nasty gnawing little teeth, which seemed to grin maliciously at him from the end of the broom.

That could be my arm, he thought, or my fingers. Or worse. He felt his genitals wither and shrink up between his legs.

Maybe it was rabid . . . there was that smell . . . slipped through Customs on the bloody Shuttle.

It dropped to the floor, stood upright on its hind legs and gave a threatening, guttural hiss. Tony screamed.

'What the hell is going on!' Minty switched on the light and saw Tony waving a broom in the air. 'Have you gone completely gaga or something?'

His mouth gaped and his hand went to the light-switch. 'But it wasn't working . . .'

'Well, it is now.' She stared at him. 'What are you doing?'

'There was something in the room.'

Minty looked over his shoulder. 'What? Where?'

'It was a weasel or something.'

'A weasel?'

'Yes. It was after Harry,' he blundered on, 'knocked his bloody cage off the table.' Tony turned round and became very still. But the cage was on the table. Across the room the seventies cane chair still hung from the ceiling, and the shutters were closed; he could hear the wind outside beating on them with relentless enthusiasm. In fact the room was spotless, untouched and in perfect order. 'I don't understand,' he said weakly, 'the cane chair had fallen, there was plaster . . . and the shutters were wide open and making a hell of a row – that's what woke me.'

'I closed the shutters before I came to bed. There was a gale warning on the news . . . I even put the bar across to make sure they'd stay put.'

'They were open.'

'No.'

He wandered over to Harry's cage and peered in. 'He's asleep,' Tony said with relief and almost to himself. 'Give me a cigarette.'

'Have you been on something?'

'Like what?'

She shrugged.

'Good old acid? L-S-fucking-D?' he suggested bitterly. 'You mean have I been "tripping" – like one of those glorious old-fashioned sixties things that made a few half-wits jump out of windows because they thought they could bloody fly?!' He stiffened with rage. 'Isn't that what you mean?'

Minty made no answer, but she wondered if he realised what a ludicrous picture he made, standing there starkers, fists clenched, little John Thomas bobbing up and down. Even some of his precious hair stood on end, as if he'd just received an electric shock.

'Well?' he demanded.

She fished into her robe pocket for her cigarettes, lit one and passed it over to him. 'What do you expect me to say?' she said. 'That it's normal to find you up at three in the morning dancing about naked with a broom?'

'There was something here!'

'Where is it then – dived back through the window where it apparently came in – despite the fact that it's been closed all the time?'

'I don't know, I don't know . . .'

With an extravagant sigh, she began making an irritating pantomime search of the room – peering under tables, behind chairs, even opened the bureau drawers and looked inside.

'All right, all right,' he snapped, 'you've made your point.'

'Can we go back to bed now?'

Tony took a long, trembling drag on his cigarette. 'Maybe it was a dream . . .'

'Some dream.'

'Well, nightmare then?' Except that it had seemed frighteningly real.

'I'll give you one of my sleeping pills,' Minty said, turning round and heading in the direction of their bedroom. 'Actually I think I'll make that two. I can't stand any more of this.'

For a few seconds Tony didn't move; he still couldn't take it in: the shock of everything being normal had been as big a shock as seeing the weasel-thing worming its way through the remains of his sitting-room. You imagined it, he told himself firmly. Dreamt it. And suddenly he felt very tired.

He took a last peek into Harry's cage and switched off the light, trotting meekly after Minty.

'I should have known that going within throwing distance of that bloody woman would mean trouble,' he murmured, getting into bed.

'What woman?'

'Who do you think? Your fat friend – the clairvoyant.' He pulled the bedclothes up to his chin.

'You can't blame Immaculata for this.'

'Can't I?'

'Don't be so damn stupid.'

'It's like seeing a horror movie, or reading a spooky story – it sows seeds in your mind . . . sets things in motion.'

'I think sane people would call it the result of an over-active imagination.' Minty handed him two tablets with barely concealed impatience. 'And stub that fag out, I don't trust you to do it on your own.'

'Charming.'

'Shut up, switch that lamp off and go to sleep.' She rolled huffily on to her side and away from him.

Tony dutifully got rid of his cigarette, popped the tablets into his mouth and turned the light off. He lay staring into space, enduring the dark and the *tap-tap* of the wind on the glass as his mind ran on, going over and over everything in minute and unpleasant detail. If it didn't sound like the ravings of a madman, he could almost believe that his unfortunate experience was more like someone's idea of a very sick joke.

Crazy idea, really. Perhaps it wasn't only his body that was fraying around the edges, maybe his brain was too. God, and his heart – it was going berserk! He laid a hand on his chest and took a deep gulp of air. What a night, he thought, what a bloody awful night.

He found his eyes wandering reluctantly to the open mouth of the doorway and the black tunnel of the hall beyond. Things look so different in the dark, his mind said, unhappily different.

When he was sure Minty was asleep he reached for the lamp and switched the light back on. Then Tony waited for the tablets to work, but they didn't take effect for a very long time.

'Why haven't you opened your letter?' Andrew was standing at the dressing table, putting on his tie. 'It's from your mother, isn't it?'

'Yes,' Eve said, 'but I don't need to open it. She sends me the same letter, the same time, every year.'

'Why once a year,' he said, puzzled. 'I mean, why can't she come over more than once – and at a different time? Come to that, why can't you go and see her?'

'We don't get on.' She paused and looked down at her hands. 'We've never got on. Besides, it's not me she's coming to see.'

'Who . . .?'

Eve drew an exasperated breath and Andrew should have taken that as a warning. 'For heaven's sake . . . she'll be arriving on 25 September for her annual visit to the lake house, in the hope that my brother will turn up for his birthday on the 27th. Which he won't.'

'Why won't he?'

'Because he hates ritual and I think he hates my mother, come to that.'

'That's a bit strong, isn't it? Why does he hate her?'

'Because she adores him.'

Andrew darted a glance at Eve. She was sitting on the far side of their bed, her back to him. 'That doesn't make a lot of sense.'

'She smothered him,' Eve said, expressionlessly. 'She never gave him a minute's peace. And when he was old enough I suppose you could say that he took his revenge.'

Andrew pulled a face. 'That sounds weird – and not very pleasant.'

'You reap what you sow – isn't that how the saying goes?' She shrugged. 'Anyway, my mother still adores him, so however badly James behaved, it didn't damage her feelings for him.'

'And you?' he asked. 'How do you feel about him?'

'He's a lot older than me,' she said in that same flat tone. 'We were never very close.'

'But you lived with him for three years – didn't you – at the lake house?'

'I was away at school most of the time, Andrew.'

'Even so, it's odd that you don't hear from him.'

'I do hear from him. Not often, it's true, and usually only in the form of a postcard.'

'You never told me.' Andrew looked at his wife. She was standing up now, slipping on her robe and looking back at her reflection in the glass of the dressing-table.

'Why would I? There's nothing to tell.'

'I'd like to meet him one day.'

Eve laughed in a humourless sort of a way. 'I don't think so.'

'Why not?'

'You wouldn't like him.'

'How can you tell?'

'You just wouldn't.'

And he wouldn't like you. In fact, he would despise you. He would come here and wreck your life and think it the height of hilarity.

'Now if you've finished with this interrogation,' she said stiffly, 'I'd like to take a shower.'

'Hey, that's not fair,' he protested mildly. 'I was only asking some innocent questions . . .' but she was already making for the bathroom and a few moments later had closed the door.

Andrew drew a breath and said wryly: 'Now that's what I call a great start to the day.' He looked again at the offending letter, picked it up and ripped open the flap. It was just as Eve had told him it would be – a list of arrangements: the same day, the same time and that was it, no 'love' before her signature, no love sent to her only grandchild, nothing at all really. Perhaps that didn't necessarily mean anything; some people just weren't capable of expressing love, it didn't mean that they actually failed to feel. Did it? Andrew sighed a little. Two weekends away. He looked out of the window, the weather had cleared up and the wind had finally dropped. Maybe the sun would come out.

Eve slipped out of her robe, took off her watch and peeled away the sticking plaster beneath. The wounds were healing.

She picked up another of Andrew's razor blades and lifted her arm. The skin which circled the area around her armpit was smooth and silky and very pale, like a baby's. It is a region of the body that is of little interest sexually or aesthetically, in fact it does not often even see the cold light of day, let alone the eyes of another human being.

Eve leaned over the basin and this time she didn't cut, she sliced – a crescent shaped piece of flesh which bled profusely and hurt so much she had to stop herself from crying out. When, eventually, it stopped bleeding (and that wouldn't be long in the general scheme of things), the raw wound under her upper arm would howl with pain every time it rubbed against the side of her body.

It probably wouldn't heal very well, perhaps it wouldn't heal at all.

Seven

It was a spoof on *Andy Pandy*, except the version Pansy was watching at TJ's would hardly be considered suitable for children. In fact, it made her cringe. As usual she found herself wondering how Frank could bear all of this, but knew it was the money; it was twice as good as the bit-part he had recently been offered.

She would take a bit-part (quite frankly, my dear, she would take any part), yet nothing had come her way – at least 'not anything suitable' – according to her agent. But she wouldn't give up and privately had started studying stage management, just as a sort of exercise in staving off the boredom and broadening her options. She wouldn't tell anyone at the moment, and definitely not Frank, he would probably tell her to stop pussy-footing around and go for cabaret or a bit of stripping . . . 'learn to relate to a real audience'.

She glanced around her. God, no. If this was 'a real audience', she'd rather forget the whole idea – do a secretarial course and put her father out of his misery; backpack around Europe; learn Chinese. Something. For an instant she felt an odd surge of despair, but she pressed the feeling down and made her eyes rove across the packed night club, looking for Frank.

Tonight, he wasn't on stage, he was taking his turn waiting at the tables. The troupe all did this on one night of the week because the management believed it was good for business, but judging by the expression on Frank's face on this particular evening he certainly didn't think so.

Pansy observed the usual giggles and stares as the punters tried to figure out how the members of the troupe achieved that so-smooth pelvis look. She could hear the same old question being asked of Frank, and usually accompanied by a lurid grin – 'where do you keep your three-piece suite,

145

then, love?' or 'where are the rude bits hiding, sunshine?'

He was approaching Pansy's table, a solo job, stuck right in a far corner because she hated being near the front with the gawpers and gazers. To Pansy's right sat a group of women on a hen-night, and to her left three men in suits halfway to getting plastered. As Frank wended his way through the closely packed tables, one of the men – who distinctly reminded her of her old headmaster on a bad day – laid a hand on the big red satin bow sticking from the rear of his costume.

'How about a smile then, beautiful . . . ?' the man leered.

Frank paused abruptly, the two drinks on his tray sloshing on to the metal surface. He whirled around and looked directly into the man's heated gaze. 'Have you ever tried smiling with your giblets stuck up your arse? Now take your greasy paws off my backside, or I might do something you'll regret . . .'

'Okay, okay,' the man said, bringing his hands up as if to ward Frank off, 'I was only trying to be friendly.'

'Well, don't bother, man,' Frank shouted into his face, 'just don't fucking bother.'

He seemed in an ecstasy of rage, out of all proportion to what had happened. After all, it was no more than they experienced each and every night – it was an accepted part of the job, and something Frank had never complained about before. For a long time now he had treated TJ's as a joke, but perhaps the funny side was finally beginning to wear a little thin.

He stormed past her with barely a glance, still carrying the tray which jagged against the swing door as he pushed his way through. She winced at the sound of breaking glass, as the tray crashed to the floor, and wondered whether she should go, or stay. Wait, she told herself nervously, give him a few minutes to cool down.

When Pansy did finally pluck up the courage to seek him out he was in his dressing-room and already out of his costume.

'What are you doing?'

'What does it look like?' He began removing his make-up with angry relish.

'You'll lose your job.' She sat down and looked at his stony face in the mirror. 'Don't you care?'

'No,' he said. 'Not any more.'

'What about your contract?'

'Stuff my contract.'

'You can't do that.'

He stopped what he was doing and glared at her. 'I don't care. Okay? I just don't care.'

'But why now – tonight? You've never given any indication that you felt like this . . .'

'Like what?' The words seemed like a sneer, bitter and furious.

'I just mean . . .' She began, 'well . . .'

'I don't need your opinion, Pansy. This isn't the time.' His voice was low, almost bleak. 'Have I got you so wrong that you really can't see that?'

She looked back at him in bewilderment.

'And don't look at me like that – it drives me crazy.' He laughed, but in a cold way, there was no humour in it at all. 'Look, I'm just having one of those days,' he stood up and waved a hand into the air in a gesture of frustration, 'in fact one of those weeks, months, years . . .'

Her eyes reproached him. She had come tonight longing to see him, even here, in this farcical place, and now he was ruining everything with this strange mood – this hostility. She cleared her throat. 'What will you do then?'

He shrugged and slipped out of his robe. He was totally naked underneath and she swallowed hard – tall, black and broad-shouldered; Frank was perfect, even down to skin texture, the shape of his head, the tilt of his eyes. Was he, like Eve, also unaware of his undoubted attractions? There was that feeling again, the one she had had too often lately, of being out of her depth.

She looked away, her eyes roaming down the long room with its battalion of light-bulbed, fringed mirrors; masses of extravagant costumes hanging against the wall: wigs and sequins and frills and lace and plumes and tiers of high-heels; its mess and its smell of grease and smoke and stale perfume.

'I've got to get out of here fast, before anyone realises what I'm up to. Do you want to come back to my place?' He was hastily putting on his clothes: zipping-up and tucking everything in.

Slowly she shifted her gaze back to him. 'Do you want me to?'

'Jesus, Pansy,' he swore impatiently. 'What is this insecurity thing with you? I wouldn't ask, would I, if I didn't want you to?' Frank looked at her harshly. She was wearing a long black pinafore with a tee shirt beneath, her hair was loose and hung in two dark curtains either side of her face. She looked too young, suddenly, and irritatingly vulnerable.

147

'I don't know,' she said softly, hating the way his sharp eyes flicked over her.

Frank picked up his jacket, thrust his arms through the sleeves and pulled the collar up around his neck in swift jerky movements. And the routine action was done in complete anger. Amazing, she thought dully, how much feeling could be put into slipping on a jacket.

'Are you coming?'

She stared at him for a long moment, trying to fathom the change in him. 'I suppose so.'

He opened his mouth to speak, but then closed it again.

In the background she could hear the troupe launch into a Madonna number, which would be followed by several more routines taking awfulness to hitherto inconceivable lows. Pansy could picture them so well: mincing about the stage, wiggling their backsides and waving their pom-poms, pouting skilfully sculpted androgenous lips . . .

Funny how quickly the future can change, because now she wished she was still out there amongst all the weird and wonderful punters, just sipping her drink and waiting for Frank.

Outside the night air seemed slightly chill, as if autumn was already creeping in. A few people walking the narrow streets of Soho folded their arms or pulled jackets close around them to fend off the sudden cold.

'August's finished, isn't it? Frank remarked abruptly.

'Three days ago.' She was walking beside him, but apart. It took her back to that walk across Putney Bridge, the one they had taken together after her mother's accident at the lake house. 'The day you came over.' Events had come a full ironic circle.

There was something in her voice and he frowned, glancing at her set face.

'What are you getting at?' He thought of Eve, and not for the first time, of course: he just couldn't help himself.

In fact, Frank couldn't sleep, either, or concentrate, or think straight, or eat properly. His longing, his need seemed like an addiction or a sickness and he despised himself for it. Despised her in an odd sort of way.

'You wanted to see me on Tuesday,' Pansy's voice broke into his endless, aching thoughts, 'at least I think you did – presumably that's why you came.' She sighed deeply and pushed her hair back from her face, 'But tonight you're like someone else and you give a very good impression of really not wanting me here at all.'

He drew a sharp breath. 'Not this bullshit again.'

Wearily Pansy shook her head. 'Not bullshit – and you know it.'

'I seem to remember us having this argument once before.' His voice sounded hard and clipped, almost bored.

'Yes,' she said. 'I was thinking the same thing myself.'

'So – can we talk about something else?'

'I don't see the point.' His mood-swings coloured everything for her now. When it was good, it was very very good, but when it was bad, it was not just wicked, but awful, terrible, stomach-churning.

'I just don't feel so good, that's all,' he said. 'Why make such a big deal out of it?'

She wanted to say that it hurt, that his attitude, his tone of voice stayed in her ears, in her head, pressing and drumming and would probably stay with her long afterwards, but instead she said, 'Because it's tiring and depressing . . .'

'Anything else?'

'Self-indulgent.'

'Thanks very much.' But all true, he told himself. Little flower was very perceptive, yet not perceptive enough to have guessed the guilty secret that lay between them like a piece of rotting meat. Frank thought it should show – be completely visible every time she looked into his face, his eyes – and a pathetic part of him longed to confess like some abject and feeble sinner.

You only had a quick grope in the hall, Frank. Just a grope. Yet he had replayed that grope over and over in his head like a piece of film on repeat – saw and felt and smelled her again and again – that touch of her soft, seeking hand, her breast, her cheek, her mouth, her tongue. The sensation of her hair tumbling over and rubbing against his skin.

Replayed it in exact and perfect sequence.

In his dreams he had had much more than that. In his dreams Eve had played a leading role in every obscene and absurd male fantasy ever invented. Some of them had even had the power to shock him, as if they weren't his own fantasies at all, but someone else's . . . someone who was using the screen of his mind like a movie theatre.

'I don't know what you expect me to say,' Pansy said.

He dug his hands in his pocket, but made no answer.

'On Tuesday,' she continued hopelessly, 'you were . . .'

'What was I?' He fumed. 'Christ, why do you have to nag me like this?!'

'Frank?' She gaped at him. 'That's not fair – you're not fair.'

He threw his head back and screamed silently at the sky.

'She . . .' he whispered, and the word was uttered like something made of magic, something that had slipped stealthily from his mouth with a will all its own.

She.

Pansy froze, literally. A couple walking straight towards them grumbled as they were forced to circle around her.

'She?'

He couldn't believe it himself. 'I didn't mean it the way it came out.'

'Yes, you did.'

He tried to think, fast. 'Why do you always read something into what I say?'

'Because it's there to be read,' she began with subdued anger, 'because you have no self-control and probably don't care too much if I notice what you do or what you say.' She paused for breath. 'At least when you're feeling like you are now.'

'What do you mean?'

'I mean when you let loose an atom bomb like you did a moment ago.'

'I didn't let loose anything.'

'Well, now I know. Which is something.'

'You don't know anything.'

'That's something else you said before.'

'Oh, cut it out, will you?'

Pansy said nothing in response. She was looking down the street at the glowing golden rectangle of a taxi moving towards her. She raised her arm, signalling it to stop.

'What the hell are you doing?' Frank protested.

'I'm going home.'

'Don't be ridiculous.'

The cab drew up and Pansy opened a door and climbed in.

'Pansy, don't be . . .' His voice trailed off as she closed the door in his face, but she turned and looked at him through the window, watched his mouth moving and was glad she couldn't hear what he was saying. Then, with great deliberation, she rolled the window down and saw relief ripple across his handsome black face.

'Look, Pansy . . .' he began.

Her eyes were blazing, glints of steel. 'Fuck you, Frank,' she said quietly. 'Fuck you.'

His face crumpled and he held his hands up, palms outward in a gesture of regret, but she ignored him, and he felt his pointless fury ebbing away too late. And he really hadn't wanted this to happen. So why? What the hell did he think he was doing? Frank closed his eyes as the cab drove away from him, pinched the bridge of his nose in resigned disbelief.

She knows, he told himself, but she doesn't know who.

The key turned, but the door wouldn't open; the latch must be up because they had thought she wasn't coming home tonight. Pansy cursed softly and stepped back, looking up at the house. There was dull light at the very top, probably in Jack's room, but otherwise everything was in complete and depressing darkness. She could knock, of course, or telephone from a phone-box, but then she would only succeed in waking the whole house and they would see the state she was in. And she was in a state. Even now her hands still shook and there was that ghastly breathless feeling in her chest which she knew heralded tears. Emotional turmoil, her father would have called it. Too true. There would be questions too – all that probing and prying when she could least stand it.

The cab had dropped her at the top of the street and she had walked home blindly, head down, with no desire to reach where she was supposed to be going. And now she couldn't get in.

How very appropriate.

Perhaps she should have stayed with Frank and had an almighty row, but that would have achieved very little in the end. It wouldn't even have cleared the air because he would simply have repeated what he had told her from the beginning: his tired litany on polygamy – that he liked having more than one woman in his life.

Why was it then, she asked herself, that this honesty of his felt so dishonest? More to the point, why was it that, despite having told him exactly where he got off, she didn't feel any better?

Pansy leaned her head against the door in despair, but there was a part of her which was beginning to feel too tired to care and she was glad of that.

She sighed with resignation and switched her attention to the locked door and her immediate predicament. Perhaps if she could squeeze her arm through the letter box (which was more or less on a level with the lock) she might be able to push the latch down.

She tried, but it hurt; even as she slipped her hand through and sideways, the mouth of the letter box began to bite into her flesh and any room for manoeuvre was pathetically restricted. Maybe, just maybe, if she fished her Biro or something similar out of the bottom of her bag it might reach where her fingers had failed.

As she withdrew her hand she heard the sound for the first time, a soft muffled whispering and she peered through the letter box expecting to see her father, or Eve.

'Daddy?' she whispered back. 'Helloooo . . . it's me.'

But the hall was silent and black, except for a shaft of moonlight spilling on to the rug from the window above the door, a pale square of illumination where Eve had stood and laid her hands upon Frank.

Pansy stared at the pallid pool of light and shivered; she was getting cold. And there was that noise again; it came tip-toeing out of the kitchen – little mutterings, a milky sigh, followed by a soft mouse-like cry of anguish.

'Eve?' Pansy called apprehensively. What was going on? She glanced at her watch, the luminous dial told her it was almost two. 'Eve?'

Someone laughed, a cynical mocking titter that seemed to hang on the air for a long time and the strange, not-quite-sane undertone of that laugh made her arms gooseflesh.

She picked up her handbag, which she had dropped on the step, and began trawling through the bottom for her pen. Once she had found it she pushed her left hand and lower arm through the letter box and felt for the latch. With her right hand she wriggled the key around in the lock, as if the action might aid in releasing the catch.

Something worked because the door clicked and swung inwards with Pansy's arm still caught in the gaping letter box. She lurched forward, retrieving her limb at the same time and swore out loud, but the word died on her lips as she looked into the tangle of shadows at the end of the hall. Eve stood there, utterly motionless, her white satin robe billowing up and open as if a wind were running wild through the house.

Pansy stared, wide-eyed, uneasily reminded of that famous pose of Marilyn Monroe's, when she had stood over a subway grating, hot air rushing up her thighs, white skirt blown out like a spinnaker above her waist. Unfortunately the parallel ended there because Monroe had not only been laughing, but also safely clad in underwear.

Eve wore nothing at all, even the robe hung off her upper arms like a pair of angels' wings.

For God's sake cover yourself, Pansy willed her silently, horribly embarrassed. There was a physical opulence about her stepmother that was almost too lavish; her creamy skin seemed to gleam in the half-light, pale and marmoreal, like a statue. Except for the dark moons that were the coronas of her breasts, and lower, where the black lustrous shadow of her pubic hair nestled. Between her thighs it was red.

Pansy frowned, lifted her bewildered gaze to Eve's face and saw that her eyes had a curiously dead appearance, lids half-closed, but looking upwards.

Pansy lowered her gaze again; the redness was blood. It was blood trickling down Eve's legs.

'Eve,' she said gently, 'what's the matter?'

Eve said nothing. She stood woodenly, as if waiting for something, but then moved and so abruptly it made Pansy jump. She began climbing the stairs and Pansy walked quickly down the hall to watch her go, but there was no relief in her scrutiny only dismay. What on earth was going on?

'Eve?' Pansy called, baffled and a little scared at the same time. She looked back at the still open front door and returned to close it, and when she arrived at the bottom of the stairs again Eve had gone.

Pansy ran softly up the first flight of stairs and then the next, hovered on the landing where her father and stepmother slept. There was a light under their door and Pansy moved up against it, listening for any sound, thought she heard the gentle rustle of her stepmother's robe and tapped lightly on the closed door.

Eve opened the door, a very different Eve from the one Pansy had observed in the hall.

'Pansy,' she said easily enough, 'you startled me – I thought you were staying out tonight?'

'No. I decided to come home after all.'

'Is there something wrong?'

'Oh, no.' Little liar. 'I saw you downstairs . . .' she feigned a soft laugh, 'you didn't answer when I called. For a moment there I thought you might be walking in your sleep.'

Eve looked over her shoulder at Andrew, who was safely sleeping, and stepped outside the door. 'Really?' she said. 'How odd. Are you sure?'

'Yes,' Pansy said, a little irritated. 'Why?'

'I did go down for a drink,' Eve lied, 'I was probably still half-asleep.' In truth she couldn't remember leaving the room. She had awoken to find herself in her robe, sitting on the edge of the bed with staring eyes, and listening. For what, or whom? She had been nervous and frightened and found herself looking quizzically around the bedroom, at her sleeping husband, the half-open windows, their bathroom which was lit up like a Christmas tree because all the spotlights had been left on – as if she were searching for something, like a blind woman groping her way across an unfamiliar room. Eve blinked at the memory, saw Pansy's partly bowed head: she was looking at her feet.

It was only for an instant. Pansy had to look, had to see if she had been right, but Eve's feet were bloodless. Not a spot or a stain. Even the white satin wrapped around her was bloodless.

'You obviously didn't sleepwalk, then?'

Eve smiled in a funny sort of way. 'To be frank, I'm not sure.'

Pansy looked back at her, puzzled. 'What do you mean?'

'When I was a child I used to sleepwalk on a regular basis apparently. I didn't remember anything about it, of course.' She took a deep, weary breath. 'I couldn't get to sleep tonight. I read until my eyes had to close.' That much was true. 'I can remember waking up and feeling thirsty . . .'

'Yes,' Pansy pressed. 'And?'

Eve shook her head. 'It's sort of blurred after that.'

'So you could have been sleepwalking?' Pansy wanted Eve to say 'yes' because it would simplify everything. She didn't like to think of her stepmother wandering around the house in the middle of the night looking like an escapee from an old Hammer film.

'Perhaps.' She pushed her hair back from her face with a trace of impatience. 'I don't know.'

'Really?' Pansy exclaimed. 'But how can you not know?'

'You'd have to ask an expert, Pansy. Not me at two, or whatever it is, in the morning.' She was tired of this now, she wanted to be left alone. In peace.

'Isn't it dangerous?'

'I've never come to any harm.' At least not walking in my sleep. No. That was the easy bit, that was like floating on air. Dreaming on a cloud. Running. Running. Far away.

'You didn't see me,' Pansy said with disbelief. 'I know you didn't and yet I still find it hard to take in.'

'People sleepwalk all the time,' Eve replied as mildly as she could. 'It's really nothing to get worked up about.'

'I suppose not.' Pansy longed to add that if you had been standing in that darkened hallway and seen what I had seen then maybe you wouldn't seem so relaxed about it.

'Look, there's no harm done,' Eve said gently. 'It's just one of those things.'

Pansy nodded, but her mind was busy focusing on the word 'harm' and she began again, awkwardly: 'I thought I saw . . . well, I thought you were . . .'

Bleeding. There was a blue vein throbbing in Eve's neck, it stood out from the creamy skin like an unhappy echo.

'What?'

Pansy shook her head, felt herself blushing an uncomfortable crimson. 'Nothing. It doesn't matter.'

'I'm sorry if I frightened you.'

'Not really.' Oh, but she had.

Eve leaned across and gave Pansy a kiss on the cheek. 'Don't think about it any more, please,' she said. 'And don't tell your father, he'd only worry.'

'If you're sure?'

'I'm sure.'

Pansy hesitated for an instant. 'You are – all right?' Had she imagined the blood? In the dark, in the rippling shadows it could have been anything.

Liquid chocolate dribbling darkly down Eve's thighs, her calves, puddling on to the quarry tiles. Blood looked like that in half-light, Pansy mused with a squirm of distaste.

'Of course.' Eve pressed her arm. 'Are you?'

Pansy nodded. 'Yes. Sorry. I just felt a bit strange for a moment there.'

'Go to bed. You look tired out.'

'I am.' She smiled with an effort. 'Goodnight, Eve.'

'Goodnight.'

Pansy paused at the top of the stairs, then rubbed at her temples before making her way slowly back through the house. She would pour herself a glass of milk, take some painkillers for the headache which was brewing and wouldn't think about Eve's sleepwalking. It was just a little too unsettling at this time of night. The whole thing had been weird. But sleepwalking would explain it, she supposed half-heartedly. Perhaps she had been talking to herself, too, which would explain the voices.

Voices. Plural.

She had forgotten about that. Or had she imagined them along with the blood? Pansy reached the bottom of the stairs and the still darkened hallway, switched on the light and moved down the remainder of the passage to the kitchen, and turned on all the lights in the large room.

The French doors were standing open.

Fear, or the lurking tip of it began to grow big in Pansy. And she didn't really know why. After all, what was so terrifying about the doors to the patio being open? Eve had done it, of course, left them swinging on their hinges in her half-awake state. Her fingerprints were probably still fresh on the fake-gold door knobs, and outside in that black-walled garden they glinted like ice-picks in the light cast by the kitchen. Pansy thought they looked like eyes.

'Don't be stupid,' she said aloud and walked stiffly across the room, not allowing herself to think or imagine or look beyond the yellow square of light spilling out on to the small paved enclosure. She took one brisk step outside and brought both doors in, and together. As she bolted top and bottom she slowed down, feeling brave enough to risk a wary glance into the dark now that something solid stood between herself and the little silent garden.

As if something, someone, was abroad in the night – hiding amongst the creepers and ivy growing thickly against the brickwork.

Eve looked down at her sleeping baby. She stood a step away from the cot and when she drew close, tentative hands on the wooden rail, Jack seemed to stir and fret.

Even in his sleep he knows I'm here, she thought, and he doesn't like it. I am not like other mothers, I don't feel like other mothers; he could be someone else's child and not mine for the lack of bonding that divides us. And I breastfed him, she argued wordlessly, I held him close up against my warm mother-love flesh, but the only thing he absorbed was the fluid drawn from my body.

'My fault,' she whispered. 'Not yours.'

Then the milk dried up and Pansy had come.

And the divide had become bigger.

She frowned, the faint lines in her wide, intelligent forehead deepening sharply. Yet in that other, far away time she could fall into sleep and wake up with milk seeping from her untapped breasts, wake up saturated and cold and full of sorrow, her nightie clinging to clammy milk-wet skin.

She stiffened, tightening her grip on the rail of the cot. It was as if she was reliving a dream, or some strange memory that she had forgotten or put away, which was now drifting slowly and inexorably to the surface of her mind. Hounding her like a nasty secret and trying to tell her something in a maddeningly obtuse, unpleasant way.

Eve took her hands away from the cot, face set, and walked out on to the landing where the window was, the one overlooking the rear garden. Immediately beneath her the kitchen roof sloped downwards and beyond the slope she could just see the end of the patio where it met the high, ivy-covered wall rising twelve feet or more. At the top, pieces of glass had been inserted into a layer of concrete, and in the poor light they gleamed like jagged, irregular teeth.

A difficult, even dangerous climb. Only a fool or a mad man would try.

Eve stared at the wall for a long time before finally turning away and going back to bed.

Harry was dead.

Minty had found him with his little head sticking half-in and half-out of his nest of straw, as if he had been trying to extricate himself and had finally given up the ghost in the attempt.

He had lain in her hand, cold and stiff like a tiny stuffed dummy of a hamster. She had stroked him with one finger, then laid him back into the straw and covered him over.

That had been the morning after the night before, the night of naked men and broomsticks.

She hadn't told Tony, of course, and for two reasons: the first that he would put the blame fair and square on Immaculata, and the second because he would be inconsolable and would very likely cry. She couldn't bear that – it moved her in an odd sort of way, but made her feel excrutiatingly embarrassed at the same time.

She wasn't used to seeing a man cry so easily. Andrew had, but only once as far as she could remember. Her own father never; he had been of minor aristocratic origin (and never let her forget it, well at least only the minor bit . . .), brought up in India during the dying days of the British Empire: the sort of man who would rather die than be seen pushing a pram or wielding a carrier-bag full of shopping. Women's work. Apart from the other stuff women were supposed to do: like opening their legs for

England and providing a few lusty kids to carry on the family name. Naturally, he had been hellishly disappointed in his only child.

And the mere sight of Tony would probably have made him physically sick.

Not that Tony would have cared, in fact he probably wouldn't even have noticed. Women and hamsters were far more in his line.

Her heart sank as her mind switched back to Harry. Tony would definitely blame the other night for his pet's demise, or rather their visit to poor old Immaculata – *if* he ever found out. Minty sighed and looked again at the shutters just as she had looked at them that night and the following morning. There had been nothing obviously wrong, unless being distinctly closed could be construed as wrong. Nothing could have got in, or out, of the windows.

Yet Harry had died.

But he was quite old for a hamster, she told herself, well past two, and had probably succumbed to natural causes; it was just an unfortunate coincidence that it had happened then.

After all, he had had no bite or scratch marks, she had examined him quite carefully – and the cage had shown no sign of being tipped over, no matter how hard Tony might have convinced himself.

Minty stared through the bars and looked at the new Harry who was busy filling his fat, pouchy cheeks with sunflower seeds. He looked exactly the same as the original version, the same pretty shade of caramel, the same splodgy white patch under his chin. She just hoped to God Tony thought so, or she would never hear the end of it.

He would harp back to all that nonsense about Immaculata and his 'nightmare' – which would lead into dubious theories and unpleasant recollections.

There was one theory that she hadn't really allowed herself to think about, in fact it had been brooding darkly in the back of her mind since she had found the body of the little hamster. It was silly really, ridiculous, but she knew Tony wouldn't think so.

Harry could have died of fright.

She bowed her head just a little, ran the fingers of her right hand down the lapel of her jacket in a distracted sort of way and shook her head slowly.

'What's the matter with you?'

Minty jumped and swore at the same time. 'Don't creep up on me like that.'

'I didn't,' he said, surprised. 'I just wondered why you were shaking your head. Got a flea in your ear?' Tony chortled.

'Oh, very amusing.'

'How's Harry on this bright and beautiful morning?' he asked, moving towards the cage.

'Harry's fine.' Minty stood with her back to the cage and continued rapidly, 'I thought you were going to take me shopping?'

'When the hell did I say that?'

'Last night – after you had finished the gin.'

'That figures.'

She scrutinised him sharply. 'What's that on your face?'

'I think it's a cold sore.'

'Ugh.' Minty wrinkled her nose. 'Well, you can keep it away from me for a start.'

'Christ,' he said sheepishly. 'It's not the bloody plague.' He stood in front of the mirror above the bureau and studied his reflection. 'It's come up so fast,' he complained. 'Funny, really, last night there wasn't a sign, not a thing . . .'

'You'll have to put something on it,' Minty broke in. 'I'm not going out with you looking like that.' She reached for her handbag and rummaged around for a concealer stick. 'Put some of this on, it will still look ghastly, but at least it won't be so obvious.'

With a sinking feeling he applied the pale make-up, rubbing it in delicately with a finger. He grimaced at the result and handed the concealer back to her.

'I don't want it back for God's sake, it's probably crawling with germs now. Keep it.'

'Thanks, Minty,' he said sourly.

'We'll hit Sloane Street first, then lunch – lightly,' she emphasised, 'at Daphne's, finishing up at Brompton Cross.'

Tony groaned. 'I thought you didn't have any money?'

'I cashed a few of Daddy's shares.'

'He's probably turning in his grave. You're supposed to be keeping those for your old age.'

'Shut up.'

'In that case, you can give me back what you owe me.'

'Later.'

Tony raised his eyes to heaven. 'I know what that means.'

'Good.'

'I don't want to go to Daphne's,' he whinged. 'It's full of Nigel Dempsterites.'

'Well, that's just too bad.'

'If you want me to go with you, we lunch where I say.'

'No.'

'Langan's',' he said firmly, 'or that's it.' It was his favourite eatery; he had discovered that there was nothing quite like their black pudding grill.

'No. I never eat outside of Knightsbridge.'

'For God's sake. We're talking Green Park here, not Tooting Broadway!'

'I said no.'

His eyes narrowed. 'Look what happened the other day when you made me go where I didn't want to go . . .'

She held his accusing glance for a long moment and thought of Harry. 'Oh, all-bloody-right,' she snapped.

'Good,' he said, and made a face at her back as she strode past him and out of the room. The concealer stick was still in his hand and he took another look in the mirror at the offending cold sore; it appeared larger now, raised and crusty. He thought it seemed less like a cold sore and more like some pallid and alien species of wart.

'I must be run down,' he said to the empty room. 'And tired.'

Tony glanced into Harry's cage and raised his eyebrows in weary resignation at the hamster. The little animal stopped what he was doing and regarded him steadily, and his look seemed to say that he understood everything.

She didn't see him coming. Eve was standing outside the main church door, shading her eyes and looking up at the building. Frank thought she looked desirable, even from two hundred yards. In fact his whole body felt a bit shaky just at the sight of her.

With an effort he switched his attention to the church; it was a pretty building: square-turretted, grey-stoned, surrounded by swaying green grass and weathered grave stones. Quiet and a little wild. His feet crunched on the gravel path as he walked through the gate and Eve turned to look; she didn't smile, in fact her face didn't move at all. She wore sunglasses so he was unable to read her in any way; he wondered if she were deliberately wearing them for that very reason. Perhaps it was true, he mused, about that saying, that the eyes are the gateway to the soul. Eyes can be soft with pity, eyes can be outraged and furious, eyes can be unhappy, or grow dark with excitement – change from serenity to desire. Not one little word need be said.

'Is this about Pansy?' Eve asked as he drew close.

'Partly.'

'You said it was on the telephone.'

'Where is she?'

'I told you – she's taken Jack to a friend's. Do you want the address?'

'No.'

She stared at him for a long moment and then slowly looked away. 'Why here?'

'You said you were taking a walk – it seemed as good a place as any.'

Her eyes were resting on the church doors again. How could Frank know that she had intended coming here; in fact she was coming two or three times a week now, but not to the services. Oh, no. How could she? When she ventured inside this place it was to find it empty and then she would select a seat in one of the pews at the back and sit in the shadows, in the silence and coolness, looking at the tired statues and gilded angels.

Perhaps she should find a priest and confess. Now, that would be funny. He would probably have her certified insane.

'Why are you smiling?'

Eve looked back at him, her smile fading, her smile gone. 'You wouldn't understand.'

'If you don't mind me saying, that sounds a little clichéd.'

'Does it?' she said flatly, her careful expression seeming to say that she wasn't concerned what he thought, as with an indifferent shrug, she shifted her gaze back to the church. He stared at her stony profile, feeling uncomfortable and out of place.

'Do you think Jesus ever laughed?' she asked suddenly.

'Jesus?'

'Yes,' she said expressionlessly, 'I mean one of those good belly laughs, head thrown back, that sort of thing.'

Frank looked puzzled. 'Well, why not? He was supposed to be a man – even if it was only temporary.'

'And a man who was not in the least ordinary . . .' she drew a breath and he watched her lips part, 'he looked like an ordinary man – drank and ate like one, just like you and me . . .'

'So?'

'There are people, rare people, that we meet and talk with who appear ordinary, but inside they're not what they seem at all.'

'Everyone's like that to a degree.'

'I said rare people.'

'But they're not Jesus-freaks though – weird, maybe, but not holier than thou.'

'That's not what I meant,' she said quietly. 'Perhaps it was a bad analogy.'

'No,' he said, a little annoyed. 'I understand what you're trying to say. Everyone's got secrets to hide – big ones, small ones.'

'Something like that.'

Frank darted a glance at her, knowing that he had somehow missed the point, stirred the ground with his foot.

'Not much of a church goer, are you, Frank?'

'Are you?' he asked, defensively.

'I was once.'

He looked at her a trifle petulantly. 'What happened?'

'I lost it,' she replied softly. 'Or, to put it more accurately, it lost me.'

He fell silent for a moment, then, 'Did you tell Pansy where you were going?'

'I told you on the phone that she'd already left.' Eve removed her sunglasses, there were dark rings under her eyes. 'What do you want, Frank?'

'You have no idea?' he said pointedly.

She had the grace to blush, but she still looked at him as if she were confused or didn't quite understand his persistence. 'Sometimes things happen . . .' she began, 'but we don't have to add to them – make them bigger, or worse.'

'Why not better?'

'For whom?'

He closed his eyes for an instant then said slowly, almost angrily, 'I know what you're saying – I really do, but I just can't help myself.'

'You sound like a little boy.'

'Then why didn't you tell me to get lost? Why did you agree to see me?' he demanded. 'Ask yourself that, then maybe you can stop trying to dismiss what happened between us so easily.'

'I'm married, Frank. I love my husband.'

He looked outraged. 'How could you do what you did then? How could you?'

'I don't know.'

'It doesn't make sense.'

'What about Pansy?' she asked quickly, hopelessly, sensing that her fragile guard was beginning to slip.

He shrugged. 'I don't know either.'

She averted her eyes and said, 'Perhaps we should walk.' There were people approaching, people who would move through the gate and come up the path. She sighed softly, a milky resigned sort of a sigh that excited him, and somehow far more than any touch could have done.

Little tracks wended their way among the gravestones and square tombs like small houses, and they followed one, and the one led into the other until it looped up and around two trees which screened out the sun and the probing face of the church. The air was still and heavy here and smelled faintly sour, the odour of grass cuttings and weeds left to run riot.

She knew as soon as they came beneath the spreading branches that it was a mistake; there were too many echoes here, even the breeze seemed to brush the grass and creamy foxgloves in the same way as it did, and had done, at the lake house. A mesh of thick vines grew upward from the moss-covered base of the two trees, crawling up the trunks, sinuous and serpentine, as if searching for something. Opposite the two trees scrub and blackberry bushes intertwined with the black iron pilings to form a wall between the path and the park beyond the church grounds, where the flat pink faces of dog roses grew.

There was no lake, of course, no sheet of still water to cast murky dreams. She laid her hand against the bark of the first tree, felt its coarse texture beneath the tips of her fingers.

He had had her up against a tree like this one. Chased her through trees like this one, through the thickets and saplings and long grass, hiding and leaping out at her by turns. She could remember hearing a small pitiful cry, as if from a distance, but which had come from her own mouth as he snatched at her dress.

Chased her.

And in that place of secrets and abrupt endings she had let him – given in, submitted, yielded. And the yielding hadn't been so bad, not after the terror of the chase.

163

There had been a sort of contagion in his touch, terrible and yet merciful at the same time.

So when Frank placed his hand on her shoulder she turned to him with no calculation at all, her eyes resting on his for a long silent moment and Eve thought she knew recognition in those few heated seconds, thought she saw the other man behind the fine dark features – felt the other man as he pressed her down on to her knees and made her take him in her mouth, filling it, ramming his sex to the back of her throat so that it made her gag.

His hands pulling her hair.

She endured the ordeal in total silence, accepting it as she had always accepted it, but then she was free and he was drawing her up and forcing her against the tree, and she was that girl again in the pink gingham dress with his hands on her, the thick, fissured bark gnawing its way into her back and buttocks. His hot laughing breath on her face. Her hot asking mouth open and hungry.

Oh, yes, that was just the way it had been; there was no fooling herself. In fact, in that far off time she had discovered that the primitive reaction of her body could resist her mind's frantic advice, that it could switch the adrenaline caused by a heightened state of fear to another level. It could make her come. Except the scream breaking free from her young throat at the point of climax had been much more than mere pleasure, it had been guilt and revulsion and regret all rolled into one hot ball of loathing. And most of the loathing had been for herself.

She closed and opened her eyes and saw something beyond Frank's tense feverish face, felt something beyond the pain of this strange muted sex which rubbed and chafed at the self-inflicted wounds between her legs. Eve was suddenly very frightened.

The past was alive to the day, and its nature was such that it would grow and develop and have a fruition all its own.

'There's a man following us,' Tony said. 'I keep seeing him.' At least he thought he did, sort of bleary glimpses, but when he looked, really looked, there was no one there.

'What?' Minty replied vaguely as she lovingly fingered the silk cuff of a Max Mara jacket. It was a deep salmon colour, almost orange, and she was busy wondering whether the tone might clash with her pale skin. Age her.

Tony rubbed at his eyes and wondered if he was seeing things. 'Oh, it doesn't matter.'

Minty lifted the jacket from its hanger and held it against her. 'What do you think?'

'Great.' Tony's voice was clipped. 'Take it.'

'You're just saying that.'

'No, I'm not,' he lied. 'It looks fabulous. The colour's just you.'

Minty promptly put it back. 'Sometimes, Tony, you're pathetically transparent.'

'I preferred the blue really . . .' he admitted sheepishly.

'Blue?'

'The blue thing you ummed and aahed about for ages in Armani,' he said, aware that his patience was beginning to fade fast.

'That was hours ago.'

Exasperated he walked away, over to the window and looked out onto trendy-too-too-rather Sloane Street. There were a lot of ladies-who-lunch trotting about, dripping with designer carrier bags; directly across the road an old dear was letting her dog crap on the pavement. Tony shook his head in disgust and then pulled a face as some Japanese with cameras dangling from their necks obscured his view, followed quickly by a group of school kids with back-packs and street maps. They were laughing with outlandish mirth and he was suddenly stung by envy. How long had it been since he had laughed like that, been so carefree? Sometimes he had the feeling that he had never been young at all.

Tony found his gaze drifting away, up and down the street, staring into the cars trapped in the heaving traffic and all the time there was that growing, languorous sensation of being watched. He hit the side of his head with the heel of his hand as if the action might allay the feeling, but it didn't, and when Minty came up behind him and prodded him in the back he jumped.

'What on earth's got into you?'

'Nothing.'

'Come on,' she said, guiding him firmly towards the door, 'we'll try Nicole Fahri – I love her stuff – and we could nip into Hermès on the way for a few bits and bobs.'

Bits and bobs that would probably cost an arm and a leg. 'Well, it wasn't his bloody money. Tony groaned aloud, but let himself be led, it was simply much easier than protesting; rows were so debilitating and he had felt debilitated enough over the past few days.

'I'm hungry,' he said lamely as she steamed ahead of him.

'We'll eat soon,' she said unconvincingly, 'after I've spent some money.'

Tony fixed his gaze on her exquisitely tailored back and sighed deeply, his mind clinging hopefully to the word soon. 'Oh, please, God,' he murmured to no one in particular.

Langan's did not have the new chic of Daphne's, but it was still Langan's and Tony always felt at home here. He liked everything from the scores of pictures on the walls to the books and quirky figurines. His favourite spot was a table in the corner by the window where, almost unobserved, he could usually stuff himself freely – when he came on his own, that is. Sometimes, and unbeknown to Minty, he had come here with one of the girls from his old ad agency. Of course, they had only been after a nice lunch in a nice place, but nevertheless being seen with a girl half his age did his ego a power of good, and there were one or two who let him have a quick feel under the table. Although these days, he admitted with a sinking feeling, that was usually as far as he got – more to the point, as far as he could manage.

He looked at Minty as she sat down. Magic fingers. Magic mouth. There was definitely something to be said for experience and he wondered if she realised how grateful he was for the other day. Naturally, he would never dream of telling her.

'I'll order,' she said, picking up the menu.

'You don't know what I want.'

'The prawns are very good . . . with a green salad.'

'I don't want a bloody salad.'

'Have you seen your waistline lately?'

Tony reddened. 'You bitch,' he swore in a stage-scream whisper, but there was also a part of him wondering what mean gift Minty possessed that made her so skilful, so deft, at homing in on his weakest and most sensitive spots.

'Don't be childish,' she retorted mildly.

You wait, he thought vengefully, for the old hot flushes and the glad tidings of the menopause and then you'll be sorry . . . but I'll be nearing sixty then, he realised bleakly and unthinkingly touched his face, tracing the contours of his mouth and jawline for signs of slackness and sagging.

'Well, why shouldn't I be bloody childish,' he started petulantly, 'you've been treating me like a child all morning. And in case it still hasn't sunk in, trailing around designerdom is hardly my idea of fun.'

'Oh, for God's sake . . .' she said with obvious boredom and waved a disparaging hand at him. 'Besides, I want you to look your best when we go to the lake house.'

Tony stiffened and said, puzzled, 'Lake house?'

'Yes. You've definitely been looking a bit seedy lately.' She grimaced. 'Probably your diet. And what with that repulsive cold sore . . .'

'What have you been up to?' he asked apprehensively.

'Eve's mother's coming for her annual visit in a couple of weeks, if you must know. I called in on Andrew at the agency and wheedled it out of him . . . everyone will be there for the weekend.'

Everyone. What on earth did that mean exactly? Tony was struck by a ludicrous vision of Princess Di and Bill Clinton, with Mick Jagger and Ivana Trump thrown in for good measure. Sometimes he wondered where Minty's head was coming from. 'But we're not invited.' He wondered why he bothered to mention it; since when had the mere issue of an invitation stood in Minty's way?

'Don't be so naive.'

'I don't want to go.'

She sighed theatrically and looked away from him.

'I won't go, Minty,' he repeated firmly. 'I won't.'

'It'll do you good.'

'Oh, no.' He shook his head with grim fervour. 'I doubt that place can do anybody any good.'

'God,' she said exasperated, 'you're such a bloody old woman. It's got running water, electricity, a telephone . . .'

'That's not what I mean.'

'What do you mean, then?'

Tony averted his eyes, looked out of the window. 'I'm not sure, but I'm not going.'

'We'll see.'

'You don't think I mean it, do you? You think you'll be able to persuade me, that I'm being a soft-headed prick as usual. Well, I'm not.'

'Shut up. Please,' she said wearily. 'You're making me tired.' Thrusting the menu into his hands she stood up. 'I'm going to the loo, but if you need to order in my absence don't forget what I've said: the prawns, green salad and two mineral waters.' To reinforce the point she gave him one of her steely looks and said finally, 'No cod and chips and definitely no weird and wonderful fatty grills. I was nearly ill the last time you brought me here. I can't imagine how you can eat congealed blood with such disgusting fervour – no wonder you're looking seedy.'

'Fatty food isn't the problem . . .' he began lamely.

'I mean it, Tony.'

He replied with a thin, humourless smile which stayed on his lips as Minty disappeared from view, but was swiftly transformed into an inviting grin as he beckoned frantically to a nearby waitress.

'One black pudding grill with bread and butter, and one prawns plus green salad please,' he ordered triumphantly, 'but bring a G and T – ice and lemon – and a mineral water straight away. Thank you.'

He tittered happily to himself, wondering if he could make this fit of rebellion a permanent fixture, and then turned to the window and his mouth fell open in appalled surprise. A man was pressing his face right up against the glass and so hard that all his features were flattened and distorted like some horror out of one of his worst nightmares. Tony's eyes grew huge and almost comically terrified, but he couldn't look away. His gaze remained fixed on that awful face even as it shifted and changed, oozing and squirming soundlessly into something resembling a smile, a big fat gleeful smile that made goosebumps run all the way up Tony's back.

There was a light glinting in the man's dark eyes and a voice whispered in Tony's head that it was the light of madness.

'Shit,' he mumbled incoherently. 'Shit.'

His nostrils twitched at some smell, a warm abnormal smell that made him think of stale, rotting things – and wasn't it familiar that smell, hadn't he come across it in another place, another time?

Somewhere in the back of his mind he heard the drinks he had ordered being put on the table and then Minty's faraway voice asking him what was wrong.

'Tony!' Minty said again and poked him savagely in the shoulder.

Dazedly he looked round and then back again. The man, the face was gone, there was not even the remains of his breath on the glass.

'What the hell is wrong with you?' Minty snapped and then cursed as the waitress delivered their food order. 'I thought I told you no fatty food.'

Tony rose unsteadily to his feet, feeling sure his legs were about to buckle and give way, but then his eyes fell on the offending black pudding. He swallowed deep in his throat, awash with nausea and unease and tried desperately to stop himself from being sick all over his shoes.

Eight

Pansy saw them before they saw her; Frank and Eve. A stunning black man and a beautiful white woman. She suddenly felt very small somehow, insignificant and uncomfortably aware of the pram she was pushing. Pansy fingered her denim dungarees and compared them unhappily with Eve's white summer shift and wished she had thought to put on something less child-like. But she hadn't known Frank was coming and he would never do anything so ordinary and straightforward as telephoning in advance.

She stopped at the top of the street and watched them, unobserved, as they walked towards her and then Eve looked up and waved.

Pansy didn't move, she stayed where she was, leaning on Jack's pushchair, just looking at them, until Frank left Eve at the gate of the house and came to meet her. She stood woodenly, waiting. Nothing in her seemed to be functioning very well and she wondered, again, at the power he had over her.

'I was looking for you,' he said.

'Were you?' she replied, desperately trying to keep out the eagerness in her voice, and it was working, she could hear the veneer of scepticism very well. It sounded horribly realistic.

'Yes,' he said, stopping a few feet away. 'Eve said you were out, so I joined her on a walk to Bishop Park.' He had to look away then, unable to meet Pansy's eyes, because he thought she would see the lie and his guilt gleaming slickly like sweat on his skin. A part of him still couldn't believe what he had done.

It had all happened so fast, over almost before they could loosen their clothes. Afterwards Eve had been so strange. When he looked into her face it had been blank, expressionless, like there was a wall of nothing behind her eyes. Then she had smoothed down her dress and walked on, as if they'd merely been admiring the view, not fucking up against a tree.

And it had only been fucking, he couldn't fool himself that it had come close to anything else. In fact, there had been no satisfaction in it at all, nothing, the most empty sex he had ever had and yet he couldn't stop thinking about it – her. He darted a glance over his shoulder; she'd gone, of course, back into the safety of her cosy house.

'What did you come for?'

He blinked, snapped out of his thoughts. 'Let's not play games, Pansy,' he said, glad of the surge of irritation because it helped blank out other, more disturbing emotions. 'I was out of order the other night.' And not only then Little Flower.

'Yes,' she said simply. 'You're beginning to make it a habit.' She regarded him steadily and Frank thought he saw suspicion in her eyes, and hurt, as if she had read his mind. She began moving the pushchair down the street so he was forced to step-in beside her.

'It wasn't what you thought,' he said quickly, 'it really wasn't, but you were determined to believe the obvious.' He tried to listen to the tone of his words, but was still unable to gauge whether they sounded sincere or not.

'Which was what?' she replied tersely.

He swallowed. 'That there's someone else.'

'There is.'

'Not in the way you think.' And in a twisted sort of a way, that was true. He couldn't kid himself that he was any sort of consideration in Eve's life, he was something incidental, a passing whim.

'There's always someone else in your life, that's how you like to play it, you've told me that often enough.' Pansy stopped walking abruptly and looked at him. 'But it's not how I like to play it, so I asked myself why I had put up with it for so long and there's only one reason . . .'

He frowned. 'Which is?'

Pansy's face was incredulous. 'You don't know?' She stared at him long, full in the eyes until he was forced to drop his gaze. 'I suppose the fact that I have to ask says everything, doesn't it?'

Startled, he countered, 'Stop this, Pansy.'

'Why?' she asked. 'Because it makes you feel uncomfortable?'

'I came over because I wanted to make things up to you,' he said lamely.

'What?' she said with disbelief. 'Like last week? You just cause me grief, Frank. I thought I could take it, but I've discovered I can't.' She shook her head. 'Funnily enough, it's not even the other woman . . .'

Frank blushed (but, of course, she couldn't see).

' . . . or – correction – women so much, it's you and your attitude towards me, all this blowing hot and cold stuff.' She looked away from him, her voice becoming hushed, too gentle and low. 'I don't need it. More to the point, I don't want it any more.'

He examined her calm, set profile and was touched by a sensation that was both discomfort and shame. 'I'm sorry, Little Flower.'

She turned on him sharply. 'I told you not to call me that. I'm not your Little Flower – I'm not anyone's bloody flower. When you say that you sound like my mother, like I'm still in nappies or something.'

He held up his hands. 'Okay, okay . . .'

'You know, what I really don't understand about all of this,' she began again, studying him carefully, 'is why you seem to want me as well.' Her eyebrows came together in an indignant frown. 'Is it safety in numbers? Greed?'

'Why couldn't it be because I actually like you?'

Like. The word sounded half-empty, a poor thing, and she longed to say something harsh and fatal so that she might hurt him as he had hurt her.

'Eve said it was fear of intimacy.'

'Eve said what?' He felt a gauntlet of emotions stampede through his outraged body: anger, embarrassment, hatred even. Discussing him like some school kid, like someone retarded or in need of therapy.

'I don't know why you're so upset – you must have asked yourself the same question.'

'Let's just leave it – shall we?' His eyes were blazing. 'You see it's no one's business but my own. Okay?'

'Fine.' Her voice was clipped, offended. 'And that just about sums you up, Frank.'

'Does it?' he said furiously. 'What the hell do you know?'

She looked back at him a little stunned, wondering how it was possible to be so angry with someone and still love them. Her eyes smarted with tears of frustration and hurt and she started walking again, suddenly wanting to get home, more than anything.

For a moment he watched her move away from him, then, 'Look, I'm sorry.'

She made no answer.

'Pansy,' he called after her. 'We can't leave it like this.' He was burning his boats, every single one of them.

'Yes, we can,' she said over her shoulder, but heard him draw close, felt his hand on her arm and thought she might cry out.

'Pansy . . .' he pleaded softly.

And she could almost let herself believe in that softness, it touched her more than any words could have done.

'Don't,' she made herself say.

'Why not?' There was that pleading again and she wondered if he knew what he was doing to her.

'Go away, Frank.'

'I can't.'

Wordlessly she pulled her arm free of his grip and walked down the street.

'I suppose I'd forgotten that your mother likes to make a long weekend of it,' Andrew said, watching Eve carefully as she pushed some meat half-heartedly around a frying-pan with a spatula.

'I hadn't.'

'You know I opened her letter?'

'Yes.'

'You don't mind?'

'No.'

'Everything's very precise with her, isn't it?' his voice ran on. 'She's got all the arrangements down to the finest detail, rather like a military exercise. Is she really such a cold fish? I mean, she didn't even ask after your health, or Jack's, come to that.'

'We never got on. I came along at a bad time, when she thought her child-bearing days were over. Besides, my brother was the focus of her life – and my father's up to a point. I was just a nuisance.' Eve stopped what she was doing and stared into space; the spatula was raised, hovering uncertainly above the semi-cooked food. 'James used to play me off against her.'

'Did he?' Andrew looked puzzled. 'How?'

'You'd have to know him to understand.' She shook her head. 'And I didn't realise what he was doing; I was too young, too innocent.' Things she had learned to suppress resurfaced in a bleary worrying haze. Perhaps

174

her mother, too, had used her in the play of those unspoken adult games. But why? Why had she done that?

Andrew raised his eyebrows. 'I know I only met her briefly last year, but she didn't strike me as the type who'd be manipulated by anyone, let alone her own son.'

Diana Sanqui made Andrew think of the sort of woman he imagined to be behind every great man – intelligent, controlled, shrewd. She was also amazingly preserved, despite the fact she was in her early seventies and had managed to survive two husbands.

Mother and daughter were physically quite different, except for their height and facial features. Eve had inherited Diana's wide-set eyes and heart-shaped face, and they were both taller than average, but Diana's figure was remarkably slender, even boyish. She had none of the generous curves of her daughter, nor the rich dark hair and dusky skin which had been passed to Eve from her father's side, and his French origins.

Diana was very English, very dignified and composed. Austere, really – no, cold – he thought meanly. He remembered that she spoke in a peculiar way and had assumed that her years in the US had given her one of those odd cross-over sort of accents, but she had been no great conversationalist and most of the time he had found her hard work and certainly not a woman to waste words on mere pleasantries. Andrew wondered what she would make of Minty.

'I think she blames me for his leaving in some way,' Eve said abruptly.

He watched her for a long moment. 'She strikes me as the sort of woman who would blame anyone else, but herself.' He moved across to her and laid his hands on her shoulders and she shuddered. 'What's the matter?' he asked.

'Sorry.' she said. 'Just a shiver.' Other hands had laid their hands on her shoulders that day and Andrew's hands felt the same somehow which wasn't fair, but she didn't want to be touched or stroked or caressed right now. Not even by him. 'Sit down,' she continued steadily. 'I'll pour you a drink.'

He kissed her unwary lips as she moved to pass him and felt her fist clench more tightly around the spatula she still held which became caught clumsily between them.

'What sort of day have you had?'

'Okay,' she said noncommittally.

'What did you do?' he persisted and didn't really know why he did.

'This and that – nothing in particular.' She veered away from him.

'You seem on edge . . . is it talking about your mother?' he probed. 'Your brother?'

'Oh, don't, Andrew,' she pleaded, turning round and looking back at him. 'I'm fine. Just fine.'

'If you say so.'

'I do,' she said. 'I do.' And then, overcome by remorse reached for him and this time the feel of his arms around her was warm, comforting, safe. All those things. 'I'm sorry.'

'There's nothing to be sorry for.' He rubbed her back, up and down, up and down, like a good parent with a fretful child. 'And if you want I'll see to your mother, I'll meet her at the airport and take her to the house. You don't have to be involved at all.'

She said nothing immediately, but then: 'No, I couldn't let you do that.'

'Why not? You didn't go last year.'

'I was being pretty sick with Jack then.' That had only been an excuse, of course, but she could still remember the wonderful relief at not having to go. Eve took a deep, steadying breath. 'I couldn't do it a second time, it would be cowardly, and she'd know.' She moved free of his arms and back to the stove where the delicate pieces of meat she had prepared were busy sticking to the bottom of the pan. 'I suppose this annual visit of hers has become a ritual, a sort of duty of mine . . .'

'That's silly.'

'No. Just the way it is.'

'Other families get together at Christmas and New Year, but the Sanquis decide on the end of September.' He was trying to lighten the atmosphere, make her smile. 'There's nowt so queer as folk.'

She turned round and met his gaze. 'It's his birthday. That's what makes it special for my mother.'

'I understand that. It just seems rather overdone, that's all.'

'I suppose it does to an outsider.' Her words weren't designed to hurt him, but they hit home as surely as if they had.

'I could help,' he said quietly.

'Thank you, Andrew,' she said. 'But no, it's only a matter of three days. I'll manage.'

Andrew looked at her sharply and wondered.

'Where's Pansy?'

'Upstairs,' she said. 'I think she and Frank have had another row.'

Frank. The letters of his name stood still in her mind like a sign or a symbol of something and Eve felt her throat tighten up. What did I do? And there was a part of her that really didn't know. 'What have I done?' she uttered softly, helplessly.

'Did you say something?'

She didn't reply.

'Eve? Are you all right?'

'Your drink,' she said vaguely, 'I forgot.'

Andrew gave her a searching look. 'I'll do it – and I think I'll make you one at the same time. You look as if you could do with something a little stronger than tea.'

'Thanks. I just felt a little giddy, that's all,' she lied.

'I think you should go back to Dr Brass,' he said gently. 'Just for a check-up.'

'I'm fine, Andrew,' she said. 'I told you.'

'Feeling giddy isn't fine.'

'If it happens again, I'll go. All right?'

He sighed heavily and poured their drinks and placed a glass next to the stove, at the same time darting a glance into the frying pan. 'That meat looks as if it's been around the block a few times.' He lifted her hands away and took over. 'Sit down and drink.'

Eve looked back at him gratefully and did as she was told.

'Anyway,' he began, 'what's this about Pansy and Frank?'

Eve quickly swallowed some of her gin. 'I think they've rowed again.'

'Obviously not the perfect match.'

'And how would you know, Daddy?' Pansy exclaimed resentfully from the doorway.

For a moment Andrew closed his eyes in frustration, hardly able to credit the bad timing of his remark. 'Well, I don't know – do I? But if you keep arguing, or whatever, it hardly bodes well for the future. Does it?'

The face Pansy turned to her father was strained and miserable. 'I suppose not.' She sat down at the breakfast bar. 'Anyway, it hardly matters now.'

'Why?'

'Because I decided enough was enough.'

'Do you want to talk about it?' Andrew looked back at his daughter warily.

'No.'

He rolled his eyes and wondered how it was that the women in his life seemed so loth to communicate in a real way, extracting anything worthwhile from them was about as hard as getting blood out of a stone. Except Minty, of course. Minty let him know everything and usually in lurid detail, always had done, and if she didn't, he only had to scrape the surface a little before he either found out, or her motives became transparently clear.

This thing about the lake house, for instance . . . Minty wouldn't rest until she'd got it out of her system. Like her 'I was just passing, so I thought I'd pop in and see you' routine at the agency. Ironically, he was glad now that he had let it slip about Eve's mother and her visit. Perhaps if Minty turned up at the lake house as well, it would take some of the heat away from Eve.

Weird, this birthday thing about her brother. Sad. Perhaps he actually might turn up. Now that really would surprise everyone and despite what Eve had said, Andrew was still very interested in meeting her brother, even eager.

'Bishop Park, Frank said . . .' Pansy's voice broke into his thoughts and Andrew looked around.

'Bishop Park?' he queried.

Pansy looked back at her father in irritation. 'Yes. Eve and Frank were there this afternoon.'

Andrew flashed a glance at his wife. 'You didn't tell me.'

'There was nothing to tell.' She shifted her eyes away. 'I met him in the park, I was looking at the church.'

'But Frank said he bumped into you outside the house,' Pansy said, puzzled.

'Did he?' Eve said vaguely. 'How odd.' She rubbed at her temples. 'Well, perhaps he did, it seems a bit of a blur right now. I've had this headache . . .'

'A headache as well as giddiness?' Andrew interjected. 'Will you do as I ask and go to the doctor's, or do I have to make the appointment for you?'

'All right, all right,' Eve said rapidly.

'You're still not sleeping, are you?' he pressed and was reluctantly reminded of her last nightmare.

'It's not so bad,' she said deliberately unconvincingly. 'Really.'

'You'll do as I ask, though, won't you?'

'Yes,' she said, and then more emphatically, 'yes.' Eve felt the sly spectre of guilty relief percolate through her body. The subject of Frank and Bishop Park had been conveniently eclipsed and the panic scrabbling inside her head was beginning to subside. Except there was not only panic, she realised with bewilderment, but also a sort of dreadful, distracted excitement, as if she were slowly filling up with something outside herself, something unbidden, un-nice.

And Frank was in there somewhere. Yet he and Pansy were no longer seeing each other apparently, so surely he wouldn't be coming to the house and she would be free of him? But there was a part of her that doubted it could really be that simple – left in peace and not delivered into temptation, (Sister Rosemary would have undoubtedly admired the phraseology).

Eve licked her lips and looked down into her glass. Tempted to what?

Her face was worried, confused, but once again she had unwittingly steered her way through the dangerous shoals of thought which had begun to haunt her, away from the jagged reefs and rocky shores where her monsters dwelt.

She didn't see the shadow of uncertainty and suspicion in her stepdaughter's eyes. It lingered there for a long moment like those small changes which shock produces; a subtle look, fading as quickly as it appeared.

Andrew stood on the gravel path and looked up at the white sky and then across at the lake. The water was utterly still and thinly covered with a transparent skin of dusty scum; it seemed bigger to him just then: wider, blacker, as if it had grown in his absence. Well, the weeds certainly had, springing up between the flags of the stone-paved terrace, along the verges and over and under the bulbous roots of trees. The lawn looked decidedly hairy.

He had arranged for a local handyman to come and tidy the garden in preparation for the visit of his mother-in-law. There was an old shed at the back of the house where the mower and shears were kept, but it was locked and the key was in the kitchen, hanging on a nail. So he had come to let the man in and also to check the house over because it would certainly need airing and dusting at some point, but that could wait until next week and nearer the day.

Andrew had not told Eve he was coming because there was no real need, he had simply left the agency earlier than usual in the belief that he could probably still make it home at more or less the same time. She wouldn't even guess where he had been, even if she bothered to try – which she wouldn't; Eve wasn't into light-hearted banter these days and certainly not guessing games. In fact, most of the time Andrew had the distinct impression that she was preoccupied, or at least that her mind was elsewhere and he had no idea what to do about it. He didn't want to dig too deep; there was a part of him which was anxious only to keep things as they were and conscientiously refrain from acknowledging that there was anything really wrong with his lovely wife except a trace of lingering post-natal depression. Maybe it was just that, he told himself firmly. Just that. Why look for ghosties and goblins when they didn't exist?

He had managed to make her promise that she would see the doctor again, so perhaps he could also persuade her to consider going back on Prozac once more – with a little judicious pushing, just to tide her over.

Andrew swept a hand over his hair, fighting away a dragging weariness. There was something melancholy about this place, he decided, something sad and lonely abiding in its unnatural stillness, in its deep moist shadows. 'Because no one lives here any more, you fool . . .' he said aloud.

Perhaps places where people once lived did get lonely; after all, no one could actually prove that it wasn't so. He smiled at the thought as he began walking across the lawn towards the jetty. He hadn't been here since the night of Minty's accident and wondered, again, how she could have let things get so out of control. But that was Minty and her love of exhibitionism, notwithstanding a few man-made chemicals pumping through her system.

His footsteps made a ringing, hollow sound as he moved along the narrow wooden walkway to the end, where he stopped and looked into the water and its lush, verdant forest of weed. A pale sun was doing its best to shine through a stubborn bank of cloud and the light which seeped down turned the lake a shimmering silver.

What harm could come to any sensible person in a place of such beauty?

It seemed to him that he stood there a long time before making his way back to the lawn and walking slowly around the edge of the water, skirting a long bank of reeds and passing over a section of soft marsh by means of two large, and probably very old, stepping-stones before reaching higher ground and the right side of the lake. If he had paused long enough on the correct spot, he might have seen the sheltered inlet where Pansy had stood and fancied she'd seen someone struggling in the water.

There were fewer trees on this side, consequently the grass was thicker, speckled with seed-heads and poppies and when the wind blew it made moving patterns of red and black play across the rough meadow. Andrew was looking ahead, to the top of the small rise, so he did not immediately see the piece of half-buried stone which happened to lie directly in his path. He managed to save himself only by taking a clumsily large stride over the obstacle and when he brought his foot down on the other side Andrew screamed.

The mole-trap had been lying just below the surface of the soil, its three metal spikes which should have been pointing downwards to ensnare an unsuspecting mole, had somehow twisted out of sync, so that they poked skywards like two lethal arrows aimed at heaven. Except they claimed Andrew's foot, not heaven.

The pain was instantaneous. He fell sideways, moaning helplessly, his foot a fiery bolt of agony. Some swallows, alarmed, took flight abruptly, dipping and swooping across his dancing vision like a waking dream.

The spikes had speared his shoe and gone deep into muscle and tissue before forcing their way through the delicate meshwork of bones which make up the upper part of the foot and then out the other side, so that a good half of their length now protruded into empty air. A fragment of navy sock waved at Andrew from one of the tips.

He lay on his back, legs drawn up, staring in shock and incomprehension at the three glinting stilettos which had skewered him with such horrific ease. They were joined at the base by a spring mechanism of some sort, but his foot obscured its true nature and therefore also a way in which he might release himself, even if he had been foolhardy enough to try. In all probability he would only succeed in tearing half his foot away, or maiming himself for life in the process. He was not James Bond or the Last of the Mohicans – whipping out bullets or arrowheads with his teeth. And this was not the movies.

He felt sick.

Andrew closed his eyes tight for a second, fighting a brief struggle with his stomach before retching into the grass. When that was over the pain seemed to worsen in a horrible, tear-jerking sort of way, as if some invisible notch had been turned up a thousand-fold. He tried to control his breath, found himself rolling around in the grass, gritting his teeth, as if it was his body's own answer to the pain.

'God, God . . . oh God . . .' He let out an anguished sob, throwing back his head and looking frantically about for help, but there was no one. No one at all. His hand found a large rock and he hauled himself into a sitting position which caused another wave of agony to cruise unconcerned through his body. Only when he felt able to look round did he realise that it was not a rock but a headstone his fingers grasped, an old headstone encrusted with lichen, the writing indecipherable. In fact, he was sitting in a virtual cemetery of headstones, albeit a very small one. Through a haze of pain he saw that the name carved on the one in front of him was clear and readable, Bonzo, the one next to it (the one he had fallen over), Jester. How very apt. He leaned his head back and stared bleakly at the distant sky.

A dog cemetery.

Quaint, really.

But painful. With a deep shudder, he prepared himself to rise, using the headstone behind him as a prop. Once on his feet he could hop back to the car and use his mobile phone, but even as the idea took shape he was seriously doubting its viability. Hopping wouldn't be very easy downhill and on rough, grassy ground. And what if there were more mole-traps? Lovely.

Andrew looked reluctantly at his skewered foot and whimpered. The pain had reduced marginally to a deep agonising throb, and as he sat there a large red ant walked up his ankle and began moving towards the blood oozing, slowly but surely through his sock and down the side of his injured foot.

'Grub-up? Is that what you think you little bastard?' Instinctively, Andrew moved his leg and was stunned by a huge lancet of pain. He lay still for a long time until something like bearable agony resumed in his injured limb.

The insect's action had at least decided him; he would shuffle along on his backside using a stick to explore the ground immediately ahead of him. He glanced weakly at his watch, realising that the handyman wouldn't be arriving for another half-hour – so he could wait and endure the pain, and the ants; or move, which might take his mind off his predicament. Not a great choice.

Andrew took a deep gulp of the hot breathless air and moved.

He covered the first few yards surprisingly well, and even the next, but by then he was approaching the bottom of the small rise where the ground began to grow unsettlingly soft; beyond this lay the stepping-stones, which now seemed precarious and even dangerous for a man with a broken (more likely fractured) foot which was swelling up like one of those sausage balloons magicians use to make funny animals.

So he stopped moving and decided to wait because the handyman would be here soon; it was almost four-thirty.

But the handyman didn't come. Not at four-thirty, not at five-thirty, by which time Andrew was beginning to realise that he was probably not coming at all.

And no one knew he was here.

For a long moment he sat there: thirsty, sweaty and tired, sprawled in the long grass while a few butterflies bobbed indifferently about his head. He stared in silent frustration at his car parked far far away on the gravel drive; he swallowed hard and shifted his gaze to the lawn, then back to the lake. It did not hold particularly pleasant memories for him, Andrew realised; there had been that incident with Eve just after they had married when he had coaxed her in and she had blacked out. Her head had literally gone under and for a moment he had panicked before dragging her back to the bank. He could recall with odd, searing clarity how his feet had sunk deeply into the silty mud, the pond weed wrapping itself about his legs and arms. Everything slipping away.

And what of Minty and her grotesque 'dip' the night of Eve's party?

Sell the place perhaps, but her mother would never allow it.

He pinched the bridge of his nose and leaned weakly back on his elbows; across the water a slight breeze was ruffling the black line of trees on the far bank. It would be cool there, he thought, silent.

He had never felt so alone in his life.

For the hundredth time Andrew looked at his foot, his poor bloody foot, and wondered what had possessed anyone to plant a mole-trap amongst the graves of old family pets. And it must have been there a long time, but when he looked at it hard, the trap didn't look old at all, it looked almost new, the spikes even gleamed in the fading sunlight. It should be rusted, he told himself, flaking with weakness and years old decay, but the metal rising out of his foot was young and strong and unpleasantly robust.

How then? Who?

Andrew felt an unreasoning flicker of panic, a disquieting feeling of vulnerability and nervousness which grew steadily worse.

Across the lake, close to the sheltered inlet where his daughter had stood, a shadow shifted its length and something slouched through the long grass.

Andrew peered anxiously around him, but his gaze seemed ultimately drawn to the trees on the opposite bank, their branches inextricably woven together into tight knotted patterns, the branches moving, the patterns changing, forming pictures . . .

So when a car beeped its horn long and hard, he nearly jumped out of his skin. The handyman had arrived.

'I'm sorry, Andrew,' Eve said. 'I couldn't put them off.' She knelt down beside her husband who was propped up on the sofa, his injured foot propped even higher. 'They'll be over about nine.'

'Minty and Tony.' He sighed deeply. 'Just what I don't need, but at least we won't have to feed them. What's it all about anyway?' It would no doubt be something he would find excrutiatingly boring, or stupid, or just plain infantile.

'Well, apart from wanting to see how you are . . .'

Andrew raised his eyebrows.

'. . . Minty has a home video she wants us to see – said it wouldn't take long.'

'Oh, God . . .' Andrew sighed again. 'I bet that's the one Bob's been hawking around.'

Eve frowned. 'Bob?'

'You remember Bob Cahill and his famous camcorder at your birthday party?'

Eve nodded. 'That Bob.' That night.

'Right,' Andrew agreed. 'Well, he's been nagging me for a couple of weeks to take a look at the video he recorded there, said he got some good film in – whatever that's supposed to mean. I think he must imagine he's Ridley Scott or something. Frankly, I thought his persistence in rather bad taste considering Minty's accident, but you know what he's like, and he did say that it might help . . . and I don't know what that's supposed to mean, either. Personally, I'd rather forget all about it.'

'So would I.'

'Although, if Minty doesn't mind,' he added with weary inevitability, 'I hardly think we can have any real objections. Do you?'

'Not really.'

'And she's made a brilliant recovery. In fact, you could almost say the accident has worked an improvement.'

'Why?'

'She's not drinking, my love. Didn't you know?' He shook his head. 'God knows how long it will last, but let's be thankful while it does.'

'How strange.' Eve said abstractedly, as the events of that night reluctantly began to unspool in her mind. Not again, please not again. The memory was causing an unfurling inside, a strange unsettling thrill which made her feel a little sick.

Andrew fell silent before speaking again; he was staring at his broken foot. 'When I was sitting so pathetically in the grass looking across that lake of yours, it felt like I was the only person left in the world. Do you understand?'

Oh, yes, she understood. 'You were badly hurt,' she said, remembering how that same awful understanding had trickled through her shock when she had learned what had happened. 'And exhausted and with no immediate help at hand. Anyone would have felt the same.'

And there would be more nasty little treats in store, of course, she was sure of that now. Eve was glad Andrew wasn't looking directly at her just then because he would see the dread there, and beginnings of panic.

'Would they?' He reflected quietly, but in truth he wasn't really saying what he wanted, because what he wanted to say was best left unspoken. He had been sure someone was there, you see, hiding amongst the trees and scrub, watching him, and for a few appalling seconds he had been very scared.

It had not made him feel much easier when John Hardy had given his opinion on the mole-trap. The handyman had told him that it was, indeed, new – if a somewhat outdated model and he, too, had had no idea why someone might have laid it in the grounds, particularly in a pet cemetery. It didn't make sense.

'Did you always bury your dogs with such formality?' Andrew asked with forced lightness. 'After all, apart from anything else, carved headstones are expensive.'

'It was traditional as far as I can recall and by the time I was old enough to ask any questions, it was pretty pointless; we virtually had no animals. My parents seemed to lose interest once my brother left home.' Eve picked a tiny speck of fluff from the black silk of her trousers. 'And they're not all dogs, you know, James caught all sorts of things and kept them.'

'Caught?' Andrew frowned. 'Like what?'

'Well,' she began slowly, 'we had dogs, of course, a few cats too, but he liked to snare things. I can remember a squirrel and a rat, birds . . . a badger, stoats and weasels – things like that.'

'He caged them?'

'Yes.'

'Wasn't that a bit cruel?'

She shrugged. 'Yes.'

'And your parents didn't mind?' He was beginning to feel a little outraged.

'I suppose not.'

'That's terrible.'

'But he looked after them very well,' she said, defending him, 'he really cared about them, odd as it may seem, and sometimes he let them go.'

'Yet caging wild things . . .'

'I know, but he was very fond of them.' She continued, remembering, 'He had a weasel, a pretty thing, it used to go with him everywhere – inside his jacket, his jumper; it was so tame.' She turned her face to him, a finger curled, childlike, in her hair and said brightly. 'They make very good pets, you know.'

'He could hardly be fond of moles if he trapped them.'

'That was my mother's idea. She hated the way they ruined the lawn.'

'So your big bad brother does have some good points?'

Her face clouded and her mouth made a bad imitation of a smile. 'Everyone does, don't they?'

Andrew caught her wrist and stared at her intently. 'What is it about him – or even your mother?'

She shook her head. 'It was so long ago, and I was very young . . .'

'What was?' he asked gently.

She swallowed thickly, felt a jolt, a little twist in her chest. 'When I was growing up there was such a feeling of isolation about the lake house, as if it wasn't part of the rest of the world, that the rules and laws beyond the gate didn't apply somehow.'

He frowned. 'Yes?'

'I don't know,' she said helplessly and looked down at her empty hands. 'I'm not quite sure what I'm trying to say.'

'Sorry,' he said, sensing her distress. 'It doesn't matter, I'm just interested, that's all. Now, subject closed.' He caught hold of her hand. 'Are you sure you don't mind about tonight?'

'No. I'll be fine.'

He saw the relief in her eyes and wondered.

But he wished he could say the same himself because he didn't really want any reminders of his accident right now, yet perhaps it would help in some way; get it out of his system by next week when her mother arrived. In the meantime he would get his secretary to chase up John Hardy on checking the ground for more traps. Andrew was sure he didn't really need to. Before driving him to the nearest hospital, the man had even been good enough to take a walk into the copse of trees on the other side of the lake and had found nothing, or more to the point, no one.

And that had been that. Three days ago. It seemed more like years.

Except now Andrew didn't want to go back.

Of course, anyone, including Eve, would tell him this was a natural reaction given the circumstances, but it was absurd, childish even.

'Stop thinking about it,' Eve said softly.

He smiled, still not used to the ease with which she could read him and lifted the tips of her fingers to his lips.

'We'll both grin and bear it,' he said. 'And tomorrow I'm going to see about us taking a holiday.'

'Oh, I'd like that, Andrew.' Eve said and kissed his soft warm cheek. 'I'd like that very much.'

Tony had brought all the equipment, hired it from a place in Tottenham Court Road, and when he and Minty arrived, she had made him carry everything except the video. Minty had breezed in, clad in drapey pale blue, with Tony following a few dutiful paces behind. Before he had even had chance to draw breath she had instructed him to set everything up in the drawing-room. Andrew found himself thinking that this comic scene was almost worth the inconvenience of having them descend so dramatically on the house.

'State of the art stuff, you know.' Tony said seriously.

'Is it?' Andrew said doubtfully.

'I'm not an expert, of course, but . . .'

'Shut up, Tony,' Minty said from the back of the room. 'You're tiring Andrew.'

'No, he's not,' Andrew retorted. 'I've injured my foot, not had a bloody stroke.'

'There's no need to snap.' Minty gave Eve a meaningful, if poor rendition, of a sympathetic glance. 'Where's Pansy? I thought she'd be here.'

'She's in her room, said she might come down later.'

'She hasn't even said hello, for God's sake. Is she all right?'

'She's broken up with her boyfriend.'

'I didn't know she had one,' Minty responded, aghast. 'At least no one important. That girl never tells me anything.'

'If she didn't live with us,' Eve remarked, 'I don't suppose we would have known, either.'

'It's Tony's fault, of course.'

'My fault!' Tony protested.

'You know she can't stand you.'

'Thanks very much.' But it was true, he told himself sullenly. They had hated each other on sight, well, at least she had, he thought, feeling wounded, and he couldn't recall a single word or act that might have set off her dislike.

'All children hate their step-parents.'

'Christ,' he said. 'We're not even married.'

'Yes, but we're living together, that means practically the same thing to Pansy's generation.'

'Yes, but you're living with me.'

'Stop splitting hairs.'

'It's my-bloody-flat!' he complained.

'For God's sake, you two,' Andrew said in exasperation. 'Can't you save this until you get home?'

Minty pulled a face and then stood up. 'I'm going to fetch my daughter.'

'Leave her in peace,' Andrew argued.

'She should see this,' Minty insisted. 'She was there. Besides, I want to see her – a girl needs her mother when she's miserable and particularly if that misery involves men.'

'Oh, God, here we go,' Tony said gloomily, finally giving in to his nicotine craving and reaching into his jacket for a much needed cigarette.

'Well, there does happen to be a man involved,' Minty declared ominously. 'No doubt some inconsiderate, totally selfish, two-timing shit who wouldn't know a good thing if he fell over it.'

'You know women can be just as . . .' Tony began feebly, lighting-up.

'Balls.'

'All right,' Andrew broke in. 'All right.' With some difficulty he shifted around to look at Minty, who was standing behind him, and said in a conciliatory tone, 'Why don't you leave Pansy alone right now. I just think she might need . . .' but Minty was already halfway through the door even as he spoke, and he wondered why he bothered. He turned to Eve and said thoughtfully. 'I wonder why she always assumes men are two-timing shits? I wasn't.'

'Well, bully for good old you,' Tony interrupted petulantly, scrutinising him through a cloud of smoke. 'That must make you eligible for The Bore of the Century Award . . .'

'Oh, very funny,' Andrew said and looked dismissively past him to the window and the evening sky beyond. 'Frank wasn't two-timing Pansy, was he?'

Eve felt her cheeks burn and darted a glance at her husband's set profile. She cleared her throat. 'I don't know.'

'Sometimes I'm rather glad that's all behind me.'

'Youth, you mean?' Tony said with disbelief. 'You must be joking. Once you hit fifty, forget it, mate.'

'Oh, give it a rest,' Andrew said, looking back at him sharply. 'And what's that on your face?'

'That's exactly what I mean,' he whined. 'I'm falling apart! Have you ever seen me with a cold sore before? No. I've never had one in my life until now – and look at the size of it for God's sake!' Even his doctor had had to admit that he'd never seen quite such a large one before, and it still showed no signs of shrinking or fading. Tony was getting worried.

'It'll go. Cold sores always do.'

'Well, it's taking its bloody time.' Tony touched it gingerly with the tip of a finger. It felt huge, as if a mountain had suddenly decided to sprout from his upper lip. And what with that weird dream . . . and that guy, that horrible, creepy guy pressing his face up against the restaurant window . . . it didn't bear thinking about.

'Are you all right?' Eve asked. Tony looked pale suddenly, even unhappy.

'No. Not really,' he said forlornly, as his mind reluctantly called up the things that woman, Immaculata, had said. He was thinking about them often now, they nagged at him like a half-forgotten message. Every day. He took another nervous puff of his cigarette and then his eyes shot to the open door, Minty was striding back in the room with Pansy in tow. He smiled weakly.

'Shall we begin?' she said triumphantly.

* * *

The darkness made the screen seem larger and Eve was struck by the clarity of the film, the detail, and she thought how strange it was to look back and watch the past. It was literally like taking a step back in time and in a way it was like memory, too, but far more vivid. Yet neither medium had the power to alter what had already taken place: opportunities missed, the slights and unwise compliments, the ache of love gone. That secret joy when a burden dies and leaves you safe.

If only it could be that simple, she wished silently, to call things back, change them – let the consequences of a deed end with the deed itself.

She was suddenly swept by anguish, knowing that the memory of her own deeds waited just out of sight to ambush her. One faltering step from the daily tightrope she walked and they would have her. She sat very still, open eyes staring sightlessly at the screen, but in the darkness her hand was reaching out for Andrew's, as if in an uncertain world he was the anchor that would keep her sane and safe. With an inaudible sigh of relief she felt the reassuring pressure of his fingers on the back of her hand.

'Give me a nudge if I fall asleep,' he whispered and she smiled despite herself.

The film wobbled too much at various points and Bob had clearly been unable to resist sneaking up on people and taking unflattering views of their anatomy, but otherwise it was watchable. Eve even began to relax a little, even found observing herself not entirely disagreeable, simply because she felt she was viewing herself from a distance, almost as if what she saw wasn't really real. So it didn't matter – wouldn't matter.

They are like cardboard cut-out figures, a voice in her head said, playing at living. She cringed a little inside herself, the thin veneer of well-being she had felt only a moment ago fading fast. It was as if the voice was at her ear, its whispering lips ready to linger and tease. 'Evey,' the voice said, 'Little Evey.'

The camera had shot to the lake and she thought of him, invoked his image in her mind's eye and felt the old despair touch her with its light black wing.

He would never let her go. Never.

She shifted in her seat and winced, clamping her mouth shut on the moan that almost broke free from her lips. She hurt: beneath her arm the wound she had made had reopened again, but further down her labia only burned a little from the cuts she had inflicted.

Itched.

190

It was healing. She knew she would do something about that later, she wouldn't be able to help herself.

If Eve had had a hair shirt, she would have worn it, let it rub and chafe her body, her soft creamy skin.

Sometimes there are things held captive in the subsconscious too long, where they grow big and then finally break free to assume distended, or grotesque proportions, which can equally become the stuff of magic, or of nightmare.

Eve stared at the familiar images on the screen and waited.

'There's that little tart.' Minty said frostily.

'Oh, Mum, don't.' Not a scene, please, Pansy begged silently.

Bob had honed in on the girl Tony had met at the party, the one Eve had found him with in the house. Even as they watched the girl was smiling and taking his hand and leading him up the lawn. 'Oh – my – God.' Minty seethed.

Halfway up the lawn the giggling girl slipped, revealing a bottom almost naked except for what looked like a piece of string.

'Oh – my – God.' Minty said again.

Tony closed his eyes.

The video camera followed them across the terrace and around the side of the house until they disappeared from view.

'You disgusting, cheap little bastard . . .'

'Shall we stop now?' Andrew warned. 'Or continue? It's up to you.'

There was silence for a long moment before Minty finally gave in and said: 'All right, all right. Continue.' She'd forgotten about Tony messing around at the party, but at least it was a record, if a distasteful one, of what a creep he could be and once they got home she would make sure that he didn't forget it in a hurry. She took a deep breath in an attempt at controlling her temper. After all, she told herself, you've come for the other stuff, the stuff that will come soon. Tony isn't even in it, he's just a dumb instrument, an empty insignificant vessel with something working through. And that made her smile.

Did she need a reminder of what a fantastic stroke of luck it was that Bob Cahill had videoed the party at all? Naturally he'd filmed her, too, he'd told her amongst all his gibbering enthusiasm on the phone. Down on the jetty, he'd said, you and some man . . .

Minty's smile widened in anticipation.

Pansy eyed her mother warily and drew in a breath, wishing she was anywhere, but here. She'd let Minty have her way, partly out of duty because she didn't see her very much, but mostly because the thought of opposing her was just too tiring to contemplate. Besides, she hated rows, and she supposed walking away from Frank was avoiding confrontation, too, but it was the only thing she had felt capable of doing. And there had been no sign of him since, not even a telephone call, so perhaps it had worked better than she'd expected. For all her fine words she wondered if he were to call right now whether she'd have the strength to turn him away.

And Eve, where was she in all of this? Had they been discussing her when they had their 'walk' in Bishop Park? Pansy twisted her fingers in her lap, sensing that there was something which she could not yet grasp, a maddening kind of thing that would not let go. Eve. Did he fancy her? Was that it? No, she was her stepmother for heaven's sake, married. Frank would know he was wasting his time, and he hated doing that. But it didn't make the thought go away.

She sighed softly and tried to concentrate on the video, but only saw a group of grinning people, one woman had a gherkin sticking out of a thin red mouth. In the background (they were inside the house now) she saw her father telling a story to a couple she knew vaguely, he was drawing something in the air with his hands. And then the picture wobbled, but almost continuously this time as Bob moved into the hall before coming to a stop in the doorway.

Down on the jetty there was her mother and she was not naked. Yet. Even from this distance Pansy knew it was her. Minty's dress gleamed in the moonlight like a sheet of gold and she was talking to someone.

'Who's that?' she heard her father say. 'I don't recognise him . . . mind you, it's difficult to see amongst all that shadow.' He turned to Minty. 'Who is it?'

Minty made no answer, she was too busy staring in fascination at the screen.

'Eve?'

His wife wordlessly shook her head. In the darkness Andrew failed to see the way her hands gripped the arms of the chair, the way the blood had left her lovely, frightened face.

'Do you know, Tony?'

'Yeah,' he said carelessly. 'That's Michael Harwood – the

photographer. I'd know him anywhere, tall bloke, did a couple of covers for *Vogue* . . .'

'I didn't know he was invited.'

'Well, he was there. I saw him.'

Suddenly Minty whirled round. 'It wasn't Michael-bloody-Harwood, you idiot!'

'I saw him,' Tony said.

'And I didn't.'

'You were too pissed out of your brains to even see straight.'

'I know who I was talking to,' Minty's voice trembled, 'and I don't need you to tell me.'

'Who the hell was it, then?'

'He didn't tell me his name.'

'You wouldn't have remembered even if he had.'

'I wasn't that far gone, for Christ's sake.'

'You were so far gone,' Tony said smugly, enjoying himself at last, 'that you nearly drowned yourself. Or have you forgotten that bit?'

'God, I hate you.'

Andrew lifted up his hands. 'For heaven's sake. Calm down.'

'I know what I saw . . .' Minty said, but her words sounded unconvincing even to her own ears, an odd mixture of fear and shrewishness.

Tony turned back to the screen, shaking his head in a particularly irritating kind of a way, and let the hand holding his cigarette dangle nonchalantly over the arm of the chair. Minty wanted to kill him.

Her knuckles were bunched into fists of thwarted rage, but out of the corner of her eye she saw that the film was already moving on and she didn't want to miss anything. Maybe, just maybe if she could see him again? The man. Her man. Everything would be all right.

She stared at the screen, her gaze avid, hungry, but Bob had clearly retreated back inside the house because the camera was busy focusing on people going up and down the stairs, until a young man (very drunk) came right up to the lens and gave it a long lingering kiss before moving back a step and sticking one very stiff finger into the air.

Tony was unhappily reminded of the ghastly face at the restaurant window and took a long drag on his cigarette. 'What a wanker that guy is . . .' he said with contempt. 'Didn't he lose the Prada account?'

'No.' Andrew said. 'He won it.'

Tony blew out a mouthful of smoke. 'He's still a wanker.'

Minty wanted to scream at him to shut up.

The next few minutes of filming were tedious repeats of similar shots, all taking place inside, at least until Bob stuck the camera out through a window and the lawn came into view again. It was a rapidly emptying lawn and Pansy realised they were probably leading up to the point where her mother decided to take her famous dip in the water.

'I think I'll make some coffee.' Eve said and stood up.

'Oh, don't go,' Minty pleaded, 'it's not finished yet.

'I've seen all I want to see. Thank you.'

'Look -- there's you!' Minty said wildly. 'With me!'

Eve's eyes were inevitably drawn to the screen, but the camera jolted away suddenly and then shot back, as if it had abruptly decided on a double-take. Belatedly Bob had realised that Minty was standing there stark naked, but by the time he focused on the scene again it was too late because Eve was standing alone and Minty was gone.

The camera hovered there, its lens a curious scanning eye, falling on the water for a long silent moment before the image shrank and was lost as Bob withdrew into the house once more.

On screen Eve could see Andrew picking up a few glasses and through the facing doorway some people leaving. A waiter crossed the room and gave a thumbs-up sign to the camera.

And that was all.

There would be no repeat performance of Minty in the lake, no feverish shrieks of joy, no sudden movements in that black water as Minty's naked body was jerked upwards, out of it, like some lurid life-sized puppet.

'I'll make that coffee, then.' Eve said, and switched on the lights.

Nine

'**Y**ou saw him,' Minty insisted, 'didn't you?'

She had followed Eve into the kitchen, determined to extract something worthwhile from the evening, something at any cost that would not send her away empty-handed.

'Who?' Eve said flatly.

'That guy – the one at the lake.'

'I didn't see any guy at the lake.'

'You did, I know you did.' Minty felt a sick sheen of sweat begin to break out on her cheeks and forehead, and for the first time in weeks longed for a drink.

Eve had her back to Minty, but suddenly she turned round and faced her. 'I didn't.'

'Who is he, Eve?'

'For the last time, I didn't see anyone. I don't know what you're talking about.' Her hands were shaking and she put them aside, but Minty had seen.

She swallowed hard. 'You're lying.' Her throat felt like sandpaper, there was a small pain in her back like a sharp prod, a finger, goading her on.

'I think you should go home.' Eve reached for the jug of coffee, intending to place it on the tray she had prepared earlier.

'What is it?' Minty caught hold of her arm. 'What are you afraid of?'

'Mum?' It was Pansy.

Minty swung round and fetched up a strained smile. 'What do you want?'

There was an embarrassed silence as Pansy's uneasy gaze came to settle on her mother's hand, which still gripped her stepmother's arm. 'We wondered where the coffee was.' And it wasn't a gentle grip, she realised. In fact, her mother's hand clutched Eve's flesh so tightly that the knuckles had turned white.

'It's coming,' Minty said dismissively.

Pansy didn't move.

'I said, it's coming.'

'Can I help at all?' She looked at Eve.

'We don't need your help,' Minty snapped.

Pansy's eyes returned to her mother's face, which had twisted into an expression of fury. 'Whatever's the matter?' She was puzzled and a little angry.

'Can't you see that you're intruding?' Minty was becoming strident. 'Isn't it obvious?'

Pansy darted a glance at Eve, 'Am I?'

Eve began unfurling the fingers of Minty's hand from her arm. 'No. We'd just finished.'

Minty turned on Eve and demanded hoarsely: 'But you didn't answer my question.'

'There's no question to answer,' she said reasonably. 'I think you're confused about something.' Eve picked up the jug of coffee and placed it finally on the tray and made to move past her.

'Don't patronise me,' she shrilled. 'And I'm not bloody-well confused.'

'Minty,' Eve warned. 'We'll have Andrew and Tony in here in a minute if you don't stop this.'

'What do I care about them, for Christ's sake?' She threw her head back and an unpleasant, scornful sort of laugh jarred out of her. 'I mean, when have they ever cared about me?'

Pansy stared at her mother as if she'd gone mad. Minty's startling mood-change was like being tossed back into her childhood, when her mother's emotions had been up one minute and down the next, but the downs had never merely been downs, they had been dark pits full of alcoholic bitterness and recrimination. 'Calm down, Mum. Come and have some coffee.'

'I don't want any bloody coffee,' Minty said with grim fervour, watching Eve like a hawk as she moved across the kitchen. 'I want an answer.' She couldn't bear the disappointment, the sickening and irrational sense of loss which was beginning to make her head spin.

Pansy looked quizzically at Eve, who closed her eyes for an instant and shook her head before walking through the door.

Minty watched them both in sullen silence until Eve had gone and there was only Pansy standing there, her face full of reproach.

'And you needn't look at me like that.'

'I'd just like to know what's going on.'

'It's none of your damn business.'

'Eve looked upset.'

'So what? Perhaps she has every reason to look upset, perhaps our precious Eve has something to hide.'

Pansy sighed and thought how truly awful this day had been. 'Stop it, Mum.'

'Don't tell me what to do. I'm still your mother, even if you do prefer to live with your bloody father.'

'That wasn't my fault.'

Minty scrutinised her daughter sharply and said condescendingly, 'You even look like him, don't you – not like me at all.'

Pansy blushed, stung by the implied criticism.

'Mr Clever-Dick, Mr Bloody-Goody-Two-Shoes . . .' Her mother's voice ran on spitefully.

'He is good, actually,' Pansy said, unable to help herself.

'Don't you mean boring?' her mother sneered.

'At least he's always been there for me.'

'What the hell's that supposed to mean?' Minty had finally switched targets now. 'That I wasn't?'

'You know what it means.'

'I want you to tell me.'

Pansy watched her for a long moment, touched by a growing and ominous sense of inevitability. 'Your drinking.'

'Oh. Yes,' her mother said in bitter triumph. 'I wondered when we'd get around to that. Blame it. Blame me. Blame everything on me. Why not? I'm always the one in the bloody dog-house!' She pointed her finger savagely at Pansy. 'Never you, oh, no, and not your dreary father and certainly not your saintly stepmother.'

'Shut up, Mum.'

'Don't tell me to shut up.'

'I was too young to tell you to shut up once, or even to ask you simply to "stop", but I'm not now.'

'I shouldn't be foolish enough to let it go to your head,' Minty said contemptuously.

'You were out of your mind most of the time.' Pansy's voice continued dully. 'Drunk,' she said. 'Or stoned.'

'How dare you.' Minty's eyes were dancing with rage. 'How fucking dare you.'

'You're drunk now,' Pansy said quietly. 'Aren't you?'

'Don't question me, young lady.' Minty's neck muscles stood out with strain and her face was parchment white beneath the careful make-up. 'Don't you do that.'

'Why not?' Pansy said accusingly. Everything was deteriorating fast, veering horribly out of control, but she didn't care any longer. Too late for that. 'I've never said anything before, have I? I've just put up with it all – everything – your ridiculous scenes, the embarrassment, the stink of booze on your breath, even my stupid bloody name . . .'

Minty slapped her, and Pansy's head rocked back. She put her hand up to her cheek and stared unbelievingly at her mother.

Minty was very still. She looked slowly down at her hand and then back to her daughter's ashen face. Big fat tears were coursing down Pansy's cheeks. 'Oh, God,' she said in a strange little voice and looked down at her hand again, she seemed honestly puzzled. 'Pansy . . . I . . .'

But Pansy had gone and Minty only heard her footsteps as they moved rapidly up the hall and away from her. And then Tony was there, Tony standing in the doorway with his arms folded.

'Now that was nasty,' he said, 'even for you.'

She stood there, stunned, baffled. The furious passion, the hysteria which had so consumed her a moment ago was gone, like a fever passing. 'I don't know what happened.'

'You slapped her.'

'Yes. I know,' she said falteringly. 'But I didn't intend to.' She felt as if her head was about to explode, primed by her own lethal actions.

'Have you had something?'

'You were listening.'

'It was difficult not to.'

She shook her head and said numbly, 'No. Only mineral water.'

'You'd better go and tell Pansy that.'

'You believe me,' she said and it seemed very important to her just then that he should. 'Don't you?'

He wasn't sure, he only knew that he hadn't seen her touch a drop and she didn't smell of anything. He shrugged inwardly. After all, since when had she cared whether he knew she'd had a drink or not? 'Yes,' he said.

Minty looked back at him wide-eyed. 'I've never slapped her before. Never. Not even when she was a child.' *Not even when I was drunk.*

'You'd better go,' he said firmly, suddenly and uncharacteristically sorry for her. 'Don't leave it too long or you'll be in more hot water.'

She began moving unsteadily towards him and Tony was reminded of a car crash victim he had once seen who had walked away from a pile-up unscathed, physically, that is. Minty paused as she drew parallel with him, there was a funny bewildered look on her face. 'I didn't know she hated her name,' she whispered in frantic despair. 'I really didn't.'

He found himself patting her awkwardly on the shoulder as she brushed past him. 'It'll be okay,' he said lamely. 'Pansy's a good kid.' And she was, he supposed bleakly, even he had realised that.

Tony let her go and then walked across the kitchen to the French doors. He wanted some air. Outside it was warm, almost humid, and he cocked his head back, looking at the sky: it was black and cloudless, the moon was a thumbnail surrounded by bright brittle stars. Beautiful – he knew it was beautiful, but it failed to move him.

Who was this bloody man? It had finally filtered through that Minty had become if not obsessed, then a little carried away with him – whoever he was. And it wasn't Michael Harwood, photographer extraordinaire. That had just been a mean wind-up. In actual fact, Tony could hardly remember anyone at the party, not even that little slut, because he had probably been as pissed as Minty.

He swept a hand through his hair and wondered what was going on.

Everything stemmed from the party, he thought vaguely, all the weird things. He felt as if there were something unpleasant at work, something scheming and unfriendly that seemed intent on making their lives as unhappy as possible. Unthinkingly he touched the cold sore on his upper lip.

'And that ghastly prophetic crone . . .' he muttered aloud, thinking of Immaculata. 'Her and her doom and bloody gloom.' He shuddered a little as that hideous face at the glass began to grow large in his mind, like some troll or ghoul with its claws, as yet, unsheathed.

Tony darted another glance at the heavens. A purple cloud was crossing the sky, a great blob of a thing like an enormous fist.

If I stayed out here long enough, he told himself, I would make a face out of that fist, a horrible grinning face like the one at the window.

Tony went inside.

Frank had been waiting a long time. There was a phone-box, a bus stop, a wastepaper bin and a small stone wall obscured by some dusty scrub at the bottom of the street, and he had been sitting there for almost two hours.

But Pansy had gone now, having just left with the baby. There had been a hat on her head, a great floppy-brimmed thing, pinned up at the front with a cameo brooch and because of it he had been able to track her bobbing head well into the distance. Nice hat. She had never worn it when she'd been out with him and he found that strangely irritating which was odd really, considering everything.

She could have seen him sitting on the wall if she'd looked the wrong way, but she just kept on pushing that pram, and in the direction of the park, he realised. Frank was immediately rewarded for his observation by a rush of hot blood to his face as the memory of his time there with Eve was jerked ominously into life. There was no chance of ignoring it. All thoughts of Pansy, and anything else for that matter, slipped irrevocably away as he turned his eyes on the house.

He knew she was in there and almost certainly alone. He had checked by using the public pay-phone as soon as he arrived, and when she'd answered he had put the receiver down. Of course, he wouldn't have done that if Eve had been reasonable the other times he had called, but now she was refusing to see him and even denying what had happened between them, which was crazy. She had made him feel stupid, like a complete stranger, as if he had dialled the wrong number instead of communing with a potential lover. Her woodenness had infuriated him.

In fact she had said that 'she couldn't remember', that her 'memory was fuzzy'. What the hell was that supposed to mean? How could she not remember what had passed between them?

Frank stared emptily into space, as if searching the distance for an answer, and then took a deep steadying breath before looking up and down the street, crossing the road and making his way to the house.

It was warm today, nice, and all the large Victorian houses appeared to slumber neat and peaceful in the sunshine. He noted that hanging baskets seemed to be the order of the day, Eve's house sporting geraniums and trailing ivy although, he decided as he drew closer, they looked a bit tired, a bit neglected. Obviously she had other things on her mind.

He rang the door bell. Twice.

When she continued to refuse to answer (after all, there couldn't be any other explanation), he peered through the letter box, but the hall was silent and empty. His gaze came to rest upon the place where they had stood and he felt a hot ripple of sexual desire. In his mind's eye he saw them together again – her with her fingers on the buttons of her blouse, the way the tips of her long nails had flicked open every tantalising single one.

And then she had pulled the material apart.

Nothing underneath.

Frank's eyes fixed on the spot, staring sightlessly at the patch of carpet, the place on the wall where they had stood and touched each other. He could feel prickly sweat begin to break out on the back of his neck and between his shoulder blades.

Eve had really wanted him then. She had been hot, man, a voice in his head taunted. Hot – For – You.

Frank swallowed hard, his tongue betraying the dryness of his mouth as it slid slowly around the rim.

'Eve!' he cried through the letter box. 'Eve, I know you're there.'

Why was she hiding? He couldn't understand it. Why had she encouraged him at all? Frank's forehead buckled into a frown, but he couldn't honestly say encourage, that wasn't the word; the look in her eyes on that fateful afternoon had been blank and dreaming, as if she neither saw nor cared about what she did.

Other times when he had looked into her eyes he had seen a haunted look there, a shock-look which made him recoil just a bit. Sometimes he had seen nothing at all. Sometimes when he looked at her he wanted her so badly the lust he felt was almost insupportable.

Like now. Like looking through her cosy English letter box and knowing she was there: breathing and thinking and listening and watching and knowing that I want.

I want.

'Please, Eve,' he begged. 'Please.'

His body flamed with adrenaline and he pressed himself up against the door, his cheek against the varnished grain as his sex began to harden.

'Oh, man,' he whimpered. 'Oh, man. I'll be fucking the bloody letter box next.' He laughed then, a wild sort of laugh that was so strange it scared him a little.

He stepped back, ran his hands over his face and took a deep gulp of air. After a time his breathing steadied and he felt himself once more under control, but the urge to look through that slit again was irresistible. One more look and then he would leave.

Frank crouched down and lifted the flap, thought he saw a shadow move there. 'Eve,' he called. 'Eve?'

It was incredibly quiet in that long narrow hall. A shaft of sunlight shone down through the window above the door and he could see tiny motes of dust swimming and drifting in the air. He could see the shadow too, a long grey thing which lay across the rug like a dark pool. Frank had a momentary feeling that it was a pool and not a shadow at all, and if he were to actually touch that patch of grey with his fingers his arm would disappear right up to the shoulder. And maybe he wouldn't be able to draw it out.

He swallowed deep in his throat and stood up. Perhaps she wasn't alone after all.

Pansy sat on a wooden bench facing the embankment. To her left was Putney Bridge and to her right the unrestricted sweep of the Thames. It was her favourite place in the park, away from the boating lake, the sandpit and the ice cream shop where the mothers gathered to stop and talk about their day. Here she could watch the world go by and be left in virtual peace, if Jack was sleeping as he was now. In the wire basket situated beneath the bottom of the pram was a baby-bag containing all Jack's things, a can of Coke and a book which she probably wouldn't read, at least not today.

Pansy was in a contemplative mood; in fact she was thinking about her future. She had made things up with her mother, even succeeding in papering over the cracks that would never, quite, heal. It had been cathartic that slap, she thought bitterly, like the ending of childhood or something equally dramatic. Frank had begun the process and her mother had finished it. And now she would make plans to leave.

She glanced down at her hands; she had even stopped biting her nails.

Out of the corner of her eye she saw someone walking towards her along the cement path which bordered the river. Pansy's face clouded over. Frank was not difficult to spot. He would always stand out from the crowd, and it wasn't only his height or that familiar graceful stride that made this so easy for him.

She looked at her fingers again and gave a little sigh, wondering if she hadn't been overconfident in predicting the end of her nail-biting days.

He was still some distance away, so she was able to watch him without the embarrassment of an excruciating blush and that awful breathless sensation swamping her. It made her think of Nina, a girl she had known at school, and what she had said about her addiction to crack – that, in the end, it was no longer a pleasure or a high or a fleeting taste of ecstasy, but only simple need because the drug had messed up her body chemistry. Sometimes Pansy wondered if that was what Frank had done to her.

'I wish he wasn't like he was,' she said softly, 'because it would be so much easier to let go . . .'

But then you wouldn't want him.

That was the trick of it.

A solitary yachtsman was taking his boat down the river and she forced herself to focus on him and thought of all the other boats, the ships, which had sailed down this great stretch of water for hundreds of centuries. The women had been left behind, of course – with the children, the worry and probably very little money and for months, even years. Roles had been very clearly defined then. There had been no blurring of duty, job or sex; everyone knew how they stood, where they stood, no matter how uncomfortable that place might have been.

Confusion must have been minimal, at least, Pansy pondered bleakly.

'Hi,' he said.

At last.

'Hi.'

'How are things?'

'Fine.'

He sat down. 'I like your hat.'

'How did you know I was here?' she asked, ignoring his remark.

'A good guess you might say.' He realised he was getting good at lying; his words seemed to slide off his tongue almost without rehearsal.

'Did you try the house?'

'Yes,' he said. 'But no one answered the door.' That much was true.

Pansy frowned and said, almost to herself, 'Eve should be in. Perhaps she was taking a nap or something.'

'I wanted to see you.'

She said nothing and for a few minutes they both fell silent, staring inevitably at the river and a trio of screeching seagulls swooping and diving for titbits in the mud bank.

'I was wondering,' he began, 'well, what you might be doing at the weekend.'

'I'm busy,' she said.

'I thought you'd say that.'

'Then why bother to ask?'

She was looking away from him, deliberately, and he couldn't blame her for that after the way he had behaved and, in fact, was still behaving. Of course, she couldn't know his motive for being here or, come to that, the other occasions when he had used her to reach Eve. She might try a guess, might sense something furtive beneath the surface of what had been a promising relationship, but she could have no real idea what it was. It was this lack of knowledge that would eventually allow him to wheedle his way back into her life. 'Persistence is all', someone famous had said once. He couldn't remember who or why, he only knew the words rang true and that wheedling and persisting would get him the thing he desired the most.

And Pansy could make it easy for him because she still wanted him; he could see that, he only had to look into her eyes.

The sad thing was he wanted her too, perhaps not as much, or in the same way, but neither was he immune to her sweetness, or indeed, her integrity. That, perhaps, more than anything.

He found himself wondering what would have happened between them if Eve had not been so omnipresent in both their lives.

A stupid way of thinking, he chided himself, hypothetical and pointless. Eve was omnipresent, which simplified everything in a stark, no choice sort of way, because there could be no question where his needs lay.

Frank bowed his head and stared at his shoes. The reality of his situation hounded him unmercifully. No woman had ever affected him in the way Eve did, and he knew his feelings were not rational, in fact they were running way out of control. It was like having an illness, something to be endured while the pain and discomfort lasted. And then he would come out the other side.

'I've got back my job in the show.'

'Have you?'

'They couldn't find another black guy with such good legs.'

She smiled at that.

'Why don't you make some time at the weekend and come over?'

'I can't.'

'You can't be that busy.'

'We're all going to the lake house,' she said flatly. 'It's a family thing.'

'The whole weekend?'

'Yes.'

'What's the big deal?'

'Eve's mother's over for her annual visit.'

'Oh.' He mulled this news over in his mind. 'Maybe I could come over and pick you up?'

'No.'

'Why not?'

'You know why.'

'I know that we both like each other,' he said carefully. 'I know that this thing between us isn't finished yet.'

'You're very sure of yourself, aren't you?'

This stung him a little. 'You mean about you?'

'Yes.'

'It's only what I believe.' And he did believe it. If it wasn't for Eve, well, who knows? Yet there was an absurd part of him that wanted to spill out everything, tell Pansy all that was going through his mind. What he had done. What he wanted to do.

Terrible things to her stepmother. Really bad things, things he had never dreamt of until he had met her; sometimes he would find himself lost in them, caught by their dark, imaginative allure. Even in sleep.

He had awoken one night, heart thudding, the blood shooting through his veins to find that he had come in his sleep, something he had not done since his teens. There had been nothing particularly pleasant about the experience except a sort of black relish, a sort of glee which seemed to come not from him, but somewhere outside him. The moon had lit up his room just long enough for him to look around: in the dark corners, at the lumpen mass of his clothes hanging on the back of the door, the way a sudden draught had pushed and pressed a gust of air against the heavy half-open curtains; as if they might harbour a life of their own.

And all the time he had been thinking of Eve, and sex. Weird, dark sex that had somehow been a little scary.

Frank flushed and saw how his hands shook and Pansy saw too, misinterpreting everything. She was studying him with wide, wondering eyes and he held her stare until her eyes darted away, back to the water.

Safer there.

'One more chance,' he said softly, pushing home his advantage.

She swallowed slowly, he could see how her throat moved and worked. There was a long, clockless moment.

'You could come over . . .' she began.

He closed his eyes with relief. 'You mean at the weekend?'

She nodded.

'For dinner, maybe. On Saturday.'

'Are you sure?'

'No.'

'Don't do it then,' he said calmly, heart racing, wondering what he risked.

Pansy leaned forward, adjusting Jack's parasol with great deliberation, her face hidden in the shadow of her hat. She was thinking how shallow her resolutions had been, how easily he had persuaded her and she supposed he knew, he'd probably known all along.

'Besides,' he added, 'what about your parents? And Eve?'

'What about them?'

'Won't they mind?'

'They might.' She was looking at him now, warily. 'But that's something you'd have to deal with.' She paused. 'If you come.'

'Shall I then?'

She looked down at her nails and then lifted her eyes to his face. 'Come if you want.'

'You don't want me to?' He was puzzled and a little unsettled by her response.

'I think what I want is probably very bad for me.'

He laughed uneasily. As if she knew.

Frank scrutinised Pansy's soft, uncertain face beneath the hat and wondered whether it was possible to stop everything right here and walk away from this obsession with Eve, but he had discovered that it was almost impossible to accept his mind's good and sensible advice. It just wouldn't go in, it didn't even come close to penetrating the strange wall which had grown, brick by brick, over the last few weeks.

'What time on Saturday?'

Pansy's eyes shifted back to the river. 'Seven.' Her voice was low and faintly tremulous. 'We have drinks then.'

When the doorbell rang Eve went to the window and looked out, saw

Frank and recoiled from the glass with a shocked, slapped expression on her face. She leaned back against the curtain, trying to quell the panic leaping and jostling inside, because beneath the panic and in the murky depths of her subconscious there was fatal recognition, and she didn't want that. No reminders of what she had done. Oh, God, no.

When the doorbell rang a second time she closed her eyes and placed a hand over her mouth, as if he were able to hear her breathing three floors up. She heard the disconcerting sound of the letter box flap being opened and then an odd sort of pause before he called her name. The sound floated eerily up the stairs like an echo from time past. Another pause followed, another strange silence, heavy and humid with meaning.

Those seconds had ticked away so agonisingly slowly that she thought she would go mad with the waiting, but he had given up in the end. Then she had peeped through a minute gap she had made in the curtains and watched him as he moved down the street, shoulders slumped, hands in pockets, head partly bowed before he rounded the corner and disappeared from view.

She had stood there a long moment, silent, stunned, before turning back into the room where her gaze drifted dazedly over the bed, the walls, the bookcase and came to rest on the open door and the balustrade beyond. The balustrade bordered the stairs and the stairs led down and down to the silent hallway.

She didn't want to go there.

Eve walked slowly across the room and then out on to the landing. From where she stood she had an almost unrestricted view of the flights of stairs leading to the other floors.

There was a dark spot down there, a shadow which did not belong to the inanimate objects with which she was so familiar. It moved a little, it mingled with the ornate patterns on the rug, spreading and unfurling like something sly stealing from a clever hiding place.

Eve drew back, eyes wide and terrified, before moving soundlessly back into the bedroom and locking the door behind her. She stayed there only a few seconds and then ran into the bathroom, locking that also. She looked wildly around; the window was half-open, like a little door leading to another place.

There was a part of her that wondered if that route wouldn't be easiest and best, solving everything. It was a sheer drop below, a long drop. She would fly for a few fleeting seconds – skirt billowing upwards like a cloud, hair rioting before rushing air caught and fanned it up and outwards, surrounding her face in a halo of ebony. Over very quickly.

But not here, a voice in her head said, not yet.

Outside she heard the light finger-touch of a hand on the bedroom door knob, followed by a persistent, fugitive rattle.

She came very close to screaming then, but instead clamped her hands over her ears and cowered in the niche between lavatory and bath, knees drawn up against her chest. He would go soon, she told herself; he wouldn't, couldn't stay and this dreadful moment would pass, just like all those other dreadful moments when she had listened and waited in the dark, terrified out of her wits.

But it couldn't really be. It was her sanity giving way, her mind buckling under the pressure of years. Wasn't it? Yet he had always known where and how to find her. Always, no matter what. He had once said that they were destined to be with each other, that she was his – the beautiful princess in all the magical tales he had ever cared to weave. Sometimes he had held her on his knee and sung to her in his deep, seductive voice, soft and low, close to her ear, like a prayer. Sometimes he had bathed her, soaped her, using his hands. In her mind's eye she could still see the down of dark hair on the backs of those hands, the long deft fingers which became the legs of a little man walking down her wet body and disappearing into the water. She was swept by nausea and disgust, as if everything and everyone she had ever known, or touched, was unclean.

Always, he had said.

She felt a shudder of superstition and fear, a sob catch and hold in the throat.

Her eyes returned to the window. So easy.

A breeze billowed the net curtain inward, like a piece of gossamer and outside the sun still shone, although it would rain later, the man on the news had said so.

Beneath trembling half-closed lids, Eve cautiously surveyed the locked door and waited. The silence grew long and longer. She knew he had gone, but she was still afraid to move, afraid that any sound she made might trigger some thing. Some thing. She rested her head on her knees, felt an immense lassitude descend on her, but her exhaustion was a weakness through which memory could work. As she sat there, secret thoughts of her mother began filling her mind, all those lurking memories waiting patiently in the deep dark corners – all her mother had contrived to do, and what she had done, finally – that last terrible thing. Even in her fear Eve found it pitiable, thought her heart would break with loss and sorrow.

She squeezed her eyes tight shut. For your own good, her mother had said that day, but Diana had been saying it for herself.

'I don't need this, Minty.'

'You want to,' she said, her voice rising.

Tony felt his body stonily withdraw. 'No.' She was standing on the end of the bed, legs spread, wearing only black leather crotchless panties. In one hand she held an enormous black dildo, in the other a spring clip which could be used to excrutiating effect on her nipples, or Tony's, if he was in the right sort of mood for a little dose of pain.

'You've never turned this down before,' she said shrilly, and he thought she looked like some mad woman, some harpy from a sex dream gone horribly wrong.

'I'm tired,' he said.

'Not too tired for this, though,' she said, a mocking grin on her face, and began making nasty pinching noises with the spring clip, 'never for this.' There was something in her voice that told him she would turn mean very quickly if his responses were not up to par.

'My cold sore is throbbing,' he said feebly.

She smiled with feigned sympathy. 'Poor old Tony, poor old boy.'

'It's true.'

'You've never let something like a silly old cold sore stand in your way before.' She pouted in a hopeless, hapless imitation of a lewd and precocious child.

'For God's sake, get down.'

'I want to play.'

'No, you don't,' he said wearily. 'You're drunk.'

Her eyes bulged with outrage. 'Don't ever say that again. And if you do, you'll wish you hadn't . . .' she drew a sharp hissing breath, 'because I'll do something you'll really regret.'

She began to sway.

He closed his eyes and enjoyed one brief blissful moment of peace.

'I mean it, Tony.'

'I don't doubt it.' He sighed and wondered what the next stage would be in this peculiar and insane week. Minty had not been the same since the video night at Andrew's place. In fact the only word that came close to describing her deteriorating behaviour (apart from pathetic) was regressive. She was like a woman who was busy losing half her brain, he mused dully, but then most people who were pissed nine-tenths of the time acted like half-wits.

'What would you like me to do?' she purred unappetisingly, as if he hadn't spoken.

'Get off the bed.' She was making him bounce and jiggle in all the wrong places and the bedclothes were beginning to fall off.

Minty tucked the titillating apparatus she still held into either side of her panties, put her hands on her hips and glared at him. She made Tony think of a very bad B movie: a science fiction cowgirl with both holsters primed and ready for some weird sexual encounter. Her make-up was smudged, there was a blob of mascara lying halfway up her cheekbone and some of her eyelashes were stuck together; a thin line of red lipstick rimmed her upper teeth. He hated that.

It was awful, he thought, to be sober when the person you were with was grotesquely drunk – ugly, irritating and sad. And he wondered why he hadn't realised quite how sad. Did he look sad when he was stoned? he wondered bleakly. Did people smirk and chortle behind their hands?

Minty began to turn round, wobbling about on first one leg and then the other, and then her backside was towards him and she was stooping down in a familiar panty-removing gesture, the black leather knickers slipping to her feet along with the dildo and the nipple pinchers. The dildo rolled to one side and fell on the floor with an ominous clatter.

Tony swallowed uneasily as his eyes ran back up her calves and thighs to the carefully honed orbs of her pale bottom. She was bending over now, deliberately, and he could see the little brown puckered hole she was offering so readily.

He felt his throat contract and his penis shrink. The prospect was singularly unappealing and he hadn't the slightest idea why, or what he was going to do about it. Once upon a time, he knew, it would have been different; once upon a time she could have been standing on her head, juggling and playing the mouth organ, and he would have gone for it.

'Come on then, you bastard.' Minty shrieked making him jump.

'I can't,' he said.

'On, no,' she wailed with a derisive snort. 'Not that again. I'll have to kick you out and get myself a bloody toy boy.'

My place. He cried silently. This is my place.

'Actually, I don't feel like it,' he added miserably. Even if I could. 'I don't want to.'

There was a horrible sickening silence, and then she whirled round like a cat, her face contorted with rage, taut and stretched as if the skin might break. He was reminded again, and all at once, of that face at the window. Instantly he drew back, feeling the brass fittings of the bedhead digging into his naked back.

Minty began crawling towards him on all fours, her lips were strained over her teeth into the strangest of smiles and he was appalled. When she came too close for comfort he brought up his knees, knocking her under the chin so that her mouth snapped shut and she howled in pain because she had bitten into her tongue. With a yelp of agony she lost her balance and fell off the bed.

Everything stopped and the sudden quiet was eerie, but then she began to cry.

Tony watched her with wide, bloodshot eyes; she was lying curled up on the floor, holding her hand up to her mouth with blood seeping slowly through her fingers.

'Are you okay?' he asked tentatively.

She shook her head.

'I didn't mean that to happen,' he said. 'It was a knee-jerk reaction, you might say . . .' he tried to laugh. 'I know this might sound stupid, but you scared me.'

She sat up and looked back at him uncomprehendingly through big tear-bright eyes. He thought that all she needed was a thumb stuck in her mouth to look like a child who has lost something precious and been spanked for it. He was struck by pity, and then, a moment later, by an idea.

'You want to go to the lake house this weekend, don't you?' he said.

She nodded.

'And you want me to go with you?' He didn't want to go, of course, if he never saw that godforsaken place again, it would be too soon.

She nodded again.

'You've got to start behaving,' he said firmly, 'and cut out the drinking.'

Minty became very still.

'Besides, Andrew will turn you away if you don't. You know that – and it's what you want, isn't it, to go back to that place?' He thought he could almost feel his words sinking slowly into her beleaguered brain. He stared at her for a long moment, and she stared back and then removed her hand.

Blood began running steadily down her chin in a thick lonely trickle; a loop of gleaming pink saliva stretched from thumb to lip.

'And I definitely won't come if you go on like this.' He finished and reached for the kleenex. 'It's that simple.'

'Do you promise?' Minty said abruptly, ignoring the pain in her mouth and the blood which was falling on to her chest and staining her small breasts the colour of blackberry juice.

He didn't answer immediately.

'Do you promise?' She pleaded, lip trembling.

He swallowed, not allowing himself to think. 'Yes.'

'All right.' Minty said, and he was surprised at the amount of relief he felt, it was a little like swooning.

She started to cry again and Tony leaned forward to dab at the blood and the tears with a tissue.

'That was nice of Minty.' Andrew said.

'What?' Eve replied, and began searching through the cupboard for the tin of powdered chocolate she knew was there. Milk was heating in a pan.

'The flowers.'

'On, yes,' she said vaguely, as if she had forgotten.

'Well, it was good of her to apologise,' he pressed, 'once upon a time she wouldn't have bothered.'

'Perhaps she should have sent them to Pansy.'

'Okay,' he said carefully, 'I take your point, but I think they've made their peace remarkably well, and I read Minty the riot act once I realised what had happened.' The following day and on the telephone; not very satisfactory.

He still found it hard to believe that Minty had actually slapped Pansy; for all her faults his ex-wife had never really been violent – she had thrown a glass occasionally, even the odd ashtray, but there had not been any physical stuff, except towards herself. He could remember one appalling time when she had thrown herself at him in a sick and twisted rage, the time when he'd finally plucked up the courage to ask her for a divorce, but that had almost been understandable. Pansy was a different ball-game altogether, and the annoying thing was that no one seemed able, or willing, to tell him what, exactly, had happened. 'Funny,' he continued, 'and she hadn't been drinking, either.'

'There are other things besides drink.'

'Maybe,' Andrew reluctantly agreed, 'but Tony phoned me today, says she's a changed woman.' And he prayed silently that it was true. He'd made Tony swear that it was; they were coming to the lake house on Saturday and were to be on their best behaviour. Andrew darted a cautious glance at Eve; she needn't know until the last minute. It was better this way, because he considered that, as far as her mother was concerned, there was safety in numbers. He wondered why it had taken him so long to realise that Diana had such a bad effect on Eve; she had been so distracted this morning that she had nearly sliced off the top of an index finger with the bread-knife and it was now swathed in a bloodstained bandage.

'I hope you're right,' Eve said, her soft voice breaking into his thoughts.

'Well, let's be positive anyway,' he said, with more lightness than he felt. 'And talking of being positive – Bill says we can have his villa whenever we want. In fact we could leave after your mother's visit if you like.'

Eve paused for a moment, her hands wrapped around the tin she had found.

'That's kind of him.'

'Yes,' Andrew frowned, puzzled. 'And odd, really – he never lets anyone borrow his precious villa, but he insisted we use it when I told him that you'd been – well – a bit under the weather.'

'Did he?' she answered dully and began spooning the chocolate powder into mugs.

'Yes.'

The milk was boiling and she lifted the pan from the gas ring to make their drink.

Bill. Somehow the word, the name, sounded like Frank.

She stared at the steam rising from the milk and closed her eyes against inescapable reality.

'Eve!' Andrew's arm shot in front of her and pushed the saucepan to one side. 'You nearly scalded yourself.'

She shook her head like someone coming out of a daze. 'Sorry.'

'Don't be sorry,' he said gently. 'Just be careful.'

She looked down at her hand. 'I expect it was this finger. I can't grip properly.'

'Let me do it.'

'No,' she said, more sharply than she had intended. 'I'm not an invalid.'

He drew back, wounded. 'I just don't want you to hurt yourself again.'

She looked away from him so that he wouldn't see her expression. He knows nothing, she thought, he knows nothing at all. And if he did, what then? The horror of losing him was almost too much to comtemplate, much worse than all the other, uglier things.

'We were talking about the holiday,' he said a little stiffly, 'I'm not sure how to get there . . . we could drive, of course, but it's a hell of a long way and I don't think I could do it with this foot, unless we took it in turns.'

'Where is it again?' she asked, not caring.

'Marseille is quite near, but this is an island, set off the coast between Toulon and St Tropez, it's called Porquerolles. Unspoilt apparently and, come to think of it, no cars are allowed if I remember what Bill told me correctly, so we'll have no choice but to fly. Good.' Andrew rubbed his hands together and limped over to the French windows. His foot still caused him a lot of discomfort; he had discovered that by the end of the day the pain had a way of escalating, as if it were crying out for rest. 'The weather should be perfect. I know it's the end of the summer here, but it will still be very warm there, even hot.'

'Will Pansy come, do you think?'

'Why not? She could probably do with a holiday as much as we can and especially after recent events.'

'I'd like her to come,' she said. 'And not just because of Jack.' Eve began to stir the sweet dark mixture she had prepared, luxuriating in the smell and its association with Andrew and the time he had taken her to Vienna. It had been November and cold, and each cafe had been a place of cosy refuge from the elements, where they had sat and talked and whiled away the hours over delectable pastries and steaming chocolate topped with cream. Before their marriage, before Jack, before everything.

'She'll come,' Andrew said with conviction, 'and maybe get that boy – Frank – out of her system at the same time.'

'I'll go on up then,' Eve said abruptly.

'You okay?' He glanced warily at her and eyed the steaming drinks in big friendly mugs she had placed on a tray. 'Rather quaint,' he ventured, 'having hot chocolate in bed . . .'

'I wanted to,' she said and felt herself blush, 'it makes me think of Vienna.'

'Does it?' His face lit up, obviously touched by her admission because he considered it one of their happiest times together. 'Do you remember the ride we took on that massive ferris wheel – and how windy it was. I was terrified.'

'Were you? You didn't say anything.'

'What? And have you think you were marrying a wimp.' He shook his head and grinned. 'Not on your sweet life.'

'I wouldn't have cared.'

His grin faded a little as he looked back at her. There was an expression of confusion and helplessness on his face and it pierced her heart.

'What's the matter?' she asked softly.

'Nothing.'

'Yes, there is.' She hovered uncertainly before walking over to him. 'What is it?'

He reached for her, almost reverently, lifted a lock of the thick dark hair which framed her serious and lovely face.

He shook his head.

'Tell me,' she whispered and put her hands on his face, exploring the contours and features slowly, carefully, like a blind woman.

He was unable to speak, he felt suspended in space and time seemed very slow.

'I love you,' she said.

Eve awoke in the night. There had been a dream, but she couldn't remember whether it had been good or bad, or just simple dreaming. She lay in the dark for a while, hot and sweaty, staring into space, listening to the sound of the traffic and thinking of the coming weekend. What else would she think of? It loomed in her mind like an oncoming train, a truck over-burdened with filth and debris waiting to drop its load.

Her mother would arrive tomorrow evening, Andrew was picking her up at the airport and then dropping her off at the lake house. Diana intended spending the first night alone as she always did, and then they would join her on Saturday.

What did she expect, that he would come whilst she was keeping her solitary vigil? Her long lost enigmatic brother turning up out of the blue like the proverbial prodigal son – with Diana waiting for him, of course, standing on the gravelled drive, greedy arms open wide, ready to rein him to her so that she might clutch tight his lean long body.

Eve's heart took a high, frightened leap in her chest. But it wouldn't be like that at all.

She pushed the covers back and got out of bed before padding across to the bathroom and closing the door behind her. She wanted to wash herself, shower, be clean. The need was urgent, just like all the other desperate coping mechanisms she had manufactured over the years, so enabling her to endure the terrors and the shame emanating from her past.

And when she was clean and the water had seeped into every crevice, every tiny sore and open wound, she examined herself.

Eve sat on the floor, in much the same way Minty had done only hours before, in fact there was the same childlike air about her, even as she opened her legs. She could almost have been a little girl sitting there, scrutinising herself with all the fleeting innocence only little ones have.

And inside where the folds of fine flesh are moist and tender it was still raw and red, but healing. No burning agony now when it was touched or stroked; but she could make it hurt again, of course, she could make it bleed like that unfortunate night when Pansy had seen her in the hall. A strange night that, full of blurred imagery and secret sounds; there had been a voice, too, and a leering sort of laugh that had made her skin crawl with loathing and desire.

Eve's eyes flicked whiplash quick to Andrew's store of razor blades. She looked at the spot for a long time and then very gradually pulled her gaze away and leaned her head back against the wall to stare at the ceiling. A small fly was circling the light.

'I have been a victim all my life,' she said.

Ten

The trees seemed richer, more full as they passed beneath them, and a little into the distance a cloud of birds rose in flight and circled, cawing, to the tops of more trees. Crows, Eve thought, there had always been a large population in and around the land bordering the lake. She could smell the water now, that earthy moistness and scent of wet grass and weed carried on the still air.

This would probably be one of the last balmy days before the autumn took hold and broke up the green monotony, touching the trees with russets and reds and golds, thinning the shadows.

When she was a child she had seen elves and fairies in those shadows, where there had really been only the movement of a branch or the stir of a sleeping bird.

There had been good days after all, she realised with unsettling surprise, little peaks of tranquillity when she had been left in peace. The peaks had been few, though, slotted between great troughs of despair like the highs and lows on a weather graph.

'Nearly there now,' Andrew said.

'Daddy . . .' Pansy said from the back seat.

'Yes?'

She closed her eyes for an instant, hating the moment. 'Frank's coming later. I said he could stay for dinner.'

Andrew lifted his eyes heavenward. 'Nice of you to give us so much notice.'

Pansy blushed furiously. 'Well, you didn't tell Eve and I about Mum and Tony arriving until this morning.'

'True,' he sighed, 'and I'm still wondering about the wisdom of my

decision, but your mother is a little difficult to dissuade when she has made
her mind up about something.'

'I'm aware of that,' Pansy said with a trace of impatience. 'All I ask is
that you try and be civil to *my* guest.'

'Frank,' he said flatly.

'Yes. Frank.'

Eve stiffened, leaned her head back on the seat and shut her eyes.

'I thought you'd broken things off?' Andrew said, peering along the
side of the high hedgerows, searching for the right turning.

'I don't know,' Pansy said in a lacklustre kind of a way, I'm just not
sure.'

'Well, I'm sure about one thing,' Andrew said firmly, 'I don't like him
messing you around.'

'I haven't said he was.'

'Well, he'd better not be . . .'

'Daddy, please.'

'All right, all right.'

'Does it really matter?' Eve broke in suddenly, 'after all, what
difference can one more body make?'

'I don't suppose your mother will be too keen, but blame the
arrangements on me if she complains – say I handled everything.'

She nodded, not caring. Let them all come, every one, she told herself,
and play the games we plan to play; the ones we think we want.

But God laughs at people who make plans.

Her brother had said that, big bad beautiful James who loved to break
all the rules.

She felt a hand on her knee and jumped.

'Hey,' Andrew said gently, 'it's only me.'

'Sorry,' she said. 'I was miles away.'

'Are you sure you want to go through with this? I couldn't give a damn
if you want to change your mind.'

'It's okay . . .' she said, 'really . . . and you'll miss the turn-off if you're
not careful.'

He switched his attention back to the road, saw the turning almost
immediately, and swung the car into the drive. 'Here we are then,' he said
with forced levity, 'back at the ranch.'

As they drew up beside the house he was unhappily reminded of his last
visit here, and his eyes inevitably sought out the place where he had

mortally injured his foot, that deceptively serene place lying amongst the long grass and weathered head-stones. He felt the aloneness creep over him again, that peculiar sense of isolation which had so unnerved him. Silly, really, he said to himself. Daft.

'Where's your mother?' Pansy probed. 'Why hasn't she come to meet us?'

'I don't know,' Eve said, her stomach churning. 'Displays of emotion, no matter how nominal, are not her sort of thing.'

'That sounds ominous,' Pansy said, pulling a face.

Eve shrugged and turned round to look at Jack, touched a little booteed foot. 'He always sleeps in the car, doesn't he? Must be the continuous motion.'

'She's never seen him, has she?' Pansy persisted.

Eve shook her head, kept her eyes on Jack.

'Let's not go into all that,' Andrew said briskly, 'I want to get off my backside and have a drink of some sort.'

Pansy looked up at the house and then at the garden and the lake beyond. 'I think I'll take Jack down to the water.'

'I'll come with you,' Eve said, not wanting to go inside. Not yet, not until she was ready.

'That leaves me to look for your mother, I suppose,' he smiled wryly. 'I get all the dirty jobs.'

He waited until they had all climbed out of the car and then watched them with a protective eye as they walked down the lawn. Eve's mother was inside. He thought he could feel her gaze burning into the top of his head, but when he looked up there was no one there.

Yesterday had been classic. She had greeted him as she no doubt would her hairdresser or her gardener or the man who came to unblock her drains. On the whole a complete repeat of last year, except for her face; she had done something to it, something surgical like a facelift perhaps, because she suddenly had wrinkle-free cheekbones – two shiny unappetising knobs of bone covered by a thin layer of skin. And her mouth, that was the weirdest thing, it sort of grimaced and smiled at the same time, and perpetually, as if she couldn't quite make up her mind what she wanted to do with her lips. It made him think of the skull which lay just beneath the old, tired flesh.

She looked worse not better and, ironically, not a day younger.

The hands that had lain in her lap all the way from the airport were still blotched with liver stains, like finger-bones wrapped in withered chicken-skin.

And what would make a woman of her age have a facelift for heaven's sake? It was a bit late for serious vanity at seventy-five. Perhaps there was a man in her life, someone she hoped to charm and impress with a 'new look'. What guy? Who? Some wizened septuagenarian with prostate trouble – or maybe a toyboy with bulging biceps and a cute little ass? He found the thought faintly disgusting. In truth, he couldn't imagine Diana Sanqui simpering up to anyone, let alone mere mortal man.

Andrew squinted up at the house again and decided he had put off the evil moment long enough.

Pansy balanced Jack's baby seat carefully on the grass and sat down beside him; Eve walked on, to the edge of the water and looked across the lake and into the distance. She wished she could go away somewhere for a long time, a year or two or three, and then come back and magically start her life all over again. Be someone else, somewhere else, make different choices. She picked up a stone and threw it into the water then turned around.

Her mother was at an upstairs window looking out across the lake, just as Eve had done.

Still looking, still waiting.

And then she was looking at Eve. They stared back at each other for a long moment before Diana's head swung round as if someone had walked into the room. Andrew, of course.

Eve slumped down on the grass beside Pansy.

'Are you all right?'

'Yes,' she said. 'Just about.'

'Is she really that bad?'

'Yes.' Her voice was flat and sad. 'I suppose she is.' She shook her head. 'Do you know, I've never said that out loud before.'

'Perhaps it will do you good,' Pansy said. 'You know, like therapy. Mind you, a slap in the face is pretty therapeutic, too.'

'I'm sorry about that. I feel it was partly my fault.' Minty's furious face took shape in Eve's mind, but she had sent the flowers, apologised and the incident was now supposed to be forgotten.

'There's no need. It's probably been coming for a long time. Actually I think I'd been meaning to say what I did to Mum since I was about three.'

She laughed a little. 'So I suppose you could say there's a lesson here somewhere.'

'What?'

'Don't store things up, they have a way of going bad on you.'

Eve plucked at the grass then glanced uneasily at the lake; she didn't need to look behind her to know that her mother was coming, two sets of footsteps were making their way across the flagstoned terrace. She stood up. Andrew had begun to walk, half-limping down the sloping lawn, but Diana had paused on the terrace to watch them, her face hidden now behind huge dark glasses.

A tall woman, shoulders a little bowed, with frosted yellow hair skilfully coiffured. She wore a pristine white tracksuit that almost made Eve's eyes ache with its brilliance. Her hand rested on a massive stone urn, cracked and spotted with mustard lichen, it had been there for as long as Eve could recall. Her father had strained his back trying to lift it after a storm had knocked it from its perch. Years ago. She could hardly remember him, she realised sadly, and when she tried to conjure his face up in her mind she could not. There was a photo somewhere, wasn't there? Surely her mother had one. He had been eclipsed by Diana almost completely, a quiet ineffectual man who had died of a perforated ulcer when she was twelve.

'Said she had a good night,' Andrew remarked drawing close, 'although she seems tired to me. Of course, that could be something to do with her face job . . .' He was trying to make Eve laugh and drive away that tense, nervous expression.

'I can't believe she'd do that, I really can't,' Eve said softly, and then her face clouded, 'although . . .'

'What?'

'It doesn't matter.' Had she undergone all that pain and discomfort for James – her wayward long-lost son who would only laugh and poke fun at her face, her teeth, her appalling tracksuit? Had she learned nothing?

Diana was walking towards them now and Eve thought that she might have lost weight; there was something haggard about her appearance, something frail and brittle.

Beneath the carefully powdered and cruelly stretched skin she is old, old.

'Hello, Eve,' she said in a cultured English, but oddly American, voice.

'Hello, Mother.' Always mother, never mum or mummy.

'You look well.' She ran her tongue along her teeth and Eve was taken aback by their whiteness, like her tracksuit, an unnatural dazzling white. 'But you always look well, don't you, Eve?'

'So do you.'

'You were always a bad liar. Don't flatter me. I hate it.'

Eve blushed.

'Did you know, Andrew,' she said, turning her back on her daughter, 'that a pig farmer from hereabouts used to come to the house just to look at Eve? He used to bring a few pork chops with him every time, like an offering to some voluptuous local goddess.' She smiled, but there was nothing nice in the smile. 'And once, I remember, he even brought half a pig, a great fat thing with black hairs sprouting from its snout. Didn't he, Eve?'

Eve was looking away from her, far into the distance.

'Obviously the man had excellent taste.' Andrew's voice was wary now, he wanted to ask this woman why she wanted to say such strange things. 'You haven't met Jack yet,' he said, steering her away. 'Your grandson.'

'Yes.' Diana peered at the sleeping child with obvious disinterest. 'I thought it must be.'

Andrew began to feel irritated. 'And this is my daughter, Pansy, from my first marriage.'

'Hello.'

Pansy got to her feet and briefly shook hands.

'I have prepared some tea,' Diana said, 'or there is a selection of cold drinks if you prefer.'

'And don't worry about dinner,' Andrew chimed in, determined to remain agreeable, 'we've brought everything with us – soup, salad, smoked salmon, the works.'

'What a very organised man you have married, Eve,' Diana observed sardonically and with great deliberation ran her eyes down the full length of his body. 'You must cherish him.'

Andrew scrutinised her partly bowed head sharply. She is laughing at me. At us.

'Your foot,' Diana continued in her smooth leisurely fashion, 'a broken ankle?'

'A badly laid mole-trap,' he said. 'I stood on it when I was checking the grounds.'

'Here, you mean?' She looked faintly alarmed and he was glad of that, it made him feel better. 'Where?'

He pointed. 'Across the marshy bit, amongst the headstones.'

Diana swallowed deep in her throat. 'An old one I suppose, rusted through.'

Andrew shook his head. 'Oddly enough, no. My handyman said it was new, or at least unused.'

'I find that hard to believe.'

Andrew drew an impatient breath. 'Well, without going into all the gory details, I can assure you that I had plenty of time to study the thing and there wasn't a speck of rust to be found anywhere.'

'James is here,' Diana said abruptly, strangely jubilant. 'He must be.'

'I don't think so,' Eve responded in a small voice. She was her mother's child again, a young girl in short socks and sensible sandals unable to free herself from that same mother's tyranny.

Nothing has really changed, she thought, but everything has grown – is growing, bigger and bigger like the unseen rot in a neglected house.

Andrew saw how pale his wife had become; she looked like a frightened rabbit.

'Oh, yes,' her mother said triumphantly. 'Only he would set fresh traps. Who else could it be?'

'A poacher?' Andrew offered.

Diana scoffed. 'Hardly.'

'Where is he then?' Andrew asked, perplexed. 'I mean, why doesn't he introduce himself, for God's sake?'

Diana smiled, an unsettling, arrogant sort of smile that made him itch to slap her. 'You don't know him, that's all. James likes to tease, to have fun with people.' She clapped her hands in delight. 'And it's his birthday, remember? I knew he'd come back, I just knew.'

'Well, if he turns up he can join us for dinner,' Andrew quipped dryly. 'I'll look forward to congratulating him on the efficiency of his traps.'

'I'm afraid he finds dinner parties rather boring.'

Had this woman ever heard of a sense of humour? If James was here (which he doubted) he had a very strange way of showing it.

She was staring beyond him at the trees on the opposite bank and he found himself following her inscrutable gaze. In the stillness of that moment he felt a prickling at the base of his neck, a lifting of the hairs along his forearms. It was the same sort of sensation he had experienced sitting helplessly on the grass with his bleeding foot.

'I think I'd like that tea now,' he said, and slipped his arm around Eve. 'Let's go into the house.'

'You go on,' Diana said. 'I'll join you in a few minutes.'

They left her standing near the water's edge, but as they reached the terrace Andrew looked back and saw her walking away from them and in the direction of the woods.

'She worries me,' he said. 'Maybe she's lived on her own for too long.'

'I'd definitely go along with that,' Pansy said with distaste. The mother from hell. Suddenly Minty didn't seem so bad, after all.

Eve said nothing. She was playing with a twist of her hair, like a little girl.

Minty looked almost demure in a pastel-pink suit. Around her neck hung a choker of pearls Andrew had given her on their first wedding anniversary (she wouldn't remember, of course) and which she had never worn, at least until now. And Tony looked like an ageing version of the man out of the Milk Tray ad, plus very large cold sore.

They were hovering uncertainly around the dining table waiting to be seated. There was none of their usual unreflecting assuredness, which tended to drive him crazy, and presumably that was because they were both sober, for the time being anyway.

Pansy was in the kitchen adding finishing touches to the food he and Eve had prepared between them. Andrew sighed softly, touched by depression because, in truth, Eve had been in a daze much of the afternoon, and there had been that funny blank look on her face, the one he hated, the one, in fact, that worried him the most.

Her bloody mother, he supposed bleakly.

The doorbell rang and out of the corner of his eye he saw Pansy flash past the doorway. Frank, he assumed, trying to press down his irritation. Didn't he have enough on his plate without worrying about Pansy's love-life as well?

'Cheer up, Andrew,' Minty called from across the room. 'What's eating you?'

'Nothing,' he responded stiffly. 'Just thinking, that's all.'

'I should stop, then,' she chortled, 'it's obviously a bit of a strain.'

'Very amusing,' he parried. 'And is this the precursor of some very witty small talk over dinner?'

Minty ruffled her shoulders a little. 'I might surprise you.'

'God, I hope not.'

Tony shot him a warning look with his eyes. 'I think you could say we're keeping our side of the bargain.'

'The evening's hardly begun.'

'Okay, but there's no need to be so prickly. Cool down, for heaven's sake.'

'I don't know why you were so desperate to come in the first place.'

'Minty wanted to.'

'I know that. I just can't understand why.'

'I told you before,' Minty said, her face pulled into an appropriate expression of indignation. 'Therapy.'

Andrew rolled his eyes and began pouring himself a drink just as Pansy walked in, Frank in tow. At that moment he couldn't blame his daughter for being smitten. Frank had clearly dressed to kill and it seemed to Andrew that the superbly cut jacket only served to emphasise the wide muscular shoulders, as did the soft leather trousers, which were both sexy and tasteful. Frank couldn't fail and he knew it. Andrew studied his daughter's pretty flushed face with apprehension, felt a disquieting sensation in the pit of his stomach; it seemed that Frank also possessed the dubious gift of playing havoc with his temperamental ulcer.

'Who – is – this?' Minty squealed in delight, examining Frank from head to toe with lusty, wide eyes.

'Frank, Mum,' Pansy said, reddening, 'a friend.'

Minty let off a tinkling peal of laughter. 'How sweet.' She caught hold of Tony's arm and dragged him forwards. 'This is Tony, my toyboy.'

With a scowl Tony shrugged her off and grasped Frank's outstretched hand with as much dignity as he could muster. 'How do you do.'

'Where's Eve by the way?' Minty asked and shot a glance at Andrew, 'and that ghoul of a mother?'

'How do you know her mother's "a ghoul"?' Tony's voice was clipped and still offended.

'I saw her at the window as I climbed out of the car. She was peering at me.' Minty made a face. 'Ghastly.'

'She's probably a decent enough soul,' Tony added and looked quizzically at Andrew, but Andrew shook his head. 'Oh,' Tony mouthed silently and prayed that he wouldn't be sat next to her during dinner. He longed suddenly for a very large whisky and wondered whether he might manage to sneak a quick one in the other room. He was dealing with the lack of fags to a degree, and thought he could cope reasonably well without one through dinner. Afterwards, though, he would creep out on to the terrace and really indulge because he'd bloody well earned it.

'I'll chase Eve up,' Andrew said and moved to the door.

'And the ghoul,' Minty prompted with a tittering giggle.

'You said you'd behave yourself.'

Minty immediately straightened her face like a naughty schoolgirl which Frank saw, and he smiled. Andrew caught his stare and they just managed to nod politely to each other over Minty's head, a Minty, Andrew thought with dismay, who was beginning to get a little over-excited.

Diana was in *his* room, the only one to be located in the eaves of the house. She waited just inside the door trying to gather herself and stave off a debilitating wave of homesickness and loss.

She loved this room. It was long and low with wide oaken beams crisscrossing the ceiling. It smelt of old wood in here and perhaps (although this was probably wishful thinking) the lingering scent of cigar smoke in the unused air. When she walked across the room one or two of the varnished floorboards eased themselves out, with a mellow timber sigh, and the corners of her mouth twitched in recognition. Like old times.

The bed was still made up, a clean towel still folded on the linen basket, books on his bedside table and along the walls, and on his desk the remains of some music he had composed, and left. Diana laid her hands reverently on the paper and studied the lines of music as she had last year and the year before that; she began to hum the familiar tune, lifted a hand and made it move in time. 'He got his gift from me,' she said proudly to the empty room, 'from me.'

In a corner stood the old French wardrobe, his paternal grandfather's, and where James' clothes still were, the ones he had chosen not to take with him hanging there all alone and neglected.

She opened the doors wide and paused for a moment before running her fingers down the sleeve of a cashmere jacket and then pressing it possessively up against her face. She could smell him, even now.

Could breathe him in.

Diana unbuttoned her silk blouse, pulled it open and stepped up into the wardrobe. She cocked her head back and pushed her slack grey breasts forward, let the clothes brush and caress her skin, wrapped the jacket around her body. All the time little mewling sounds issued from those dry old lips, little feverish sighs that turned her new cheekbones to hectic blotches of crimson.

When she had finished the annual ritual Diana tidied herself with great care: smoothing down her blouse, plucking a hair from the rim of her skirt, coaxing her hair into place and then, when she was satisfied, she flicked open the gold and enamel locket which always hung around her neck. James looked back at her, dark eyes gleaming beneath the deep, intelligent forehead and rich black hair. He was smiling, a wide wicked smile that never failed to move her. She brought the miniature to her lips, her cheeks, her eyes. 'So handsome,' she murmured. 'So beloved.'

A sob caught in her throat.

'Mother?'

Diana wheeled round. 'Why didn't you knock?'

'I did.' Eve averted her gaze. Diana had been crying, but now her eyes had that look about them of anger boiling up. 'Dinner's ready.'

'I can smell it.'

Eve frowned, puzzled and wary at the peculiar response.

'I can smell him, too,' Diana added with relish. 'He's been here, hasn't he?'

'No.'

'How can you be so sure?' There was a plea in her voice, even eagerness. 'You're hardly ever here – and the mole trap – only he would have laid any more. You know that.'

Eve shook her head very slowly, a little fear had begun to press up against her stomach.

'You know where he is.'

Eve was long in answering. 'No.'

'You always say that, but I can't believe it.'

'It's been too long,' Eve said, her eyes fixing on the locket lying against her mother's blouse.

'What does that indicate?' She seemed astonished. 'When has time ever mattered over real love, or real longing?' Her fists were clenched in a gesture which rebelled against the inconsistencies of fate.

'Why would he come back now?'

'Because of you.' Diana said grudgingly. 'Because he just couldn't help himself. Besides, how do I know you haven't been in contact with him all these years? You could see him once a week, or once a month and I'd never know.'

'I haven't.'

'You wouldn't tell me, even if you had.' Diana paused. 'No, he wouldn't let you, he wouldn't want me to know.' She glared at her daughter, eyes flashing in flesh gone pale. 'You always did do everything he asked.'

'No.'

'Yes you did.'

'No.'

'Always acting Little Miss Innocent . . .' Diana swallowed hard and deep, her throat bobbing unbeautifully. 'Playing hide and seek in the long grass . . . in the woods.'

Eve's eyes were on the locket, but all the time her head was shaking from side to side like someone whose load in life has suddenly become too great.

'He was always weak where you were concerned.'

'You left me alone,' Eve said abruptly, and so quietly Diana strained to hear.

'What did you say?'

'You knew. You let it happen.'

'I don't know what you are talking about,' but there was a moment of recognition and Diana shifted her eyes away.

'I was only fifteen.' A pawn in a grown-up game considered outside her comprehension.

'You are imagining things.'

'You never listened,' Eve said dully. 'Only to him.' Her pale face was unnaturally calm, but she was screaming inside.

Diana was staring fixedly at her now, hardly aware that her daughter had spoken, pushing and kneading her hands in slow twisting pain. 'He never forgave me, did he?'

Eve took a step back, not wanting to hear any more, sickened and afraid by her mother's outburst, the sudden show of vulnerability and what it might herald if she stayed in the room.

'It was the only thing to do,' Diana's voice continued unsparingly. 'I still believe I made the right decision, even now. He didn't think I would do it, that was the thing, he thought I would go along with what he wanted like I always had. But I couldn't do that . . . I couldn't. People would have found out – there would have been a terrible scandal.'

Eve's hand was on the door with an instinct for escape.

'He didn't care about that . . . not him.' Diana laughed harshly. 'He liked the thought of notoriety.' She flashed a conspiratorial glance at her daughter. 'You, of all people, know what he was like.'

Eve looked down at the hand which grasped the door, another step, perhaps two and I will be free of her.

'I thought it was another of his games, you see. I never dreamt he would take it so hard.' She could see him in her mind's eye so clearly, it was there in an instant rising up out of the years: the same colours, the same cries, the same feeling of calamity gathering in the air.

He had come running from the woods like a mad thing, long legs loping up the lawn, his voice bellowing, 'NO . . . NO . . . NO!' and still she had stood there, unable to move, waiting for his punishment, waiting for whatever penance he was prepared to mete out. She had misjudged. Badly.

Diana's face crumpled; she might suddenly have been very ill. James had simply pushed her, lowering his beautiful head and shoulders like some strange animal. Pushed her. Pushed her all the way down the gravelled drive and out of his life.

'Hey.' It was Andrew. 'I've been looking for you two.' He looked from mother to daughter and wondered what he had walked in on. 'Are you okay?' He touched Eve's arm, made her turn to him, her face was parchment white. 'Have you had words or something – what's been going on?' He glowered at Diana.

Diana cleared her throat. 'We're fine.' She said in that endlessly calm voice. 'Just talking about old times.'

'I'll bet,' he snapped.

'There's really nothing to be concerned about.'

He ignored her and switched his attention back to Eve. 'Can you manage dinner . . . maybe you'd rather lie down and have supper in our room?'

She shook her head. 'I'd rather come down.'

'All right.' He felt a little relieved, at least she would be where he could keep an eye on her.

Only tonight and tomorrow and the weekend would be over and her hideous mother with it. Next year would be different, he promised himself. She could make her precious annual visit all on her own and the year after that, and the year after that.

Eve just wasn't up to it, but he didn't know why that should be and there was a part of him that was almost afraid to ask. Something way back he assumed, something very unpleasant.

'Gorgeous chocolate mousse.' Minty simpered.

'You've hardly had any,' Tony exclaimed looking at the teaspoon-sized skid-mark on her plate. 'In fact you didn't finish the soup or the main course.'

'I don't need to over-indulge to enjoy my food,' she retorted and wiped her mouth primly with a napkin, darting a mean sideways glance at Tony's bulging waistline. She wondered absently why it was so many older men ended up with spindly legs and a pot belly. 'I wouldn't want anyone to think my stomach had anything in common with a bull elephant – unlike some I could mention.'

Tony scowled and shot her a thin, vengeful smile.

'Pansy made it,' Andrew piped up quickly.

'No.' Pansy laughed. 'Eve got it at Marks and Spencers.'

'Well, you'd never know,' Frank remarked. 'It's superb, really delicious.'

'That's the extra cream,' Pansy continued, smiling at her stepmother and trying to draw her out of the listless mood that had descended on her since they arrived. 'Eve always adds a huge dollop when she's trying to impress, don't you?'

Eve smiled back in a distracted sort of way, felt Andrew's hand squeeze her fingers. Perhaps it would be all right, perhaps everything would be all right if she could just get through this talk and the evening and the night.

Nor catch her mother's eyes.

Nor Frank's.

She swallowed hard and took a large mouthful of wine.

'By the way, that's a super dress, Eve . . . unusual . . . something Grecian about it,' Minty observed a little resentfully, aware that she would also look good in turquoise silk, that it would set off her pale skin perfectly. 'What label?'

Eve frowned. 'I think I got it off the peg in the Fulham Road.'

'Really? You surprise me.'

'Yes, ages ago,' she said vaguely. 'I didn't know quite what to wear. I discovered it still wrapped in cellophane this morning; it seemed about right.'

Minty raised her eyebrows, astonished that anyone could be quite so blasé and uninformed about their wardrobe.

'The colour's wonderful,' Frank said, and added unthinkingly, 'you look beautiful'. He was staring at her from the other side of the circular table and, too late, realised the mild stir his comment had caused. Andrew coughed and abruptly stared back, Pansy looked down at her plate, Minty and Tony exchanged meaningful glances and Eve took another gulp of wine.

'My daughter has always managed to provoke admiration where the opposite sex is concerned.' Diana broke in like some doom-laden sibyl. 'Even when she was a child.'

'Do tell,' Minty pressed eagerly.

With difficulty Andrew pulled his gaze away from Frank and regarded his mother-in-law steadily. 'I think I've heard enough reminiscences for one day.' He had a sneaking suspicion that her dubious remark was not meant to be a compliment at all, in fact there was a bitchy note to it somehow, even a touch of humiliation. Was it jealousy? Her own daughter? He found himself dwelling on the afternoon and her seedy recollection of the pig farmer.

'It was just a remark,' Minty patronised him gently, but there was a gleam of mischief in her eye. 'I'm sure Diana has lots of interesting stories tucked away.'

'I do, as a matter of fact. We Sanquis have a very interesting family history. My first husband, Eve's father, was of Huguenot descent and Protestant, of course. My family, on the other hand, have always been strong English Catholics.'

'No wonder he died young . . .' Tony muttered under his breath.

Minty jabbed him in the midriff with her elbow. 'Do you still practise?' she asked sweetly. 'Because I know Eve is what they call "lapsed" – like me, actually. You are, aren't you, Eve?'

Eve plucked at the napkin lying in her lap, smoothed it out flat across her knees.

'Eve?'

She looked up slowly. 'I don't attend Mass any more. No.'

'Why is that? I've always wanted to know.'

'Well,' Andrew broke in sharply, 'why don't you?'

'Oh, that's easy, the local priest tried to put his hand up my skirt – shattered all my illusions in one blasphemous go.'

'Mum . . .' Pansy protested.

'Embarrassing, darling, but true.'

Diana's face turned crimson. 'You must have been mistaken, my dear.'

'Oh, no,' Minty said trying to keep her face straight. 'I don't think so.'

'Young girls often have crushes on older men,' Diana began, 'they day-dream about them, dream about them, weave intricate fantasies about them, so much so that they can often seem very real.' Diana caught Eve's gaze, held it for a long moment.

'His ring got caught in my stocking,' Minty added, winking at Pansy.

'I'm sorry?' Diana frowned.

'The ring on Father McManus' busy hand got caught in my stocking – I can assure you that was very real – actually it was a hoot!' She burst out laughing, as did everyone else.

There was a frozen little smile on Diana's face and for once Andrew was thankful for Minty's irreverence.

'Priests are human beings . . .' Minty brayed, 'men for God's sake. I've never been able to understand why people get so upset when they lose control once in a while.'

'Unnatural,' Tony concluded.

'What is?' she snapped. 'Losing control?'

'Celibacy.'

'Well, that hardly applies to you.'

'*I* hope to attend Mass in the morning,' Diana broke in and looked at Andrew. 'You will find the time to give me a lift?'

'Of course,' he said. Despite the fierce control, he thought she looked deeply upset and he suddenly felt sorry for her. After all, she was among virtual strangers and very much alone; there was a tenseness about her of someone unaccustomed to the close proximity of others. She could go back to the States tomorrow and no one would miss her, in fact no one had cared about her in a very long time which was, he had to admit, mostly her own fault if her current attitude was anything to go by.

Diana seemed to have aged ten years in ten minutes, she looked old and frail and pathetic and he wished he hadn't noticed. He supposed her religion and her missing son were the only things she considered of value, the only things she had left herself.

Eve, and even Jack for that matter, didn't count, of course, she had made that very clear; Diana had made her choices long ago and he wondered how easy it was for her to live with them; she had probably spent the last thirty years trying to justify them.

'Let's have coffee,' he suggested, unable to keep the impatience out of his voice. 'In the sitting-room.'

'That's a good idea, Daddy.' Pansy said with a meaningful glance.

'Isn't there any cheese?' Tony whined.

'You can have it in there with the coffee,' Andrew said irritably. 'I really don't care.'

'Don't worry. I will,' he said. 'And a bloody smoke.'

'It's a lovely evening,' Diana began suddenly, turning to Tony with a brittle smile.

'Yes,' Tony replied, puzzled.

'In that case, I wonder if you wouldn't mind smoking outside, on the terrace.' She was regarding him steadily. 'I dislike the smell of cigarette smoke intensely.'

Tony winced at the patronising plummy voice, except it wasn't totally plummy, he thought, there was a weird twist to it. Like her, he observed with distaste, privately likening her to an effigy in a waxworks museum. More unsettling was the way her beady eyes deliberately alighted on his cold sore.

'I could do with some air,' he said, and stood up.

Jack was sleeping. He lay on his back, head to one side, little hands open and curled. Eve slipped a finger into a palm and immediately it was grasped and she felt a little collapsing sensation in her chest, an inexplicable warmth which surprised and perplexed her with its intensity. She wanted to hold him, badly, but instead gently removed her finger from his strong little grip and smoothed his fine baby hair back from the perfect forehead, again and again. He didn't grizzle or complain, not this time. Not this time. She couldn't believe it. He even seemed to move towards her, as if dreaming of more.

The touch of her son seemed like a sweet charm, a talisman that would keep her safe.

Eve only became aware that someone was standing in the doorway because the silence had subtly changed. There are silences that breathe different things, different meanings, she thought abstractedly, they are palpable.

'Hello.'

She turned around slowly, Frank was standing in the doorway.

'What do you want?'

'You asked me that once before.' Her eyes were on him at last, the deepest, most beautiful eyes he had ever seen.

'Please go back downstairs.'

'I came to see you.'

'Just go. Please.'

'Don't make me say it.' He was growing desperate, he could feel the desperation actually crawling through him like an infection.

'You must go. Someone will come.'

'I don't care.'

She shook her head in despair and panic. 'What about Pansy? What about my husband?

'What about me?' He wanted to scream at the moon.

'It was wrong – it is wrong. Don't you see?'

'We both wanted each other.'

'No. It wasn't like that.'

'We made love,' he persisted relentlessly unable to help himself, unable to stop. 'Remember? We had sex.'

Eve squeezed her eyes shut and when she opened them again he had moved closer. 'Go away.'

'We did. Didn't we?' he said and then shrugged, helplessly, because she wouldn't let him touch her. 'I know why I did, but what about you?'

'Please, Frank . . .'

'We made love, Eve,' he repeated savagely.

'That wasn't love.' Her voice flashed suddenly, laced with contempt and he was shocked by the change in her. 'And it wasn't you.'

'What the hell's that supposed to mean?'

'You were someone else.'

He looked back at her with an expression close to disgust. 'What is this – what garbage are you trying to insult my intelligence with?'

'It doesn't matter.'

'Tell me,' he said dryly, folding his arms. 'Convince me.'

She stared at him for a long moment, as if weighing him up, like a child about to be told bad news. 'You've felt him, haven't you?'

'Who?'

'When you came to the house the other day, you saw him . . .'

Frank looked a little uneasy.

'I saw no one.'

'You saw some thing,' she pressed, 'in the hall.'

234

'A shadow.'

So he had. He had seen, she thought exultantly, as if she had been exonerated in some strange way and was not, after all, crazy.

Just teetering on the edge, my dear.

'It wasn't my shadow, Frank,' she said.

'How do I know that?'

'And that first time, in the hall, you felt something wrong, didn't you?'

'I don't know,' he said. 'What are you trying to say?' There was something in her set, blank face that was disquieting, even scary.

'I'm not sure what I'm saying.'

'Well, what do you think you're saying?'

'This is a big tease, Frank. A nasty game.'

'And you're pretty good at the game, aren't you?' he retorted sharply, hating himself. 'I'd say you were a bit of an expert.'

'Oh, I'm not talking about me.' She was staring at him, as if he were a fool, an imbecile. 'Good God, no.'

'Who then?'

Her eyes shone a little wildly. 'Go away, Frank.'

Contempt was back in her voice and he didn't like that. 'I don't understand.'

'Believe me,' she advised softly. 'You wouldn't want to.'

They stood and looked at each other until Frank dropped his gaze. He felt empty suddenly, purposeless and directionless. 'I'll go then.'

Her face was remote, under control again. 'Yes.' She said.

Pansy watched him walk down the stairs. She had watched him walk up them, too, once he had taken a quick furtive glance over his shoulder to make sure no one saw; but she had, of course, she had seen everything – it had been there on his face, all through the evening.

Her heart was beating very fast as Frank caught and held her steady gaze, there would be no pretending now.

'You've been to see her, haven't you?'

He nodded and sat down on the stairs.

'But she turned you away?'

'What do you think?' he said bitterly.

Pansy felt tremendous relief, not just for herself, but for her father and when she looked at Frank's partly bowed head she realised she couldn't forgive him for that.

'What will you do?' she asked.

He looked back at her. 'I don't know. I made a mistake.'

She sat down beside him. 'A pretty big mistake.'

He nodded. 'I thought . . .'

'Don't, Frank,' she said. 'I don't want to hear.'

'It was like being under a spell,' he continued as if she hadn't spoken, 'like an obsession, a madness.' He ran his hands over his face, feeling slow and stupid and bewildered. What had Eve meant? What weird (and definitely unpleasant) secret had she been trying to impart in their strange and unpalatable conversation?

Something told him it was better not to know.

'Did I come into this "madness" at all,' Pansy's voice cut into his uneasy thoughts, 'or was I merely a stepping-stone to Eve?'

'It wasn't like that,' he said, fighting away dragging weariness, 'at least not to begin with.'

'That's nice to know,' she said tightly.

'I couldn't help it, Pansy.'

'That's about the most pathetic excuse I've ever heard.'

'It's true,' he said lamely.

'Well, it doesn't really matter, now, does it?'

He looked down at his feet and made no answer.

'I knew something was wrong and you knew I knew,' she added in a soft, grieving voice and stared through the open door to the room beyond. Her father was pouring himself a drink and beyond him she could just see Tony smoking on the terrace. 'Even when I invited you along tonight I wondered, but I had to see it through for some reason. So maybe we have that much in common.'

'What?'

'Seeing things through to the bitter end.'

'I didn't mean to use you.'

She was silent for a moment and when she spoke again it was with a forced control. 'Even before Eve you did.'

'No,' he protested. 'That's not true.'

'There is something hollow about a man who coaxes so many women into his life and only wants a taste . . . it's rather like picking sweets, except afterwards there's a nasty taste left in the mouth.'

'No. It's not like that.' He sighed heavily. 'It wasn't like that with you.'

'You must end up with nothing,' she said. 'And I don't mean just emotionally – take your job – you hate TJ's really, but you stay there because it's convenient, unchallenging and the money's good. You have a wonderful voice, but you do nothing about it. You could do many things, but you don't. Is that what you want?'

'I don't know what I want any more.' He felt muddled and devoid of resolution.

'Well, that's where we differ, I suppose, because I do.' God, she hoped so.

At this remark he glanced at her, but her face was hidden in the fall of her hair. 'What do you mean?'

She lifted her head, chin tilted, and all at once he realised how pretty she looked and he hadn't even noticed. He wondered how long the shutters had been down over his eyes.

'I'm joining the Bristol Old Vic as assistant stage manager at the end of October.'

'I thought you wanted to act?'

'I'm not good enough,' she said and looked back at him unflinchingly, 'but mostly I'm too soft, surely you've noticed?'

He shifted his gaze back to the floor.

'Actors need to have the hide of an elephant to suffer all those "slings and arrows". I don't. I'm only a "Little Flower". Remember?'

Her words stung him and when he looked back at her he was suddenly struck by the enormity of what he had won and what, in the end, he had allowed himself to lose.

Tony was aglow with whisky and enjoying his cigarette. A hazy cloud had gathered around him and a skein of smoke was curling into the night air. He felt lulled, even relaxed, which was something he had not expected to feel here and it was a relief; neither was there a smidgin of that unsettling, 'watchedness' sensation which had dogged him over the last weeks. It was true that he no more liked this place than he had the first evening he ever set eyes on it, but it was only a place – an old, slightly neglected house set in the tedium of rural England.

And Minty had behaved, at least to a large degree. He glanced over his shoulder, meanly pleased to see that she was embroiled in conversation with Eve's hag of a mother and obviously bored. Perhaps old Ma Sanqui's stories were not so interesting after all.

His mind wandered lightly, irreverently over the last few days to this evening and the fiasco at dinner – which succeeded in making him smirk.

Down on the blue-black lake a few frogs croaked monotonously and a bird sat on the water preening its back feathers. It caught Tony's eye. Despite his rather limited knowledge of the natural world he was sure that most birds slept at night, just like he did, or rather was supposed to do. Curious and a little bored, he took a leisurely walk down the lawn towards it.

The grass was springy and grew soft with moisture as he neared the water's edge where Andrew, predictably considerate as usual (what a strain that must be), had planted a number of Chinese lanterns left over from Eve's party. To his right the jetty advanced darkly into the lake and to his left a broad band of reeds grew and the bird, a duck he realised now, sat just beyond them, staring at him. It didn't seem in the least bit afraid.

Tony's feet began to sink into the softening and waterlogged soil and he quickly stepped back; the damp would ruin his shoes. When he looked up the duck had moved further left towards the muddy bank where the reeds thinned and he followed. Was it lost? Or perhaps looking for its mate – a naughty stop-out of a duck who had gone to the pub and stayed on for one jar too many. Tony laughed, a silly drink-induced chuckle which made him cough.

The duck had stopped in the shallows and was only a few feet away, so Tony crouched down to peer at it more closely.

Even in the dull golden light cast by the lamps he could see how handsome it was. The upper part of its body was black and it had a funny little tuft sticking out of the back of its head, also black, but its sides were a brilliant white. It wasn't unlike a penguin, he thought – round and plump and rather cute.

Perhaps it was tame. He cooed at it, held out his hand as if he might coax it to him and on to dry land.

Or perhaps it could see with its odd yellow eyes that the man on the bank was no threat, only a pathetic ageing human trying to cling on to its lost youth.

Tony gawped, caught off-guard by such a wretched thought; it had leapt into his mind with no warning at all and in its wake left a lingering feeling of despondency like a thin sad cloud. He stood up and took a long trembling drag on his cigarette.

The duck looked back at him steadily and then abruptly upended in the water, making him jump. It hovered in this inelegant pose for a second before suddenly going right under, as if it had been dragged there by the force of an undertow. A ring of water rippling towards his feet was the only evidence that it had been there at all.

Tony's mouth dropped open into a slack-jawed gape of unpleasant surprise. It wasn't coming up. Even as realisation percolated into his addled brain, a movement in the trees crowding close to the bank caught his attention and in their shadow he thought he saw a weasel standing upright, grinning at him. It seemed as if a cold hand clutched at his stomach.

'No,' he said aloud. It was a trick of the dismal light, a feat of imagination a child makes when alone in a darkened room.

Tony blinked and rubbed his knuckles in his eye sockets, but it was still there. In its peculiarly human-like paws and snagged on the end of its little needle teeth there was blood where a few sad feathers hung.

'You mean shit,' he muttered weakly. 'You murdering little bastard.'

It can't be the same weasel, he told himself, not the one that had crept so stealthily into his sitting room and upset Harry. But something inside insisted that it was; something inside also told him that someone was enjoying the cruel joke, someone eaten up with bitterness and drained of human kindness who knew them all.

'What are you doing?'

Tony swung round and was swept by tremendous relief; it was only Minty.

'What's the matter?' she asked. 'You look as if you're about to throw up.'

'Nothing's the matter.'

'Yes there is.'

'Tell me,' she said, that hungry gleam back in her eye, the one that made him uneasy. 'You saw something, didn't you?'

'Let's go back to the house.' He cupped her elbow, tried to steer her round.

'Not until you tell me what you saw.'

'Don't start, Minty,' he said, and there was that firmness again, that unfamiliar mulish note in his voice. 'I'm tired.'

'Him?' she asked eagerly, ignoring the warning signs. 'You saw him?'

He sucked in a breath and almost swore. 'I don't even know who him is, or what you're talking about. I saw nothing.'

'You do know,' she said with strange relish. 'You saw him the first time at Immaculata's, that's why she said the things she did . . .'

'Can't you listen for once in your life? Look—' he said, shaking a little and pointing at his lips, 'watch my mouth move: I saw nothing. Nothing. Okay?' He wanted to go back to the house, desperately. He had his back to the bank of trees, but there was a pressing part of him that wanted to look over his shoulder and see if anything was lurking there.

Minty sniffed. 'I'm going to take a look around.'

'No.'

'Don't tell me what to do, Tony.' She threw her head back. 'And why do you think I'm here, for Christ's sake? Why do you think I've bloody behaved and lived like a bloody monk – just to please you?' Her voice was almost at shrieking level.

'I don't know and I don't care.'

'Yes, you bloody do!'

Her face had merged with the tree shadows, the glint from her white teeth and the gleam of her eyes the only parts of her which seemed to have substance. For a queasy moment he thought that if he reached out to touch her his hand would go right through and out the other side.

'I want to go back to the house.'

Minty took a deep breath and poked him in the chest.

No ghost this, no eerie phantom plucked out of the night air. It was almost a relief.

'Now you listen,' she began and poked his chest again. 'I'm going to take a look around and you are not going to stop me.'

He took hold of her wrist. 'No, you are not. You are coming back with me.'

'There is something there.' She sounded almost triumphant and he saw that the careful control she had exercised so well over the past few days was fast melting away.

'You had a nasty accident last time you came to this place.'

'So?'

'Do you want to repeat the experience?'

'Don't be ridiculous. Do you really think me such a fool?'

'Well, then – what, exactly, are we doing here, Minty? Pressing another self-destruct button?' He jerked his thumb backwards, over his shoulder, and brought his face close to hers. 'He's no nice guy, you silly bitch. He's not nice at all.'

Tony was speaking to her in a voice she had only heard once or twice in their tempestuous relationship, hard and clear and aimed straight at the heart.

'You're hurting me.'

'I don't care.'

'Let-fucking-go!'

'No.' He caught hold of her other wrist.

'I could always use my knee,' she threatened in a low unpleasant voice.

'Go ahead,' he said and wondered what he was saying.

For a few agonisingly slow seconds she actually seemed to consider his response and any moment he expected to feel white fire course through his unsuspecting groin.

'Why are you doing this?' she said morosely. 'Spoiling everything.'

'Come back to the house.'

Minty tilted her head on one side and her eyes gave him an odd look; Eve had said that to her once, that last time beside the water when *he* had come.

That wet sound, suction tight, flesh against flesh.

Sex in the water.

'It's not you he wants.' The words jolted out of Tony like an unthinking reflex and he was almost as shocked as Minty so obviously was.

'You bastard.'

She made to slap him, but it was a useless gesture, and for a long uneasy moment they stared back at each other, and she felt the desire, the feverish longing to step into that dark place drain out through her body.

Gone, her mind said. Gone. And she felt unbearably sad.

Her voice cracked on a small moan. 'I want a drink.'

He sighed softly with relief. 'I'll let you have one,' he said as he led her away. 'But only one.'

When they reached the terrace Minty stopped and pulled her hand savagely away. 'Don't ever do that again.'

Tony grinned. 'It worked, didn't it? See, all you women need to keep you in line is a bit of good old-fashioned male domination,' he parried with as much levity as he could muster.

'You goon, you cheap shit. What would you do if I ran back there now? Run after me?'

'Yes.'

Except that there would be no going back now. Whatever danger was abroad in the night had now passed – for them, anyway. He didn't know how, or why that should be, and he didn't want to know. Things had occurred which he could not understand and probably never would, but at least Minty had missed the boat, and for that he was very glad.

'Why don't I put you to the test?'

'Go ahead.' He shrugged. 'It won't make any difference.'

She stared at him mutinously, but then her shoulders slumped, her eyes giving him a strange uncertain suspicious look. As she watched him her eyebrows slowly drew together in an interested frown. 'Something's happened to your cold sore.'

Tony's hand flew to the offending spot. 'What? It's not bigger – it can't be bigger . . .'

'It's smaller,' she said. 'Definitely.'

She swept away from him, nose stuck in the air and he watched her go with something close to wonder and disbelief at his own powers; but he didn't feel particularly reassured because he didn't want to be proved right this one and only time. Not at all.

There was still something out there.

Tony stole a fearful glance at the blackness behind him; his instincts had been spot on all along, of course, he just hadn't wanted to listen. And now he didn't want to stay the night, he wanted to bugger off like that boyfriend of Pansy's had done, zooming into the night with a bloody great motorbike throbbing between his legs; leaving everyone, and everything behind.

Depressed, Tony wondered whether he might persuade Minty to go home, but knew that would be no easy task; he suspected his newly acquired skills of persuasion had already been used up this strange and stressful evening.

Across the room Diana was watching him, saw the nervous look he cast over his shoulder at the darkness.

Beyond that darkness and the first bank of trees there was a grove near some willows, rather overgrown, a secret place: clotted with saplings and scrub and where a ring of wild mushrooms had once grown. She had walked there yesterday after she arrived and it had been just like that; she had done the same thing again today, but it had changed. Someone had cleared it.

Eve opened her eyes and listened. She looked at the open window, the curtains drifted back and forth just perceptibly as a mild night breeze slipped over the sill. She got up and walked across the room. All the time

242

she could feel her heart pounding very fast, very hard. She put her hands on the window-ledge, pushed the curtains right back and looked out. He was standing by the water gazing up at the house.

No dreams would trouble her now, no telling nightmares, but for just one moment she would gladly have opened her arms to all the nightmares in the world. There is relief in this, she told herself, something oddly sweet in giving up.

'And I am so tired,' she whispered.

He was calling her name now. 'Evey,' he said, 'Evey.' And a smile crept across his face like a promise.

Eve went down.

A pale sun awoke Andrew, streaming uncertainly into the room, irritating his still tired eyes. He flung an arm across his face and turned over in the bed reaching for his wife at the same time, but there was only empty space where her body should have been, a dent in the pillow where her head had lain. And it was cold.

He sat up abruptly and called her name just like the other man had done, except it was 'Eve' this time and when Andrew said it out loud his voice shook with slowly mounting apprehension. He looked at the clock, it was just after six. He threw the bedclothes back and pulled on his dressing-gown.

She was not in Jack's room, or the bathroom, she was not downstairs, in fact she was not in the house at all. The terrace doors stood wide open and he waited in their shadow for a second and looked out across the grounds. A mist lingered close to the earth and ghosted up from the water, and he wondered why he should be so frightened.

He walked down the lawn and as he walked his bad foot began to throb. When he reached the water's edge he scoured its surface with growing dread, before turning left and following the path through the woods – the one that Frank and Pansy had taken, and Diana, and Eve.

He didn't like the silence, didn't like the crackle of twigs beneath his feet which only seemed to heighten the silence, but a wind was picking up, he heard it weaving its way through the soft and verdant undergrowth, felt it ruffle his uncombed hair as he continued his stumbling, clumsy walk and saw beyond the trees how it was whipping up the surface of the lake.

He felt extraordinarily alone and it was the kind of loneliness that made the wind and the water and the wood seem hostile and against him.

Andrew looked up through the meshwork of branches high over his head as the wind gathered force and the first sting of rain hit his face. Another hundred yards or so and he knew this side of the lake would peter to an end, so when he saw the grove of trees waiting ahead of him he increased his pace which increased his dread, and then he began to run. 'Eve,' he sobbed. 'Eve?'

The body was lying face down in the water, it had been there a long time.

She had been sitting in the grass without stirring for nearly three hours.

Sounds and sensations were beginning to seep through the wall of shock and nausea: the dawn cry of a bird, the whir of insect wings, the wind brushing the grass, and thoughts; these filtered through one by one like solitary survivors.

He had called her name like a summons, and she had gone, obeyed, as she always had.

Brother. Lover.

James had never forgiven their mother, Diana had been right about that, never forgiven her for taking the baby, the little girl her mother had removed with such breathtaking efficiency before she had even seen her.

Between them they had taken her childhood, and her child.

She had been a lamb to the slaughter where her brother's subtle caresses had been concerned – she had known nothing of his dark nature: the intensity, the force, his amorality. After a time it had become difficult for her to separate good from evil. In trying, she had been swamped by his desires, overwhelmed by his dubious code of values.

Yet the bitter irony of his seduction of his sister was that he became seduced himself. James loved, but denied and fought against it with all the strength of will and intellect he had.

Then the baby came.

Poor, pretty baby.

And Diana had taken it away.

James had been sick with grief. Mad. They say people go mad with grief.

For the first time in her young life she had seen her cynical, calculating and bewitching brother break. Until that time he had considered life a delicious challenge, a languid game – believed any emotion evoked within that life could be examined, assimilated, and put neatly away.

She had watched him lose control bit by bit by bit.

She had watched him drown in their special place, the secret place beneath the willows, his legs sucked down deep by that ancient mud and the voracious weed keeping him there with its busy green fingers.

He had called her name – shrieked, screamed, but she had only watched, torn between those two feelings he had instilled in her so well over so long – loathing and desire.

And all this time, all these terrible months she had thought he had finally come back for her.

She wondered what event, or yearning, or loneliness had finally triggered the revenge which had burst open a door and left it free to stalk.

Her mother would know now, of course, just as she would know that James was dead, that he had lain all these years in the cold and the wet and the dark without ceremony or mourning.

A trickle of water found its icy way down the back of her nightie and she shivered, her mind coming back to its present surroundings with a twinge of sorrow and confusion.

Across the lake she saw Andrew emerge from the trees, saw him limp haplessly over the lawn, calling her name in frantic, pitiable tones.

She stood up, felt the chill of the growing wind make goose bumps up her legs and bare arms, billowing her nightie upwards and outwards. Over her head the sky was darkening, but for a second the massing clouds parted and a deep blue vault appeared before the clouds swept across and it was gone. The rain fell faster, big heavy drops pummelling the ground and denting the surface of the lake. She lifted her face to the torrent, let it soothe her flushed cheeks, her neck, the memories.

He saw her then, even from this distance she could see an incredible expression of relief, the way the rain had plastered his hair flat against his head like a little cap, his sodden night clothes.

He would catch a chill, she thought, as he came towards her, and she had probably made his ulcer complain and burn, his poor damaged foot whimper and hurt.

Pity came, for him and for herself.

She would look after him now; they would look after each other.

'I have a right to be happy.' Eve said.